Introduction to Neuropsychology

J. GRAHAM BEAUMONT

Senior Lecturer, Department of Psychology
University of Leicester

BLACKWELL SCIENTIFIC PUBLICATIONS

OXFORD LONDON EDINBURGH

© 1983 by
Blackwell Scientific Publications
Editorial offices:
Osney Mead, Oxford, OX2 0EL
8 John Street, London, WC1N 2ES
9 Forrest Road, Edinburgh, EH1 2QH
52 Beacon Street, Boston
  Massachusetts 02108, USA
99 Barry Street, Carlton
  Victoria 3053, Australia

First published 1983

Set by Oxford Verbatim Ltd and
printed and bound in
Great Britain by
The Camelot Press Ltd, Southampton

British Library
Cataloguing in Publication Data

Beaumont, J. Graham
  Introduction to neuropsychology.
  1. Neuropsychology
  I. Title
  616.8   QP360

  ISBN 0-632-01103-3
  ISBN 0-632-01104-1 Pbk

Published in USA by
The Guilford Press, a Division of
Guilford Publications Inc
200 Park Avenue South
New York, NY 10003

Contents

                                         . . . And I have felt
A presence that disturbs me with the joy
of elevated thoughts; a sense sublime
Of something far more deeply interfused,
Whose dwelling is the light of setting suns,
And the round ocean and the living air,
And the blue sky, and in the mind of man.

WILLIAM WORDSWORTH, from
Lines Composed a Few Miles above Tintern Abbey

Preface

This book was born out of my frustration at being unable to find a text to accompany the courses which I teach in neuropsychology to under-graduates, graduate clinical psychology trainees and other medical and paramedical groups. Its first aim is therefore to provide a systematic and comprehensive introduction to the field of neuro-psychology for those with some, perhaps not very advanced, knowledge of psychology.

At the same time, I wanted to produce a book which would make the current advances in neuropsychology accessible to the intelligent layman, without sacrificing critical standards of good science by 'popularizing' the material. I wanted to communicate, if I could, some of the excitement which I feel about this area of investigation. Only you can judge whether I have succeeded in this ambitious aim.

In trying to cover, in a balanced way, what I consider to be the whole subject of neuropsychology within a fairly short book, I have naturally met problems. The limited space has dictated rather severe compression of the material in places, and more examples and further elaboration would probably have been helpful. However, every book has a purpose, and the purpose of this one is to provide a thorough but concise introduction to the subject. I hope that you will not feel that readability has suffered unreasonably in trying to fulfill this aim.

Throughout the book, there are both references and suggestions for further reading to enable the reader to pursue specific topics and particular areas of interest. This may help to fill some of the gaps which are inevitably left in a text of this length.

One limitation which has been accepted in preparing this text is that it deals only with adult neuropsychology. There is quite delib-erately almost no reference to children. Sadly, it is not even possible to recommend an alternative text for those whose prime interest is the neuropsychological organization of children in normal or abnormal states. That is another book waiting to be written.

Another point – in one sense an apology – is that the text uses the male gender 'he' throughout to imply male or female individuals. There comes a time when the syntactic manoeuvres required to avoid any use of 'he' or 'she' become burdensome, and until some better neutral article than 's/he' is found, it seems reasonable to carry on using 'he'. No particular stance on sexual politics is implied by this, and I hope that you will accept what has been written in good faith as simply a traditional (and I think fairly harmless) usage within the English language.

A word also about the figures. First, and most importantly, I should like to thank my talented friend Don Keefe for his excellent work in preparing these. Although all the anatomical figures are original drawings, they are inevitably in some debt to two quite exceptional sets of anatomical illustrations: the collections of Nieuwenhuys, Voogd and Van Huijzen (1978) and Netter (1962) (see references on p. 42). The example items from test material are also, with some exceptions which are noted, original drawings. They are based upon real test material but, because it is considered unethical to expose this material unnecessarily since it may undermine the accuracy of the test in clinical practice, most of the examples have been slightly altered.

There are many others whom I want to thank for their help with the book. There are those people who have kindly given permission for the reproduction of figures. Dr Jennifer Wakely was extremely helpful in arranging for the photographs of normal brain specimens. Professor Tony Gale read the manuscript and made many perceptive and constructive suggestions which have been particularly valuable. The publishers have been unfailingly patient, encouraging and helpful, and I am especially grateful to them. Lastly, my family, colleagues, students and friends have had to tolerate my reclusiveness and frequent ill-humour during the preparation of the book and they have been unreasonably understanding and kind.

It only remains to say that I hope that you not only find the book informative, but that you enjoy reading it. I especially hope that some readers may become sufficiently interested by this introduction to continue their study of neuropsychology, and may become those who will develop the subject towards solving some of the great and fascinating problems which remain in understanding the relationship between the brain and intelligent behaviour.

J G B
Leicester
March 1982

I

Introduction

CHAPTER 1

The Discipline of Neuropsychology

WHAT IS NEUROPSYCHOLOGY?

The human brain is a fascinating and engimatic machine. Weighing only about 3 lb and with a volume of about 1250 cc, it has the ability to monitor and control our basic life support systems, to maintain our posture and direct our movements, to receive and interpret information about the world around us, and to store information in a readily accessible form throughout our lives. It allows us to solve problems which range from the strictly practical to the highly abstract, to communicate with our fellows through language, to create new ideas and imagine things which have never existed, to feel love and happiness and disappointment, and to experience an awareness of ourselves as individuals. Not only can the brain undertake such a variety of different functions, but it can do more or less all of them simultaneously. How this is achieved is one of the most challenging and exciting problems faced by contemporary science.

It has to be said at the outset that we are completely ignorant of many of the things that the brain does, and of the way in which they are done. Nevertheless, very considerable advances have been made in the neurosciences over the last decade or two, and there is growing confidence among neuroscientists that a real understanding is beginning to emerge. This feeling is encouraged by the increasing integration of the various disciplines involved in neuroscience, and a convergence of both experimental findings and theoretical models.

Neuropsychology, as one of the neurosciences, has grown to be a separate field of specialization within psychology over about the last fifteen years, although there has always been an interest in it throughout the hundred-year history of modern scientific psychology. Neuropsychology seeks to understand the relationship between the brain and behaviour, that is, it attempts to explain the way in which the activity of the brain is expressed in observable behaviour. What are the mechanisms which are responsible for human thinking, learning and emotion, how do these mechanisms operate, and what are the effects of changes in brain states upon human behaviour? There are a variety of ways in which neuropsychologists conduct their investigations into such questions, but the central theme of each is that to understand human behaviour we need to understand the human brain. A psychology without any reference to physiology can hardly be complete. The operation of the brain is relevant to human conduct, and the understanding of how the brain relates to behaviour may make a significant contribution to understanding how other, more purely psychological, factors operate in directing behaviour. Just how the brain deals with intelligent and complex human functions is, in any case, an important subject of investigation in its own right, and one which has an immediate relevance for those with brain injuries and diseases, as well as a wider relevance for medical practice.

BRANCHES OF NEUROPSYCHOLOGY

Neuropsychology is often divided into two main areas: clinical neuropsychology and experimental neuropsychology. The distinction is principally between clinical studies, on brain-injured subjects, and experimental studies, on normal subjects, although the methods of investigation also differ. The division between the two is not absolutely clear-cut but it helps to form an initial classification of the kinds of work in which neuropsychologists are involved.

Clinical neuropsychology deals with patients who have *lesions* of the brain. These lesions may be the effects of disease or tumours, may result from physical damage or *trauma* to the brain, or be the result of other biochemical changes, perhaps caused by toxic substances. Trauma may be accidental, caused by wounds or collisions, or it may result from some failure in the vascular system supplying blood to the brain, or be the intended result of neurosurgical intervention to correct some neurological problem. The clinical neuropsychologist measures deficits in intelligence, personality and sensory-motor functions by specialized testing procedures, and relates the results to the particular areas of the brain which have been affected. The damaged areas may be clearly circumscribed and limited in extent, particularly in the case of surgical lesions (when an accurate description of the parts of the brain which have been removed can be obtained), or may be diffuse, affecting cells throughout much of the brain, as is the case with certain cerebral diseases. Clinical neuropsychologists employ these measurements not only in the scientific investigation of brain-behaviour relationships, but also in the practical clinical work of aiding diagnosis of brain lesions and rehabilitating brain-injured patients.

Behavioural neurology, as a form of clinical neuropsychology, also deals with clinical patients, but the emphasis is upon conceptual rather than operational definitions of behaviour. The individual case rather than group statistics is the focus of attention, and this approach usually involves less formal tests to establish qualitative deviations from 'normal' functioning. Studies in behavioural neurology may often sample broader aspects of behaviour than is usual in clinical neuropsychology.

The distinction between clinical neuropsychology and behavioural neurology is not entirely clear, and it is further blurred by the traditions of investigation in different countries, particularly in the United States, the Soviet Union and Great Britain. Examples of clinical work in these countries are discussed below and in Chapter 14.

By contrast, *experimental neuropsychologists* work with normal subjects with intact brains. This is the most recent area of neuropsychology to develop and has grown rapidly, with the invention of a variety of techniques which can be employed in the laboratory to study higher functions in the brain. There are close links between experimental neuropsychology and general experimental and cognitive psychology, and the laboratory methods employed in these three areas have strong similarities. Subjects are generally required to undertake performance tasks while their accuracy or speed of response is recorded, from which inferences about brain organization can be made. Associated variables, including psychophysiological or electrophysiological variables, may also be recorded.

COMPARATIVE NEUROPSYCHOLOGY

Although the subject of this book is human neuropsychology, it should not be forgotten that much experimental neuropsychology has been, and continues to be, conducted with animals. At one time, the term 'neuropsychology' was in fact taken to refer to this area, but it is now used more generally and the relative importance of the animal studies of comparative neuropsychology has declined. The obvious advantage of working with animals, ethical issues apart, is that precise lesions can be introduced into the brain and later confirmed by histology. Changes in the animal's behaviour are observed and can be correlated with the experimental lesions. The disadvantages are the problems of investigating high-level functions using animals as subjects (the study of language is ruled out, to take the most obvious example) and the difficulty of generalizing from the animal brain to the human brain. Although it may be possible to discover in great detail how some perceptual function is undertaken in the brain of the rat, the cat or the monkey, it may not necessarily be undertaken in the same way in the human brain. There are also basic differences in the amount and distribution of different types of cortical tissue in the brains of the various animals and of man, which add to the difficulties of generalization.

Nevertheless, animal studies continue to be of importance, particularly with regard to the functions of subcortical systems – those functions located in the structures below the surface mantle of the brain which deal with relatively basic aspects of sensation, perception, learning, memory and emotion. These systems are harder to study in humans, because damage to these regions may interfere much more radically with a whole range of behaviours, and may often result in death. One of the problems facing contemporary neuropsychology is to integrate the study of cortical functions and higher-level behaviours, which have generally been studied in humans, with the study of subcortical structures and more basic behavioural systems, which have been studied in animals. These have tended to be separate areas of research, although there are now signs of integration between the two. For example, intelligence is now being discussed not just in terms of human performance on intelligence tests, but also in terms of underlying basic processes of learning, attention and motivation which are only understood, in neuropsychological terms, from animal studies. Sexual behaviour is another area where the basic systems are only open to experimental study in animals, yet must be viewed within the context of socialized and cognitively controlled behaviour in humans.

CONCEPTUAL ISSUES

Neuropsychology suffers philosophical and conceptual difficulties no less than other areas of psychology, and perhaps more than many. There are two problems in particular of which every student of the subject should be aware.

The first of these springs from the nature of the methods which must be used in neuropsychological investigation. Descriptions of brain organization can only be relatively distant inferences from the human performance which is actually observed. The real states of the brain are not observed. Behavioural measures are taken, and by a line of reasoning which is based on background information about either the general arrangement of the brain (in the case of experimental neuropsychology) or about the gross changes in the brain of a particular type of patient (in the case of clinical neuropsychology), conclusions are drawn about what must be the correlation between brain states and behaviour. The one exception to this general rule is in electrophysiological studies and studies of regional cerebral blood flow, where actual brain states can be observed, albeit rather crudely, in 'real time' alongside the human performance being measured. This makes these studies of especial importance in neuropsychology. However, in general, neuropsychological study proceeds only by inference. It is important to remember this in assessing the validity of many of the findings claimed by neuropsychologists, and also to be particularly vigilant that the reasoning used in drawing inferences is soundly based and the data not open to alternative explanations.

The second problem is even more fundamental, and is that usually referred to as the *mind-body problem*. It is a subject far too complex to receive satisfactory treatment here, but in brief it is concerned with the philosophical difficulties which arise when we talk about mental events or 'mind', and physiological events or 'body', and try to relate the two. We first have to decide whether mind and body are, or are not, fundamentally different kinds of things. If they are, then there are problems in giving explanations which correlate the two. If they are not, then we have to be careful not to be misled by our everyday language and concepts which tend to treat mind and body as if they *were* different kinds of things. The debate has gone on for some centuries, and is far from being resolved, but there is a general position which is accepted by most if not all neuropsychologists.

This position is known as 'emergent materialism' or 'emergent psychoneural monism'. It rejects the idea that mind and body are fundamentally different (hence it is 'monist' rather than 'dualist') and proposes that all mental states are states of the brain. Mental events therefore exist but are not separate entities. However, mental states cannot be reduced to a set of physical states because the brain is not a physical machine but a biosystem, and so possesses properties peculiar to living things. The brain is seen as not simply a complex composition of cells, but as having a structure and an environment. The result is that there are 'emergent' properties which include being able to think and feel and perceive. These properties are emergent just as the sweetness of an apple is an emergent property. There is nothing in the chemistry or physical structure of the apple which possesses sweetness. It is the whole object, in interaction with the eater, which produces the quality of sweetness. Mind is therefore seen as a collection of emergent bioactivities, and this has implications for both theories and methods in neuropsychology. It means that it is sometimes quite proper and sensible to reduce explanations to lower levels of description, purely in terms of the physiology or the biochemistry involved. However, it also means that integration among these lower processes, and their description in terms of higher level concepts (concerning the emergent properties), is both feasible and valuable.

The student first taking an interest in neuropsychology should not be overly concerned about these philosophical issues; much, if not most, of neuropsychological work is conducted while ignoring them altogether. However, some position is always implied in any investigation or theoretical model, and it is wise not to lose sight of the implications of holding a particular position for a satisfactory understanding of how the brain works.

HISTORICAL BACKGROUND

It is intriguing to discover just how far back neuropsychological study may have been undertaken. Although the interpretation of the content is a little uncertain, there is an Egyptian papyrus dating from about 2500 BC which reports on some cases of trauma to the brain. Many primitive societies, and even some more developed societies, have from early times practised the trepanning of skulls, although the evidence is usually in the form of artifacts and in human remains. In trepanation large or small openings are made in the skull which may or may not be subsequently repaired. The purpose of these, whether magical, medical, religious or simply punitive, generally remains obscure, but the practice has been recorded over a large proportion of the globe, and into this century.

In classical Greece there was, as one might expect, an interest in the brain and its functions, and Hippocratic writers clearly recognized the role of the brain in mental functions from careful study of their patients. However, while these ideas passed into the Arabic world, and were preserved there until the Renaissance, Greek ideas about the brain did not hold an important place in Western mediaeval thought. Galen in the second century AD also made remarkable advances in observation of the anatomy of the brain, but his ideas on the functioning of the brain, and those developed from his work, do not form the basis of our understanding today.

Following the Renaissance, and the growth of practical human anatomy (rather than the dissection of animals which had previously been the practice) there were increasingly sophisticated and accurate descriptions of the anatomy of the brain, and by about the middle of the nineteenth century a number of factors came together to form the basis of modern neuropsychology. These factors included: the location of the cortex of the brain as the source of intelligent behaviour, the accurate description of the neuroanatomy of the sensory and motor pathways, the idea that psychological processes could be analysed and grouped into a number of associated sets of 'faculties', and the observation that specific areas of the brain could be identified which, if damaged, resulted in the loss of language abilities.

Gall, with Spurzheim, in the 1830s had founded the 'science' of phrenology, which was based on the idea that development of the various mental faculties was associated with development of certain areas of the brain, and that this in turn was reflected in bumps on the skull overlying the relevant area. 'Reading the bumps' was in fashion through much of the nineteenth century. Professor J. Millot Severn was providing 'delineations' from the person or from photographs ('verbal statement' from 2s 6d) at the Brighton Phrenological Institute up to the First World War. If the hypotheses both about brain development and its reflection in scalp topography were ultimately to be dismissed, phrenology at least planted the idea that psychological characteristics could be broken down into a number of components, and each component associated with a specific area of the brain.

Broca, in 1861, demonstrated that lesions of a specific area interfered with the production of speech, as Wernicke was to do later for the understanding of speech. From the 1860s then, there was an intensive study of the cortical lesions of patients with psychological deficits in an attempt to map brain-behaviour relationships. This approach is known as *localizationist theory* because it assigned a specific function to a precise part or location of the brain, and it had moderate but not unqualified success.

From the outset, however, there were those who supported an *equipotential theory*, believing that precise mapping of functions was impossible because damage at different sites in the brain could result in the same specific deficit. Equipotential theory states that while sensory input may be localized, perception involves the whole brain, and the effects of brain lesions depend not upon their location but upon their extent. It is not which cells are damaged that matters but how many. Equipotential theory has had many eminent supporters until well into this century, including Kurt Goldstein, Henry Head and Karl Lashley. However because it has, on the one hand, been possible to demonstrate some kind of a relationship between cortical locations and certain specific functions and, on the other hand, impossible to derive a good index of brain damage which is independent of the site of the damage, equipotential theory has proved rather unsatisfactory.

A third position, which largely derives from the work of Hughlings Jackson, and is sometimes termed *interactionist theory*, proposes that higher functions are built up from a number of more basic component skills. These component skills are relatively localized, but because of the potential variety of complex ways in which the skills are linked to form intelligent functions, then the higher level behaviour does not necessarily appear to be localized. That no single function or learning process is entirely dependent upon a particular area of cortex, and that each part of the brain plays an unequal role in different functions, would support this position. Interactionist theory, often linked with *regional equipotentiality*, which argues for equipotentiality but within relatively well-defined regions, is the position implicitly accepted by most contemporary neuropsychologists. Important modern examples of theories which express this position are those of Luria (see p. 276) and Geschwind, although Geschwind has emphasized the role of connections between the component elements rather than the elements themselves.

Clinical neuropsychology in the twentieth century has shown a steady accumulation of clinical reports and research investigations which have gradually refined the theoretical positions sketched above. A particular impetus was given to research by the First and Second World Wars, and subsequently by the wars in South-East Asia, which provided cases of fairly discretely localized traumatic injuries. Great advances were made at these times both conceptually and in the sophistication of the psychological descriptions, by Teuber, Luria, Zangwill and a host of other workers. This approach, of examining relatively discrete psychological deficits, together with the more recent development by such workers as Reitan of batteries of tests assessing a broad range of behavioural functions, forms the basis of contemporary clinical neuropsychology.

Experimental neuropsychology has rather more recent origins. It has grown from two independent, although related, sources. The first is general experimental psychology, and in particular that branch now described as cognitive psychology. Again from the 1940s, spurred in part by wartime demands to investigate the performance characteristics of people operating complex equipment, the analysis has been developed of humans as information processing systems. Some of the forms of investigation – examining the responses of subjects to briefly presented visual stimuli (see p. 15) or to complex and competing auditory messages – have been seen as relevant to neuropsychology. It has been found that a neuropsychological model of the organization of the brain can be a powerful component in explaining certain aspects of human performance, and the methods of the experimental psychological laboratory have been employed to study hypotheses about the organization of the brain. Just how these methods differ from those of clinical neuropsychology is explained in the next two sections of the book.

The realization of the significance of human performance research came about as a result of interest in the other source of experimental neuropsychology. This was the fortuitous revival (for the researcher at least) of the 'split-brain' or 'commissurotomy' operation in about 1960 (see Chapter 9). This operation, which divides the connections between the two hemispheres of the brain, was thought to produce two independent brain systems within the individual, and it enabled the study of the relative specialization of these two systems within split-brain patients. Its historical importance lies not only in the data collected in such studies, but also in the techniques developed in the course of the investigations, which could be employed in the laboratory with normal intact humans to draw inferences about cerebral organization. It is from the study of split-brain patients that modern experimental neuropsychology can be considered to date, and the very large number of studies in this area, particularly in the last decade, has established experimental neuropsychology as a significant element of modern psychology.

CLINICAL NEUROPSYCHOLOGY

Clinical neuropsychology relies almost exclusively on established correlation between damage to particular regions of the brain and relatively specific deficits in psychological functions, indexed by a variety of more or less formal psychological tests. The collection of data by which such correlations are established allows models to be constructed of how systems of psychological functions are organized in the brain. It also allows knowledge of the deficits exhibited by a particular patient to be used to suggest where brain damage might be, as well as providing a psychological description of the handicap which that patient experiences. Within this central, essentially very simple, methodology there are different traditions which influence how clinical neuropsychology is practised. These traditions are far from independent, but are characterized by different emphases in approach of which the student should be aware. The three main traditions may be said to be associated with work in North America, Soviet Russia and Great Britain.

Of all the traditions, that in *North America* has shown the most systematic approach. Allied to the general interest of American psychology in the assessment of individual differences, neuropsychological investigation has been linked with psychological models of human abilities. That is, the tests which are used (and which are illustrated in Sections II and IV) are more likely to be selected because they are believed to measure some element of a scheme of psychological abilities. This is, of course, not always entirely explicit, but theories on the structure of human abilities have been influential in selecting which aspects of behaviour are to be assessed. Because of this, it is only in America that systematic batteries (collections of tests) for the assessment of neurological patients have emerged. The most widely used of these is the Halstead-Reitan Neuropsychological Test Battery, which incorporates a range of tests covering all the principle elements of psychological abilities. It includes a full assessment of the intelligence of the patient, which yields information from the component subtests of the intelligence scale, a systematic assessment of the language abilities of the patient through a standard aphasia battery, and a range of more specialized tests to assess perceptual, psychomotor, memory, learning and thinking abilities. This enables an analysis of the overall pattern of deficits and preserved abilities in the patient, which can lead to a diagnosis of his dysfunction. Attempts have been made to improve the diagnostic efficiency of this approach by the application of the specialized statistical techniques of multivariate and discriminant function analysis, and even to automate the interpretation of the test results by computerized key analysis. These methods, together with the more recent Luria-Nebraska battery, are described more fully on pp. 278–81). Such approaches have achieved a considerable degree of success, although a penalty is imposed by the length of time required to administer the extensive tests.

By contrast, *Soviet* neuropsychology, again reflecting the general character of psychology in that country, has tended to adopt a single case study approach linked to the prevailing theories about cerebral organization. These theories are expressed in terms of functional systems which can be referred to particular regions within the brain. Rather informal, and in general unstandardized, tests are used to assess the functional status of these systems, and only those tests which the clinician considers immediately relevant to a patient will be employed. Again reflecting the interests of Soviet psychology, psychophysiological and electrophysiological measures may well be taken alongside those using more typical psychometric instruments such as standard psychological tests. Attempts, not entirely successful, have been made to extract a systematic battery out of the investigative procedures employed in Soviet neuropsychology. The difficulties which arise in such an exercise are largely due to the fact that the tests are often not formal, standardized procedures, not 'tests' in the psychometric sense at all, but are general procedures for the assessment of some function which depend on the clinical skill and insight of the investigator.

British neuropsychology stands between these two approaches. This third tradition has drawn from both the strong tradition of British neurology and the experimental biases within British psychology. In Britain there is a tendency to use standardized procedures but for the selection of tests to be more pragmatic. Research in clinical neuropsychology tends to focus on some relatively discrete aspect of performance and to investigate it by controlled procedures in an homogeneous sample of patients selected according to some criterion, which is often the regional locus of their lesion. These procedures, originally employed in experimental investigations, have often evolved into relatively standardized tests which can be used to investigate the problems of individual patients. While research has tended, therefore, to concentrate on group data, the investigation of individual patients proceeds by the selection of appropriate tests, in a relatively standard form, which are combined to elicit a description of the deficits present in that patient. This tradition, while relying upon data from standardized procedures, emphasizes the individual nature of each case, and is not averse to the construction of single case experimental investigations to clarify some aspect of the problems shown by a particular patient. A summary of the three traditions, with the strengths and weaknesses of each, is shown in Table 1.1, and more detailed discussion of all these approaches will be found in Chapter 14.

To describe the three traditions in this way underestimates the variety of approaches to be found in the practice of clinical neuropsychology. However, all approaches rely to a certain extent upon the clinical skill and insight of the investigator. Perhaps especially within the British approach, there is a strong element of scientific detective work in selecting appropriate tests and developing an appropriate investigation for each patient. There is a certain satisfaction in the exercise of a clinical skill which enables the clinical neuropsychologist to take information about the patient from other medical specialities, to evolve an investigation, to arrive at a relatively specific description in psychological terms of the patient's problem, and to contribute to the diagnosis of the patient's lesion which may subsequently respond to treatment. There is also a definite thrill in the successful solution of this kind of detective problem, which

TABLE 1.1. APPROACHES IN CLINICAL NEUROPSYCHOLOGY

North American: systematic collections of tests.

Strengths:	Comprehensive coverage of functions.
	Based on psychological model of abilities.
	Allows use of scores which combine results from different tests.
Weaknesses:	Cumbersome, and perhaps wasteful, in use.
	Based on model of normal function, rather than abnormalities.
	May be insensitive.

Soviet: single case approach based on behavioural neurology.

Strengths:	Relevant assessment instruments selected.
	Wide scope for application of clinical skill.
	Based on model of abnormal function.
Weaknesses:	Little use of standardized procedures or normative data.
	Depends heavily on clinical skill.
	Difficult to measure subtle changes in level rather than quality of performance.

British: investigation of individual cases by selection of standardized tests.

Strengths:	Focus on difficulties of individual patient.
	Can make use of statistical psychometric analysis.
	Allows development of a model of individual patient's disability.
Weaknesses:	Investigation may be fragmentary and unsystematic.
	Overemphasis on tests which happen to be available.
	Risk of over-reliance on poor and inadequate test procedures.

demands intellectual as well as clinical ability, and which may benefit a patient in danger, pain or distress.

The relevance of clinical neuropsychology is not hard to see. Despite developments in other neurological fields, particularly the development of computerized axial tomography or 'brain scan' which enables far clearer imaging of changes in the structures within the head, neuropsychologists can still make a substantial contribution to the diagnosis and localization of lesions in individual cases. In addition, although it has been a field slow to develop, neuropsychology can play a central role in the rehabilitation of brain-injured patients. In order to encourage the relearning of lost skills, the development of compensatory strategies, and to promote appropriate social and occupational adjustment, an accurate description of psychological deficits is vital. This description needs, of course, to be integrated with the application of theories of learning, memory, language and motor skill. Our developing knowledge of the neuropsychological organization of the brain enables coherent plans to be formulated for ways in which individual patients may be helped to compensate for their handicaps, and cognitive strategies to enable them successfully to circumvent their difficulties.

EXPERIMENTAL NEUROPSYCHOLOGY

Experimental neuropsychology is best understood in terms of the various methods which have been used in research studies. These can be grouped into methods which rely upon the logic of stimulus presentation, those in which lateral asymmetries in human perform-ance allow more distant inferences, and those involving various specialized techniques.

By far the most numerous are the studies which rely upon the *logic of stimulus presentation*. These employ the techniques known as divided visual field presentation (see Chapter 10), dichotic listening (see Chapter 11), and lateralized tactile presentation. In all of them, the stimuli presented for subsequent cognitive analysis and response are 'lateralized'. The brain (as will be made clear in the following chap-ter) is divided into two lateral hemispheres which are only intercon-nected at the cortical level by a number of commissures, the most important being the corpus callosum. From clinical evidence, particularly that from split-brain patients, the hemispheres can be regarded as relatively independent systems with their own particular specializations. Sensory input, through vision, hearing or touch, is

lateralized to the contralateral hemisphere, that is, stimuli presented
at one side of the body are received at the opposite side of the brain.
This contralateral mapping is complete for vision, and more or less
complete for touch and predominant for hearing, it also works in
similar fashion for voluntary motor control. Therefore, if stimuli are
presented at a selected location on one side of the body, it is to the
opposite side of the brain that the information initially travels, and
subsequent performance, generally in terms of accuracy or response
latency, can be studied according to the initial reception of the
information at one of the hemispheres. The use of the left or right
hand to respond is an additional variable which can be included in the
design. When visual stimuli are employed, the technique is that of
divided visual field presentation; when auditory, it is that of dichotic
listening, and when tactile, that of lateralized tactile presentation.

Although a very complex series of events, involving both
hemispheres, follows the initial reception of information from
lateralized presentation, it has been possible to establish a number of
asymmetries in performance, which are taken to indicate different
specializations of the cerebral hemispheres. These relate in part to the
nature of the information given to the subject, whether verbal or
non-verbal (e.g. words or faces), in part to the nature of the cognitive
task (naming, matching or evaluating), and in part to more general
attentional variables. Despite a number of methodological problems,
and some lack of clarity in the cognitive and neuropsychological
models which are used in this area, there seems to be sufficient
consistency in the data to enable conclusions about cerebral organization to be drawn from these studies. In recent years these techniques
have led to very considerable advances being made in our understanding of the principles which underlie the operation of the brain for
psychological function, and progress has been made in the construction of coherent models of neuropsychological function.

Associated with these more direct techniques (although it should
not be forgotten that they still rely upon a rather indirect chain of
inference about the brain), are some other *performance asymmetries*. One
of these concerns lateral eye movements. Many subjects, when
involved in solving a problem they have been given, avert their gaze to
either the right or left, and this has been shown to be associated with
the nature of the mental processes (either verbally or spatio-
perceptually based) required to solve the problem. This is believed to
reflect, in turn, the operation of lateralized brain systems. Some other
performance asymmetries – direction of preferred movement in drawing circles, the extent of thumb rotation, and preferences in judging

pictorial compositions, among others – have also been linked to hemisphere specialization, although the connection is rather less well established (see pp. 220–21).

More extensive research has been done on handedness. Individual differences have always been a theme of study in experimental neuropsychology, with handedness and, to a lesser extent, sex as the most important variables. It is clear from clinical and other experimental evidence that right and left handers differ in their brain organization. While there are groups of left handers who show a laterally reversed pattern of asymmetry, left handers in general seem to have less lateralized brains than right handers. Research into the relative performance of right and left handers has been undertaken to clarify these differences and to extend our understanding of brain organization in general.

Lastly there are some more *specialized techniques* which come closer to a direct association of brain events with psychological processes. In the Wada test, sodium amytal is injected into the left or right internal carotid artery, which is the principal blood supply to the brain. The effect is to suppress all activity on the side of the injection for a period of a few minutes. It is therefore possible to observe the functions of one half of the brain while its partner has been temporarily put out of action. Because of the risks involved in this injection, the test is not made on normal subjects, and is only performed as part of the assessment of patients who are to undergo certain types of neurosurgery (see p. 80). It has nevertheless yielded some valuable data.

The study of regional cerebral blood flow, or rCBF, can, however, be undertaken with volunteer subjects. Here a quantity of radioactively labelled gas is inhaled, absorbed into the bloodstream, and then tracked by an array of detectors placed alongside the head as it passes through the brain. Subjects may be engaged in some mental task during this procedure, and more active regions of the brain, by demanding more blood, show up at the recording detectors. Amounts of radiation are small, but the problem with the technique is its poor resolution. It takes some time for the radioactive elements to pass through the head and the temporal correlation with psychological events is therefore crude.

The last specialized technique of importance is one of the most promising, and is the study of electrophysiological variables. The electrical activity of the brain has for many years been recorded for clinical, neurological purposes, but it has more recently attracted attention as a research technique in psychology. Electrical activity can be recorded while subjects engage in psychological tasks and can be analysed in terms of the characteristic activity at certain sites during certain periods ('on-going' EEG), or else in terms of the typical response of the brain to some stimulus event (average evoked potentials). While there are considerable technical and methodological difficulties in this area, it offers for the first time an opportunity to observe psychological events and the associated brain events simultaneously and with a fair degree of resolution. This is a fundamental advance which holds great promise for the future.

THE FRINGE

Neuropsychology, like many sciences, has its fringe elements, and because it has recently become fashionable, perhaps more than its share. Hemisphere lateralization has been the starting point for a whole range of theories about consciousness, cultural differences, and occupational and educational adjustment. It has been suggested that consciousness originated from processes in the right hemisphere which were originally attributed to the 'voice of gods'. It has been proposed that differences in societal development between primitive cultures have their origins in the relative development of the specializations of the two cerebral hemispheres, and that Eastern and Western styles of thought reflect similar lateral differences. Occupational success has been attributed to 'hemisphericity', or the relative balance between the activities of the two sides of the brain, and questionnaires have been designed to measure this balance. Changes in educational curricula have even been proposed to develop the supposedly more creative aspects of right hemisphere function.

While many of these ideas are stimulating and exciting, it has to be said that they go well beyond the scientific evidence at present available, and may indeed be harmful if incorporated into our general cultural ideas, or translated into social policy. It is hoped that the student, having read this book and some of the recommended further reading, will be in a better position to make a balanced assessment of some of these ideas and their significance and value.

THE PLAN OF THIS BOOK

The following chapter gives a brief overview of the structure of the brain for those unfamiliar with neuroanatomy. It is necessarily rather cursory, but should be sufficient to enable the reader to understand the structures and systems which are referred to in the remainder of the text.

The fairly clear distinction, already made, between clinical and experimental neuropsychology is preserved in the arrangement of the main part of the book. Section II deals with clinical studies, which have been divided according to the main regions of the cortex, with separate sections on language and subcortical systems. In any study of neuropsychology, the student needs constantly to try to build an integrated scheme which maps the interrelations of psychological processes on to the anatomical systems of the brain. It is possible to approach the studies either in terms of the anatomical structures, or by subdividing the material according to psychological functions. There are advantages and disadvantages to both approaches. As it is expected that readers may be more used to thinking in terms of a psychological scheme of functions, the necessary integration may be easier if the material is presented according to the anatomical classi-fication, so that the student makes the necessary links across func-tional categories. This is not an easy task, but is one of the exciting challenges of the study of neuropsychology.

Section III presents some of the principal areas of experimental neuropsychology, divided by the techniques of investigation em-ployed, and enables reference to be made back to the findings with clinical patients described in the previous section. The final section presents in further detail some of the practical ways in which neuropsychology is applied, and suggests some of the advances which may soon be made in translating research studies into techniques which may be of value in both neurology and psychiatry.

Neuropsychology is a fascinating, and currently very exciting, field of study. At both the conceptual and theoretical level, and the level of practical application, there are a variety of challenges and a number of mysteries. We do not know much about the brain and must suspect that it still holds many secrets. Dramatic developments are being made and there is the promise of many to come. I only hope that some of this fascination and excitement will be glimpsed by readers begin-ning their study of neuropsychology.

CONCLUSION

Neuropsychology can be divided into two branches. The first, clinical neuropsychology includes behavioural neurology and deals with

patients with cerebral lesions. Three traditions, loosely associated
with North America, the Soviet Union and Britain, can be identified.

The second branch is experimental neuropsychology which studies
normal subjects in the laboratory by a range of techniques including
dichotic listening and divided visual field and lateralized tactile presentation, as well as more specialized physiological techniques.
Studying the brains of animals, comparative neuropsychology, makes
an important but distinct contribution.

There are fundamental conceptual issues raised by neuropsychology which include the mind-body problem. The generally accepted
position is emergent materialism or emergent psychoneural monism,
which holds that all mental states are also states of the brain, but
cannot be reduced to the properties of single cells. The historical
origins of modern neuropsychology can be traced to the second half of
the nineteenth century. Early theoretical positions included
localizationist and equipotential theories, but most neuropsychologists now accept interactionist theory with its associated concept of
regional equipotentiality.

FURTHER READING

Two books which form a good introduction to some conceptual issues:

Bindra, D., *The Brain's Mind: a Neuroscience Perspective on the Mind-Body Problem*
(New York, Gardner Press, 1980). A collection of useful and readable
papers.

Bunge, M., *The Mind-Body Problem* (Oxford, Pergamon Press, 1980). This is an
excellent introduction to the philosophical issues, with extensive reference
to the neurosciences. It summarizes all the major positions, assesses their
strengths and weaknesses, and proposes a new development of emergentist
materialism.

Some general books on neuropsychology, perhaps more for reference
purposes:

Dimond, S. J., *Neuropsychology* (London, Butterworth, 1980). An important
and stimulating book which for the first time attempts to integrate human
and animal research. Valuable as an advanced text or as a reference work, it
divides the subject according to psychological rather than anatomical
systems.

Gazzaniga, M. S., ed., *Handbook of Behavioural Neurobiology, vol. 2 Neuropsychology* (New York, Plenum Press, 1979). This is a collection of state-of-the-art
papers which cover both clinical and experimental studies. The quality of
the contributions is in general good, although this book should be used
selectively.

Three books which concentrate almost exclusively upon clinical neuropsychology:

Filskov, S. B. and Boll, T. J., eds., *Handbook of Clinical Neuropsychology* (New York, Wiley-Interscience, 1981). A rather mixed collection of contributions, but it gives some useful descriptions of clinical practice, although the examples are American.

Kolb, B. and Whishaw, I. Q., *Fundamentals of Human Neuropsychology* (San Francisco, W. H. Freeman, 1980). A comprehensive and well-illustrated text.

Walsh, K. W., *Neuropsychology: a Clinical Approach* (Edinburgh, Churchill-Livingstone, 1978). An excellent text which treats clinical neuropsychology in greater depth. Includes a more extensive treatment of the historical background.

Finally two books which concentrate upon experimental neuropsychology:

Springer, S. P. and Deutsch, G., *Left Brain, Right Brain* (San Francisco, W. H. Freeman, 1981). An introductory text, but could provide a slight expansion and alternative view to Section III of this book.

Wittrock, M. C., ed., *The Brain and Psychology* (New York, Academic Press, 1980). Almost the only book to provide a general coverage of experimental neuropsychology. The coverage is a little uneven, but it contains some valuable contributions.

CHAPTER 2

The Structure of
the Central Nervous System

The human nervous system is conventionally divided into three parts: the Central Nervous System (CNS), the Peripheral Nervous System (PNS) and the Autonomic Nervous System (ANS). The ANS is a specialized system formed from components of both the CNS and the PNS, and is concerned with general activation, with emergency response and with emotion, and is more particularly the study of the psychophysiologist.

The function of the PNS is to carry information from receptors distributed around the body into the CNS, and to carry information back out to effectors. By this system, sensations of light touch, pain and temperature are detected in the skin; pressure, pain and position sense are conveyed from subcutaneous and deep tissue; and pain is transmitted from the viscera. Similarly, instructions are carried outwards from the CNS to effectors in muscles and glands. Although the PNS is more complex than this would suggest, for our purposes we can consider it simply as forming a communications link between the spinal cord and the periphery of the body. The only specialized parts of the PNS that we should note are the cranial nerves which deal with the neck and head and the special senses, but we shall return to these later. Perhaps the most significant difference between the PNS and the CNS is that, when damaged, parts of the PNS can be regenerated and will grow back into their original configuration. If the CNS is damaged, then there is no practical degree of regrowth possible, and the damage, in structural terms, is permanent.

TERMINOLOGY

The terminology for structures in the CNS can often seem difficult to students. Two points may help to reduce this difficulty. The first is to note that many structures have Latin, or rather mediaeval dog-Latin, names which were often given by anatomists on the basis of some visual reference or joke. This helps to make the terms easier to remember, and for those not familiar with Latin, translations of some of these terms will be given in parentheses when they are introduced. The second point is to understand how the general biological system of indicating direction is applied to the CNS. In this system, *rostral* means towards the head (a 'rostrum' is raised up), and *caudal* towards the tail. *Dorsal* means towards the back, while *ventral* is towards the belly. *Lateral* is towards the side, and *medial* towards the midline. (See Fig. 2.1.)

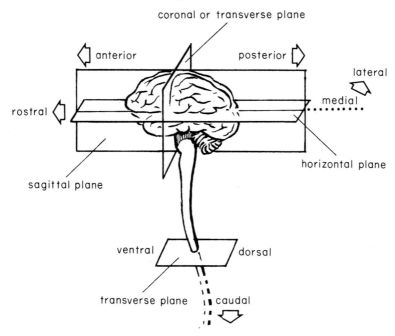

Figure 2.1. The terminology used to describe sections and relative locations in the central nervous system.

The complication with respect to the human CNS is that in the course of evolution it is considered to have bent forwards through a right angle at the level of the brain. We should therefore think of these terms as applying to the situation in which the figure is standing but with the head bent back and the eyes pointing towards the ceiling. This resolves the puzzlement often generated by the description *coronal* (or *transverse*) applied to a section through the brain, which in a standing figure would appear to be a vertical section. You must imagine the head bent back before the 'crown' is placed on top of the figure. A *sagittal* (cut by an arrow) or front-to-back section is fairly clear, although a *horizontal* section applies to the head placed in its actual everyday orientation. The terms *anterior* (towards the front), *posterior* (towards the back), *superior* (above) and *inferior* (below) as applied to the head also refer to it in the normal posture. There is sadly no alternative to learning how these terms are used, and in the early stages of study being prepared to look up them whenever you are unsure.

THE ENVIRONMENT OF THE CNS

The CNS, which is basically composed of the brain and the spinal cord, is contained within the bony case of the skull and the spinal column, no doubt because of the serious biological consequences of damage. Within that bony case it is further protected and supported by a series of membranes, or *meninges* (meningitis is inflammation of the meninges). These membranes are the *dura mater* ('hard mother'), the *arachnoid* layer (like a spider's web) and the *pia mater* ('soft mother'). An extradural block is an anaesthetic, used in obstetrics, placed outside the dura mater in the spinal column, and a subdural haemorrhage is bleeding in the space below the dura, but outside the brain itself.

The brain also has a very rich blood supply, taking about a fifth of the blood pumped by the heart. Seeing models of the brain, or illustrations of the appearance of the brain, from which the arterial and venous structures have been cleared, often allows this to be forgotten. The system extends richly around every part of the brain, and failure of part of this system in a cerebrovascular accident (CVA), either by part of the blood supply becoming blocked (in a stroke), or by bleeding into the brain and surrounding tissue, is a common cause of pathological change.

Within the meninges and enmeshed in its vascular supply, the brain floats in a fluid known as the *cerebrospinal fluid* (CSF). The function of CSF is both to provide mechanical protection by absorbing some of the shocks to the CNS and to supply certain aspects of nutrition of the brain. It is generated within the brain itself, in the *lateral ventricles*, which are large chambers within the brain, and it circulates through narrow passages into the midline *third* and *fourth ventricles*, and then out into the spaces surrounding the brain and the spinal cord, until it is finally absorbed into the venous system. (See Fig. 2.2). CSF is generated in the ventricles under some pressure in order to maintain flow in the system, and there are serious consequences if the passages in the brain become blocked. This is the cause

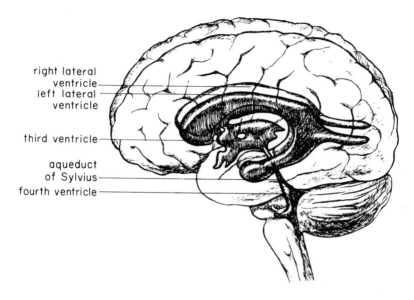

right lateral
ventricle
left lateral
ventricle

third ventricle

aqueduct
of Sylvius
fourth ventricle

Figure 2.2. The ventricular system of the brain.

of the condition known as *hydrocephalus* (water on the brain), and is the reason why the head circumference of infants is regularly measured. In some children the passages are congenitally blocked, the CSF is unable to circulate out of the ventricles, and the brain – and hence the unknit bones of the skull – begins to swell. This can be corrected by the insertion of a by-pass channel and valve, and few long-term effects are apparent if the condition is detected at an early stage. The condition can also occur in adults, and be successfully treated. However, because the bones of the skull cannot separate to allow the brain to swell, the condition may not be detected at such an early stage, and the consequences can be more serious.

The ventricular system can be made use of in diagnosis in two ways. In lumbar puncture, a needle is inserted in the lumbar region of the spine to withdraw a quantity of CSF for inspection, and in *ventriculograpy* or *air encephalography* a quantity of radio-opaque dye or a bubble of air is introduced into the ventricular system so that its outlines can be traced by X-ray photography. This can give information about either the displacement of structures inside the head, or changes in the size of the ventricles which may indicate shrinkage of brain tissue.

THE SPINAL CORD

The spinal cord is often underrated by psychologists, but many aspects of behaviour are in fact organized and integrated within it. It may be considered as composed of a series of layers, with each layer related to a spinal vertebra. At each layer there are spinal nerve roots, one ventral and one dorsal pair, by which the PNS links to the CNS, and each relates to an identifiable region on the surface of the body, which, because of the resemblance of a map of these regions to a series of horizontal slices, are known as *dermatomes*. The neurologist can make use of this mapping to determine the level of the spinal cord at which pathology is present.

Apart from carrying motor information down from the brain out to the body, and receiving sensory information back in return, certain behaviours are organized entirely within the spinal cord, principally by means of *reflexes*. In these reflexes the sensory information enters at one layer of the spinal cord, links directly in a reflex arc to a motor nerve, which then exits back out to the PNS. This is the simplest form of reflex and is known as a two-neuron reflex, but slightly more complex reflexes may extend over several adjacent layers in the spinal cord, although the principle of their operation is exactly the same. All this occurs without the direct intervention of higher levels of the CNS. Higher levels of the brain may influence the speed with which reflexes operate, or how easily they may be triggered, but control is limited to this general kind of supervision.

Reflexes may be divided into *superficial*, *deep* and *special* reflexes. Superficial reflexes may be elicited by stimulation of the skin. For instance, if the sole of the foot is scratched, then the toes flex. An example of a deep reflex is the knee jerk which follows striking the patella with a soft hammer. Here a tendon is stretched which results in a reflex muscle contraction. There are other similar reflexes associated with the ankle, elbow and wrist. Special reflexes often have a more complex organization, of which the constriction of the pupil in bright light is a clear example. Reflexes may be of developmental significance, and in abnormal form, of clinical value. For example, the Babinski reflex at the sole of the foot produces upward flexion of the toes in infants, but after infancy changes to downward flexion. Upward deflection in adults is therefore a sign of some pathological process.

One way to assess the contribution of some region of the CNS is to ask what functions remain when all other regions have been removed. This kind of experiment can of course only be carried out with animals. Clinical cases involving complete section at the very top of the spine are in any case very rarely seen since such damage is incompatible with survival. However, animal experiments have provided some useful information about this. If the section is above the fourth cervical segment (the cervical section of the spinal cord is at the top, and is numbered from the top down), artificial respiration is required, but section below that is compatible with life. Following spinal shock there is, in motor terms, a progression from some reflex activity, through flexor spasms, to extensor dominance and mass extension with all the limbs rigidly stretched out. The animal may even stand if placed upright on its extended limbs. The bladder will function, defecation may occur, as may integrated sexual activity following appropriate stimulation. Otherwise there is little which we would call behaviour, although a description of this state may underestimate the contribution of reflex activity organized in the spine to the normal functioning of the intact system.

DIVISIONS OF THE BRAIN

The *brain*, which is a rather loose term generally taken to be all of the CNS except the spinal cord, is conventionally divided into a number of regions. Outside a phylogenetic perspective, these divisions are not always very helpful, and are not of great importance for neuropsychologists. To add to the difficulty there is no complete agreement on their use. However, these divisions have been laid out in Table 2.1 and Fig 2.3 in order to show how they relate to some of the major structures in the brain, and we shall follow these basic divisions in describing the major components of the brain. It is worth noting, however, that the phylogenetic development of the brain does have some significance for understanding its structure, and thereby under-

TABLE 2.1. THE REGIONS INTO WHICH THE CENTRAL
NERVOUS SYSTEM IS DIVIDED, AND SOME PRINCIPAL
STRUCTURES IN EACH. THE NUMBERS REFER TO FIG. 2.3.

BRAIN		FOREBRAIN (prosencephalon)	TELENCEPHALON (end brain) (1)	cerebral cortex
			RHINENCEPHALON	limbic system
			DIENCEPHALON (interbrain) (2)	thalamus hypothalamus basal ganglia internal capsule
	BRAIN STEM reticular formation	MIDBRAIN	MESENCEPHALON (midbrain) (3)	midbrain
				cerebellum (4)
			METENCEPHALON (afterbrain)	pons (5)
			MYELENCEPHALON (narrow brain) (6)	medulla oblongata
SPINAL CORD (7)				

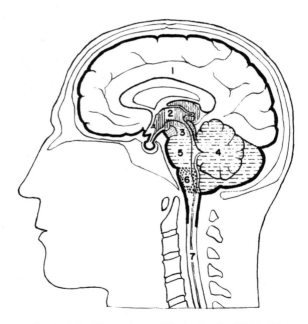

Figure 2.3. The regions of the brain. See Table 2.1.

standing the functional interrelationship of parts of the system. The brain has evolved as a series of layers wrapped around a central core formed by the spinal cord surmounted by the brain stem, and with each layer a 'higher' level of function has developed, progressively extending the functional capacity of the system. Each of the divisions which we shall be considering represents a major development in which another layer was added to the total brain system.

THE BRAIN STEM

On entering the skull, the spinal cord becomes the *brain stem*, which is formed of three principal structures: in ascending order, the *medulla oblongata* ('oblong marrow'), the *pons* ('bridge') and the *midbrain*. The *cerebellum*, which will be discussed shortly, sits astride this region and forms massive connections with it. (See Fig. 2.4).

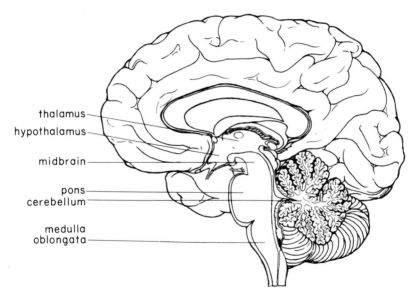

Figure 2.4. Principal structures of the brain stem and cerebellum.

The functions of the brain stem can most easily be considered if we again look at what happens when it is separated from higher control in the brain. In a *decerebrate* animal the cranial nerves (see below) are intact, allowing full sensory information into the system, and intact final motor outflow. The cerebellum is still contributing to behaviour, but otherwise the system is divorced from higher levels of control. In motor terms, the decerebrate cat has strong extensor contractions which it will maintain (like the 'spinal' animal), and its limbs will support its weight, but it is unable to move about. If pushed over, it cannot right itself. It must be fed by hand and, as temperature control is lacking, be kept at an appropriate stable temperature. Blood pressure is, however, maintained and respiration continues, slowly and deeply (as it does characteristically in many patients in coma). Certain reflexes which depend on sensory information carried by the cranial nerves also operate, so that the head and neck can be moved.

The midbrain in particular has some additional and specialized functions. Visual information is relayed to this part of the brain and some forms of visual reflex, for instance, blinking, pupillary constriction and certain eye movements, are organized here. Similarly, auditory reflexes, for example starting at a sudden noise, originate in this region.

Certain aspects of autonomic function are organized in the brain stem, so that salivation, control of blood pressure, respiration and movements in the alimentary canal are influenced through the ANS from this region. These influences may include part of the control of vomiting.

An important structure which runs through the whole brain stem is the *reticular formation* (like a little net – as in *retiarius*, meaning a Roman gladiator who fought with a net). Cells in this formation communicate with cells throughout the spinal cord, cerebellum and the higher regions of the brain. A particular feature is the *ascending reticular activating system* (ARAS). This system receives inputs from sensory pathways on their upward path, and projects on to the cerebral cortex through a variety of intermediate centres. The result is a generalized arousal of the whole forebrain, and is an important component in wakefulness, in the maintenance of consciousness and in attention. The ARAS thus forms a general vigilance apparatus which ensures that the brain is in a state ready to receive information.

As indicated above, the *cranial nerves* enter the brain at this level. They consist of a set of twelve pairs of nerves, some sensory, some motor, and some combining both functions, which almost entirely project to the head and neck. Apart from subserving sensation in this region, and providing motor control, the cranial nerves serve the special senses through the olfactory nerves (smell), the optic nerves (vision), the auditory nerves (hearing and equilibrium), and the facial, glossopharyngeal and vagus nerves (taste). Eye movements are, of course, also directly controlled by the cranial nerves. The important factor is that these nerves enter the brain directly without passing through the spinal cord.

In summary, the brain stem is concerned with the special senses, with vital processes, and with other visceral and somatic functions, all of which may be modified by impulses entering by the cranial nerves, down from the cerebellum or from the forebrain.

THE CEREBELLUM

The *cerebellum* ('little brain') is joined on to the brain stem and sits astride it, but this should not lead us to ignore the cerebellum's important direct connections with both the spinal cord and the forebrain.

The cerebellum's main role is to coordinate muscular activity, both in postural and locomotor mechanisms, all of which is carried out at a subconscious level. Perhaps because this happens without our awareness, we tend to forget what a massive control operation is required to maintain our posture and to effect both voluntary and involuntary motor movements. Most positions of the body are achieved by the antagonistic activity of opposed groups of muscles. These muscles, if not properly coordinated, are sufficiently powerful to break bones or at least to tear other muscles out of position. It is therefore vital that these groups of muscles be carefully coordinated. That we can achieve this feat of control so effortlessly, and not only avoid self-injury but also execute the most delicate, accurate, smooth and graceful movements, is a tribute to the marvellous contribution of the cerebellum in motor control.

The cerebellum achieves this control by receiving information from the skin, from muscles, tendons, joints and the semicircular canals (the organs of positional sense and balance near the ear), as well as from the visual and auditory systems. In turn, it discharges out to the cerebral cortex and spinal cord, executing control over the timing of operation of motor events. It thus ensures smooth, controlled and well-organized movement. Patients with damage to the cerebellum show jerky movements and intention tremor (tremor which only appears when a deliberate movement is made), walk in a broad stumbling gait and show loss of both balance and position sense. In fact, deprived of visual feedback, by closing the eyes, these patients readily topple to the ground.

THE DIENCEPHALON – THE SUBCORTICAL FOREBRAIN

When we reach this level of the CNS, things start to get more interesting for the psychologist, for structures in this region are centrally involved in motivation, emotion, the ANS and in states of awareness. We also begin to consider the structures which, when damaged, lead to recognizable psychological signs in clinical patients, although it must be remembered that many patients with

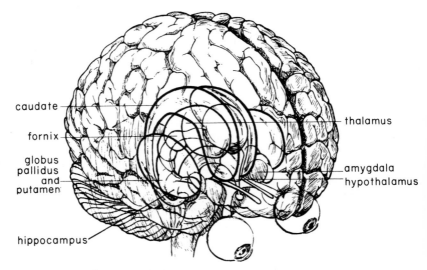

Figure 2.5. Principal structures of the diencephalon.
(Drawing after W. J. H. Nauta and M. Feirtag, *Scientific American*, 1979.)

extensive diencephalic damage do not survive, and much of our information is based on inferences from comparative studies on animals. Nevertheless, because relatively isolated injury to the cerebral cortex (the most common form of clinical damage to be studied by neuropsychologists) cannot be considered without reference to the subcortical structures to which that cortex is related, an understanding of the arrangement and function of the diencephalon is of central importance.

It is convenient to consider the diencephalon in terms of three structures (see Fig. 2.5): the *thalamus* ('inner room'), the *hypothalamus* ('lower room') and the *basal ganglia*. 'Basal ganglia' is a rather 'rag bag' term used differently by different writers, but it indicates centres of activity deep in the middle of the brain, and I am using the term in just that inexact way. Some writers include the hypothalamus in the basal ganglia.

While thinking phylogenetically often leads us to think of the cerebral cortex as the endpoint of the CNS, in a sense it is the thalamus which is the main control centre governing sensation and movement. Physiologically, all the pathways (except the direct voluntary 'pyramidal' motor pathway) travel to and from the thalamus as the terminus of the system, with an additional loop via the cerebral cortex. This loop no doubt allows more sophisticated operations to be performed with the sensory or motor information, and may be the circuit which gives us conscious awareness of sensory and motor events. However, it is unwise to neglect the primary role of the thalamus in the central registration of sensory information and the executive control of motor activity.

Righting reflexes (which enable a cat to land safely on its feet from whatever orientation it begins its fall) are organized in the thalamus, operating with visual and positional information from the head, neck and body, but the thalamus also performs more general underlying motor functions, as a list of the motor disorders which may follow thalamic lesions indicates. Damage to the thalamus may produce resting tremor, *chorea* or rapid jerky involuntary movements, and *dystonia* or uncontrolled movement. The syndrome of *Parkinsonism* is associated with thalamic lesions and includes rigidity in movement, a shuffling gait, loss of associated movements (such as arm swinging while walking), loss of emotional expression, and tremor. It is not uncommon to see Parkinsonian tremor in the elderly, and in such cases the presence of resting tremor is obvious in that it disappears when an intentional movement, such as drinking from a cup, is executed but reappears when the attention is allowed to wander, usually resulting in the contents of the cup being spilled.

Similarly, the thalamus is an important receiving centre for sensation, although the sensation is not at this stage localized in terms of associated perceptions, but is in the form of general awareness of touch, temperature or pain.

The hypothalamus (below the thalamus) is equally important behaviourally, and its functions have led certain writers to call it the 'centre of the brain'. It contains pairs of nerve centres which can be shown to influence eating and drinking, sleeping and waking, sexual behaviour, organization for fight or flight and the rage reaction (in association with the ANS), and the response to reward and punishment. Although such studies are now considered to give too simplified a picture of the operation of the hypothalamus, studies of animals in which particular centres are either stimulated or extirpated (surgically removed) suggest that there are relatively discrete centres which turn these aspects of behaviour on or off. Appropriate lesions can cause animals permanently to cease drinking, or else to drink continually and excessively. Animals will also work, in a conditioning paradigm by bar-pressing or by running in a treadmill, far more vigorously to achieve self stimulation if electrodes are placed in certain hypothalamic centres than they will for conventional rewards such as food or water.

Perhaps the most dramatic of the demonstrations of the diencephalic control of behaviour was performed by Delgado. He inserted electrodes in the appropriate regions of the brain of a fighting bull. Entering the ring armed only with a cape and a radio-controlled telemetric stimulator, he showed that it was possible to halt the bull in mid-charge. The rather confused bull merely turned and wandered away.

The remaining structures in the diencephalon, the basal ganglia, which include the *amygdala* ('almond'), *globus pallidus* ('pale sphere'), *caudate* ('having a tail') and *putamen* ('husk'), have functions largely associated with those described for the thalamus and hypothalamus. There is, however, one important system which involves many parts of the basal ganglia, as well as parts of the telencephalon, which is the *limbic system* (on the 'borders' of the diencephalon). This is a relatively ancient system, sometimes known as the *visceral brain*, and is concerned with many aspects of emotion and behaviour (see Fig. 2.6). The principal structures in this system, which is coiled around the central structures of the thalamus and hypothalamus, are the *hippocampus* ('seahorse'), the *fornix* ('a vaulted chamber') the *amygdala*, the *septal region* ('enclosing'), the *cingulate* ('belt-like') *gyrus*, and the *mammillary* ('breast-like') *bodies*, together with significant links into the thalamus and hypothalamus. The functions undertaken by parts of this system include memory and learning, taming and some aspects of aggression, some primitive features of object recognition, sexual and exploratory behaviour, and, in animals, avoidance learning, connected with the effects of frustrative non-reward (the effects on subsequent learning of not receiving an anticipated reward for performance). As there is some similarity between these behaviours and those associated with the hypothalamus, it seems clear that the limbic system in general undertakes the organization of these behaviours and the control of their execution, while the hypothalamus is more concerned with their initiation in response to the current level of motivation.

Because the cortex of the temporal lobe has direct connections with the limbic system, we shall return to discuss certain aspects of this system, particularly those relating to memory and sexual behaviour, in Chapter 4. We shall also meet the limbic system again when we discuss psychosurgery in Chapter 8.

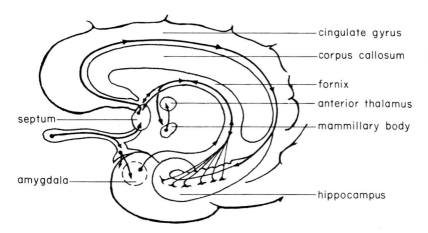

cingulate gyrus
corpus callosum
fornix
anterior thalamus
septum
mammillary body
amygdala
hippocampus

Figure 2.6. Some of the interconnections between structures in the limbic system.

THE TELENCEPHALON – THE CEREBRAL CORTEX

The *cerebral cortex* ('bark' or 'rind'; also called the *neocortex*) forms the surface of the brain. It is spongy and jelly-like, and extremely convoluted or wrinkled. Man is the only animal to have a brain convoluted to this degree, and this is often considered an evolutionary response to the need to pack an ever expanding amount of cortex in a head of given size. If the most intelligent aspects of function are organized in the cortex, and that seems a reasonable supposition (man has more cortex in relation to his body size than any other animal), then to evolve a more intelligent animal, the cortex must grow larger. However, if this were to imply an ever increasing head size, there would be severe biological disadvantages, including signifi-

cant loss of heat through the head, difficulties of balance and motor
control of the head, and vulnerability of the head to damage, either
accidental or aggressive. By screwing up the cortex, it has presumably
been possible to fit a larger cortex into an acceptable size for the
human head.

The appearance of the brain has led to its description as 'grey
matter' (although in reality it has a distinctly yellow tinge) and,
indeed, if the brain is sectioned, both grey and white regions are to be
seen. The grey comes from the cell bodies of the neurones and
indicates that nerve cells have their origins and are making rich
interconnections in these regions. The white comes from the myelin
which covers the bundles of fibres forming tracts passing about the
brain. A section of the brain clearly shows the distribution of grey
matter around the edge forming the cortex, and indicates the subcortical centres which have been described above, leaving the areas in
between to appear as white matter.

The furrows on the surface of the cortex are known as *sulci* (singular: *sulcus*, 'furrow') or fissures, and the islands between as the *gyri*
(singular: *gyrus*, 'coil'). There is surprising regularity in the pattern of
sulci between individuals, (not always apparent on casual inspection)
but only some of the main features of the cortex need be remembered.
Most of the topographical features of the cortex have been named in
Fig. 2.7, and photographs of a real brain have been included in Fig.
2.8 for comparison. The most obvious feature is the horizontal line
named the *lateral* or *Sylvian fissure* or sulcus, and the sulcus which runs
down from the top of the brain to meet it, which is the *central* or
Rolandic fissure or sulcus. These landmarks allow us, more or less
completely, to map out the four *lobes* of the cortex into which it is
conventionally divided: the *frontal, temporal* (behind the temples),
parietal (across the brain) and the *occipital* (to the back of the head)
lobes.

It should not be forgotten that from the diencephalon up, we are in
fact considering pairs of structures (two thalami, two hypothalami,
and so on), and that the telencephalon is formed of two *cerebral
hemispheres* separated by the *longitudinal fissure* and a large partition
extending down from the meninges, the *falx* ('sickle'). The two cerebral hemispheres are only directly connected by a series of cerebral
commissures: the *anterior commissure*, the *corpus callosum* ('hard skinned
body') and the *posterior commissure*. Apart from these commissural
links, the two cerebral hemispheres are quite independent at the
cortical level, an intriguing feature which has implications for brain
organization, as we shall see in later chapters.

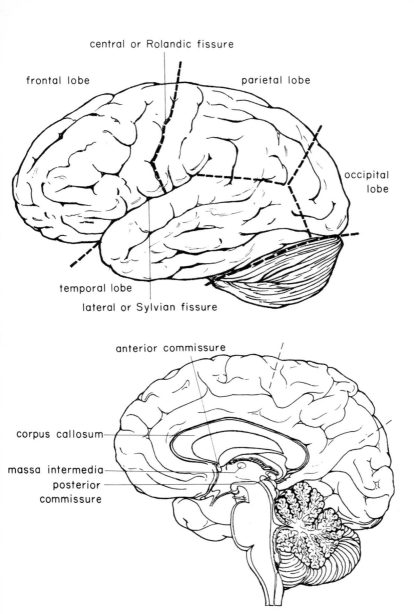

Figure 2.7 a, b The cerebral cortex: (a) left lateral view showing the four lobes and two principal fissures; (b) medial view of the right hemisphere showing the interhemispheric commissures.

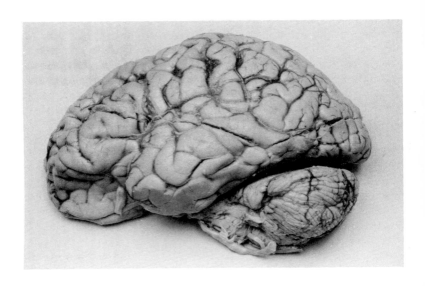

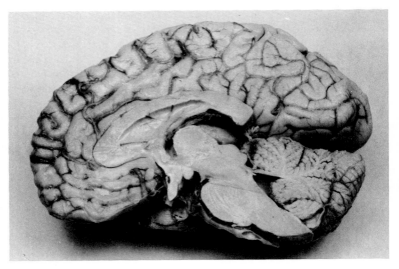

Figure 2.8 a, b Photographs of the normal human brain in the same view as
Fig. 2.7.
(Note: the two straight diagonal cuts are artifacts caused at autopsy.)

The terms introduced so far, together with the general orientational terms, will enable us to refer to areas of the cortex with sufficient precision for elementary neuropsychological analysis. More precise taxonomic systems are currently of little use in human neuropsychology, although some are used, and students must refer to more advanced neuroanatomical texts if these are met in further reading. Perhaps the only system which should be mentioned here is the numbering system for areas based upon Brodmann's cytoarchitectonic maps (where areas are delineated by the cell types they contain). This is thought to provide a surer basis for generalization across species, so that, for example, studies on area 17 (primary visual cortex) can be referred from cats and monkeys to man by reference to the area of cells in roughly the same structural location, but delineated by the presence of appropriate cell types.

The next chapters will examine what conclusions can be made from clinical studies about the function of each of the lobes of the cerebral cortex, and what follows here are some general remarks about the organization of function in the cortex.

The first principle to note is that of *relative localization*. Neuropsychologists hold differing views on the extent of localization, but the majority assume that most functions can be assigned to a region of the cortex, but without precise localization to specific cells. There is certainly no accurate mapping of specific cells taking on specific functions, at least outside the areas in which primary sensory information is received. The degree of localization appears to vary according to how 'high level' a function is, with the higher levels which involve more integration of different types of information and which serve more complex functions appearing to be less localized. This is probably an artifact of the way basic functions are linked together to produce complex behaviour: if we examine the effects in complex behaviour of a system composed of basic, relatively well localized units, the function will not appear to be well localized because aspects of it are distributed throughout the system. The higher the function, the higher the degree of integration and the less localized the system. Nevertheless, most workers still maintain that at the level of basic functional components there is a relative distribution of function within a region of the cortex.

The second principle to note is that of *plasticity*. This doctrine holds primarily that the brain of young children is plastic (less clearly localized), and that the degree of plasticity decreases with increasing age. The corollary of this is that the brain of a young child is functionally resistant to damage, as a greater degree of compensation is possible in the young than in older patients. This is clearly illustrated by the amazing preservation and recovery of abilities in children who undergo hemispherectomy, or the removal of one entire cerebral hemisphere, for some pathological condition, in comparison with the severe and persistant handicap which may follow loss of certain very specific regions of cortex in adults, particularly if the handicap involves language. Whether the degree of plasticity seen in the young reflects true compensation, in which undamaged tissue actually takes over the function previously performed by the absent or damaged tissue, or whether there is radical functional rearrangement and new learning, which may be more easily achieved in the young brain, is a matter of debate. There is some evidence for both processes, although the contribution of functional rearrangement, as opposed to structural compensation, may be the more important.

Lastly, it is helpful to consider the cortex as comprised of three zones: primary, secondary, and tertiary cortex. (This follows the division made popular by Luria, although it does not necessarily imply his scheme of functional interpretation.)

In *primary cortex* are found the primary sensory and motor regions of the cortex, each with a relatively high degree of localization. Here primary visual stimulation is received near the pole of the occipital lobes, auditory stimulation in the superior temporal lobes, and somatosensory information in the sensory strip just posterior to the Rolandic fissure. Stimulation of sites in these areas in the conscious subject results in reports of non-specific but localized stimulation in the appropriate modality. The patient may report a flash of light (to which he may point), or a touch on the arm, or hearing a particular tone. Primary motor cortex, situated in the strip anterior to the Rolandic fissure, is similarly organized, and stimulation of points in this area may elicit discrete body movements. The area of the motor and somatosensory strips dedicated to each body region reflects the relative functional importance of these regions in a most illuminating way (see Fig. 2.9). It should also be noted that the projection of sensory fields up to the cortex, and motor control downwards, is contralateral; that is, the left hemisphere receives sensory information from the right side of the body and sensory space, and controls the right side of the body, with the reverse arrangement for the right hemisphere.

Secondary cortex is formed by regions adjacent to primary cortex, so that there is, for example, secondary visual cortex anterior to primary visual cortex. Stimulation of secondary cortex results in the report of integrated percepts. The patient may describe a vivid visual scene,

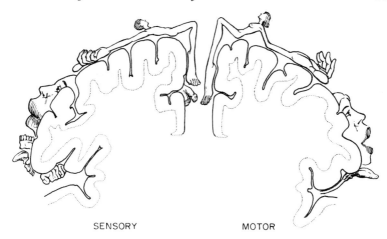

SENSORY   MOTOR

Figure 2.9. The relative representation of different parts of the body over the sensory and motor strips of the cortex as revealed by stimulation studies. (Drawing after N. Geschwind, *Scientific American*, 1979)

may say that his arm has been lightly brushed by velvet, or that he hears part of a popular melody. It is inferred from this that the secondary cortex is important in interpreting the sensations received in primary cortex and turning them into perceptions.

Apart from the specialized regions – those in the left hemisphere of right handed subjects which deal with language functions and which we shall discuss in Chapter 7 – the remaining cortex can be considered as *tertiary* or *association cortex*. We do not have a clear idea of the real function of this cortex, which forms large areas of the cerebrum, but we assume that it performs functions which contribute to intellectual processes at the highest level. Evidence for this is given in the next chapters, but the nature of these processes is still very much a matter for speculation.

The cerebral cortex may contain some of the most difficult puzzles for the neuropsychologist, but it also contains some of the greatest scientific challenges. In that the cortex holds the key to whatever it is that separates man from other animals and gives him intellectual power, insight and foresight, it is the most fascinating of systems to investigate. In the next chapters we shall see how closer examination of the effects of damage to the cortex can give us clearer insights into how the brain is organized, and how it undertakes some of the amazing feats of which it is capable.

CONCLUSION

The brain can be divided into four areas: the brain stem, cerebellum, diencephalon and telencephalon. The brain stem receives the input from the special senses and deals with vital processes and other visceral and somatic functions. The cerebellum plays a major role in the coordination of muscle activity. The diencephalon or subcortical forebrain maintains central control of sensation and movement as well as of appetitive behaviour. Motivation, emotion and the ANS are also served by this region and states of awareness maintained. The telencephalon or cerebral cortex supports high level intelligent behaviour and provides conscious experience. It can be considered as composed of three zones. Primary cortex deals with sensation and the initiation of voluntary motor activity. Secondary cortex produces perception and the integration of sensory and motor behaviour. Tertiary or association cortex serves high level thinking, planning and problem solving. In addition, there are specialised regions of the cortex which deal with language.

FURTHER READING

Almost all general textbooks in physiological psychology carry an extensive introduction to the structure of the CNS. Among those that can be recommended are:

Brown, T. S. and Wallace, P. M., *Physiological Psychology* (New York, Academic Press, 1980).
Carlson, N. R., *Physiology of Behavior* (Boston, Mass., Allyn and Bacon, 1977).

Three more specialized but readable texts:

Garoutte, B., *Survey of Functional Neuroanatomy* (Greenbrae, Calif., Jones Medical Publications, 1981).
Gardner, E., *Fundamentals of Neurology*, fifth edition (Philadelphia, W. B. Saunders, 1975).
Noback, C. R. and Demarest, R. J., *The Nervous System: Introduction and Review* (New York, McGraw-Hill, 1972).

Finally, two superb collections of illustrations, including functional systems:

Netter, F. H., *The CIBA Collection of Medical Illustrations: Vol. 1, Nervous System* (Summit, N.J., CIBA, 1962).
Nieuwenhuys, R., Voogd, J. and Van Huijzen, C., *The Human Central Nervous System: a Synopsis and Atlas* (Berlin, Springer-Verlag, 1978).

II

Clinical Studies

CHAPTER 3

The Frontal Lobes

The frontal lobes of the cerebral cortex are traditionally considered to be the seat of the 'highest' mental functions, and the centre of those activities which make us characteristically human. This is largely because in evolutionary terms the frontal cortex has been the most recent to evolve, and man happens to possess particularly large frontal lobes. However, it may also be that because of the relative difficulty of ascribing a clear set of functions to these areas, they have been attributed with intelligence by default. The large proportion of the cerebral cortex described as frontal lobe, up to about half of the total area of the cortex and an even higher proportion of the association cortex, makes it likely that significant aspects of intellectual activity are performed there, but, as we shall see, it is necessary to be a little more cautious about what functions we can with confidence ascribe to this region, which nonetheless remains one of the most interesting for neuropsychologists.

SOME METHODOLOGICAL ISSUES

Before considering just what aspects of intelligence may be associated with the frontal lobes, some points must be made about the specific problems which arise in carrying out research studies on the effects of focal damage to the cerebral cortex. These problems appear because we have to work with clinical material, which does not arise in a random way, and the points made here therefore apply not only to this chapter, but to all the chapters in this section on clinical studies.

The logic of the research design is to collect cases in which there is an identified lesion of some area, let us say in the frontal lobes, and to compare the performance of these patients with the performance of patients who have lesions in areas outside the frontal lobes. This determines whether the functions being studied are affected only by frontal lesions. However, the essential point is that we have to control in some way for all the factors apart from the site of the damage which could contribute to any deficit observed in performance. These other factors include the type of lesion: what caused it, whether it is developing ('progressive') or stable ('static'), and whether it was recently caused ('acute') or is long-standing ('chronic'). For example, tumours are usually progressive, and may develop slowly or rapidly depending on type, while a gunshot wound can be considered, after the initial period following the injury, to be static. The age of the patient is also important, as is the extent or 'mass' of the lesion and how far it extends below the cortex into subcortical tissue.

The main problem is that lesions of different types tend to occur in different areas, and in patients of different ages. Tumours of certain types grow in particular sorts of tissue, but may be fairly evenly distributed throughout age groups, while missile wounds obviously occur most frequently in young males injured during war. Vascular accidents, in which either the blood supply to some region of the cortex is lost (as in a 'stroke') or some failure results in bleeding into the brain, tend to occur more commonly in older subjects. Studies which compare lesions of frontal with parietal regions without controlling for the type of lesion may then end up by confounding the site of the lesion with its cause.

Even if the study is restricted to a comparison of lesions of one particular type, for example those caused by gunshot wounds, the lesions occurring at less usual sites may be in some way atypical. Wounds from modern high velocity projectiles yield perhaps the best clinical material for the neuropsychologist, for the bullet, if not at close range, tends to punch a very neat hole straight through the head, causing remarkably little disturbance to regions not immediately affected, and producing a clean wound which is self-sterilized and cauterized by the heat generated as the bullet passes through. In such cases, the important issue for survival is whether the bullet passes through important central subcortical centres essential to life or fundamental aspects of behaviour. If the entry and exit points are around the temporal and parietal regions, death is much more likely than if they are in frontal and occipital regions. As a result, more soldiers arrive for neuropsychological assessment with frontal or occipital wounds than with temporal and parietal wounds, and the lesions of those with temporal and parietal injuries who do survive may be less extensive than those of their colleagues and in a variety of ways less serious.

An alternative example is studies which examine differences between the left and right members of a particular pair of lobes. Here the confounded variable may be the mass of the lesion. Someone with a developing tumour in the left or right frontal lobe, will sooner or later notice some of its effects and will probably consult his GP. However, because of the much greater importance of verbal as opposed to spatial abilities in everyday life in our society, the patient is more likely to notice that he cannot remember the contents of the day's paper or an address just given to him, than that he cannot remember some drawing or route to be taken to a particular place. Since the failure in verbal memory usually results from a left lesion and in spatial memory from a right lesion patients typically arrive for surgery with smaller tumours in the left than in the right hemisphere, where they have been allowed to grow for longer. This can naturally confound the results of any study which compares the effects of tumours in the left and right sides of the head, because any differences found may not be due to the lateral site of the tumour but due to the mass of the lesion.

These examples illustrate the considerable difficulty of constructing sound scientific studies when it is necessary to work with incidentally occurring clinical material. The ideal study would involve equal amounts of the same kind of damage occurring in each cortical area, but the data is just not available for such a study. There are additional problems in that it is often assumed that the deficits observed are a reflection of more specific deficits in complex tasks which involve several basic unitary functions in their performance. The factors which contribute to methodological difficulties are summarized in Table 3.1.

It should also be realized that studies of the highest methodological standard are rather uncommon, owing to deficiencies in design and theoretical interpretation, and that many of the findings reported below are subject to difficulties of interpretation which follow from research problems of the type just described.

INTELLIGENCE

From the latter part of the nineteenth century the frontal lobes have been associated with intelligent abilities, but a controversy has raged over the last forty years as to whether these abilities may be associated exclusively with the frontal lobes. It may simply be that the frontal lobes are large, subserve many functions, and are as a result likely to affect 'intelligent' behaviour more than other lobes of the brain.

TABLE 3.1. METHODOLOGICAL DIFFICULTIES IN
INTERPRETING CLINICAL LESION STUDIES

1. Variations in: site
                     lateralization
                     extent
                     cause
                     age of patient
                     stability
                     acuteness.

2. Inferring unitary deficits from performance on complex tasks.

(Many psychologists would in any case say that 'intelligence' is no more than the abilities which determine performance on intelligence tests.) To evaluate the arguments presented in this controversy, it is important to distinguish between quantitative and qualitative changes in intelligence.

In terms of quantitative deficits in intelligence, case reports from the turn of the century reported reduced intelligence following frontal lesions, and these findings were largely confirmed by the first important research studies by Rylander in 1939 and Halstead in 1940. The finding was simply that measured general intelligence was reduced after damage to the frontal lobes. The view was expressed most clearly in Halstead's description of 'biological intelligence' in 1947. He had formulated this concept from the results of a statistical analysis of a battery of tests which had been administered to a large sample of subjects with various focal cortical lesions. Among these tests, and showing the highest 'loading' on biological intelligence, was the Category Test, which is a test of concept formation or categorization in which sets of graphical items are presented, and the patient has to indicate which of the numbers 1 to 4 may be associated with the set from the other three (see Fig. 3.1). Frontal lobe damaged patients do badly on this test.

Figure 3.1. Examples of four items presented in four subtests of the Category Test. In each case the correct response would be to press the button marked '3'.

Although Halstead's theory commanded much support through the 1940s and 1950s, it was criticized by Hebb who, largely on the basis of his studies of the effects of deliberately placed experimental lesions in animals on abilities such as maze-learning, argued that the mass of the lesion was more significant than its location. This view was confirmed in 1959 by Chapman and Wolff, who performed a re-analysis of much of Halstead's data, introducing the factor of lesion size and adding new data of their own, and found that Halstead's findings could be interpreted in terms of the effect of the mass of the lesion.

During the 1950s and 1960s Teuber, with colleagues, carried out an impressive series of studies on the war-injured, which again tended to emphasize that deficits in general intelligence are not exclusively associated with frontal lesions, and that not all frontal lesions produce deficits of this type. The majority of recent studies, particularly those which have been careful in their experimental design, have supported this view, and a good example is the study of Black (1976) on veterans from the war in South-east Asia. Even studies based upon the modern version of Halstead's own battery, developed by Reitan (see Reitan and Davison, 1974, and p. 278), and including such tests as the Category Test, do not support the idea that 'biological intelligence' is a property of the frontal lobes. There is therefore no good evidence to support the association of the degree of intelligence with the frontal lobes. But do frontal lobe injuries affect the quality of form of intellectual performance?

The change in the quality of thinking most commonly linked with the frontal lobes is the loss of *abstract thought*. This change, or the loss of the 'abstract attitude', is linked with the name of Kurt Goldstein, who published his ideas between 1936 and 1959. Goldstein considered there to be two forms of thinking, 'concrete' and 'abstract'. The abstract form was characterized by the ability to assume mental sets, to consider different aspects of a given situation, to dissect and synthesize the elements of some object, and to plan ahead and think symbolically; the concrete 'attitude' was tied to the immediate sensory data which could be derived from the object. He employed a battery of tests, which included various sorting tasks and a block design task in which coloured blocks had to be arranged to match some design presented to the subject (see Fig. 3.6 on p. 57), and claimed to demonstrate that frontal lobe lesions impaired the ability to adopt the abstract attitude, and thereby also caused a decline in conventionally measured intelligence. It should be noted, however, that Goldstein's own work was not based upon the quantitative results of performance in his tests of abstract thinking. He did not, for example, present any quantitative data upon which a discrimination between frontal and more posterior lesions could be based. His arguments rested essentially upon the nature of qualitative changes, despite the fact that they could be argued to provide the explanation for the quantitative changes in intelligence observed by some workers.

The difficulty in assessing Goldstein's views arises from both general theoretical and specific methodological problems. The theoretical problem is with the formulation of abstract thinking and its distinction from concrete forms of thought. For instance, some workers take the copying of a block design in the same colour as a concrete task, and the copying of it in a different colour as an abstract task. Others, in demanding a definition of the proverb 'The sun shines upon all alike', would take 'The sun shines on everybody' as a concrete response, and 'All men are created equal' as an abstract response. The meaning of 'abstractness' is clearly different in these two examples. This is a general problem in psychology and has been discussed in an excellent book by Pikas (1966). There is insufficient space to discuss this topic sensibly here, but few psychologists would currently accept the views implied in Goldstein's theoretical formulations.

The methodological problem arises from the nature of the tests used to assess the abstract attitude. Because the performance of subjects was not observed, recorded, scored and analysed according to the standards which we would now consider appropriate for the administration and interpretation of clinical tests, some doubt is cast upon the data collected by their application. The expectations of the examiner may have played some part in determining the results of Goldstein's tests, and it is known that their formal reliability (that is, the degree to which they yield stable and replicable measures) is unacceptably low. Normative data, by which the test results may be interpreted, is either not available or inadequate. For these reasons, the results of the tests of abstract thinking are not generally acceptable. It is also clear that patients with posterior lesions may also fail on these tests.

In conclusion, it is fair to say that there may be qualitative changes in thinking following frontal lobe lesions but the data and arguments presented by Goldstein are not acceptable evidence for such changes. It seems more profitable to enquire why patients may fail on certain tests, and to look at more specific deficits to provide a better explanation of the general difficulties experienced by frontal lobe patients.

The concept of impairment in abstract thinking is very important historically but does not feature significantly in current neuropsychological explanations.

SPECIFIC FUNCTIONS

If we reject the idea that general aspects of intelligence can be specifically linked to the frontal lobes, then what specific aspects of behaviour are controlled by them? There are, indeed, a variety of behavioural components which are affected by frontal lesions, but lacking any clear theory of the logical relationships among these components, it seems sensible to discuss the frontal lobes by dividing them into four regions, and to treat these separately. It must be emphasized that the division into these four regions, and the association of specific behaviours with each region, is not at all clear-cut, but is a way of making sense of the rather bewildering collection of data.

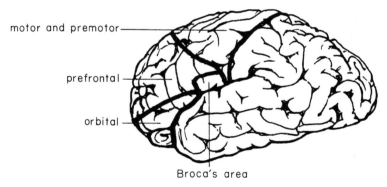

Figure 3.2. The four main divisions of the cortex of the frontal lobe.

The four divisions, which are shown in Figure 3.2, are the motor and premotor cortex, the prefrontal cortex (sometimes referred to as 'frontal granular cortex' because of the type of cells predominant in this area, or as 'dorsolateral cortex'), Broca's area, which we assume to exist in the left frontal lobe only (at least for the right handed – see Chapters 7 and 13), and the orbital cortex. We will examine the effects of lesions of each of these regions in turn.

THE MOTOR AND PREMOTOR CORTEX

When the organization of the cerebral cortex was introduced in Chapter 2, the model of three levels of control was suggested: primary, secondary and tertiary, of decreasing specificity and increasing integration. The frontal lobe control of motor function provides a clear illustration of the model.

The primary region is the *motor cortex*, or 'motor strip', which has already been described. As cells in this region connect directly with spinal motor neurons and motor nuclei in the cranial nerves, focal lesions of a specific area will lead to a loss of voluntary control over the precise area of the body which is 'mapped' on to that area of the motor cortex. The general arrangement of this mapping was illustrated in Fig. 2.9. Although there is variation between individuals, the mapping is sufficiently precise for it to have been seriously proposed that a prosthesis for spinal injuries might operate by picking up the signals which originate in the motor cortex and relaying them by wiring, past the damage in the spine, directly to the point at which they should be fed into the peripheral nervous system and on to the muscles. Damage to the motor cortex results in chronic deficits in fine motor control, which may be seen most clearly in movements of the hands, fingers and face, and in a reduction in the speed and strength of limb movements.

Adjacent and anterior to the motor cortex, the premotor cortex forms the *secondary level of motor control*. Cells in this region contribute to motor control by forming connections in various subcortical centres, particularly in the basal ganglia, and there seem to be distinct systems for limb movements and for whole body movements. Because the control is exerted by influencing the operation of these lower centres, the effects of lesions of this region are less specific and more subtle, for the basic aspects of control are still being carried out by centres in the basal ganglia, the thalamus and elsewhere. In particular, lesions of the premotor cortex (with some contribution from parietal cortex) seem to impair the way in which separate movements of the limbs, the hands, and gross body movements are integrated into fluid sequences of action.

Among the signs of lesions of this region, apart from the specific effects on particular limb movements, are some changes of a reflex kind. In *gegenhalten*, which literally means 'counter-pull', there is an involuntary resistance to movement, so that if the forearm, held in a certain position quite loosely, is moved by the examiner, a marked resistance preventing movement of the limb may develop unintentionally. Similarly, there may be an involuntary grasp of a hand or object placed in the patient's hand, despite conscious attempts not to take hold of the object in this way. There may also be changes in gait (rather similar to those seen with damage to the cerebellum), so that the patient shows '*marche à petit pas*', walking rather clumsily in little rapid steps.

The tertiary level of motor control is in the next region of the frontal lobes, which is discussed below, but there are some specific functions associated with the three levels of the motor cortex which should be mentioned here. These concern control of the face, and the data come from the study of patients who have had the motor and sensory cortex for the *face region* on one side of the head surgically removed (Taylor, 1979). These patients do not in fact suffer a lasting problem in controlling the face, or in receiving and interpreting sensation from it, largely because the motor and sensory connections to the head (via the cranial nerves) are bilateral, and are not contralaterally organized as in the rest of the body (via the spine). On recovery, the patient's face is normally expressive, and facial movements can be imitated on command. There are some expressive speech difficulties immediately following operation, but, apart from some slight residual difficulty, this clears within the first year after surgery. The patients, rather surprisingly, nevertheless show marked difficulties with verbal fluency, phonetic discrimination, spelling (especially after a left-sided operation) and design fluency (after right-sided operation).

The verbal fluency deficit is seen when the patient is asked to give a series of words beginning with a particular letter within a given time limit, usually five minutes. (This deficit is also seen with prefrontal lesions, but is reported to be less severe.) Design fluency is tested similarly, except that here the patient is asked to make as many non-representational drawings as possible within a five minute period. While normal subjects may write down 60 to 100 words beginning with, say, 'S' in five minutes, patients with a verbal fluency deficit may only manage 10 to 30. They also cannot identify, with normal accuracy, phonemes (the building blocks of spoken language, roughly equivalent to syllables) which have been embedded in nonsense words, and there is an associated impairment in spelling. These difficulties occur in the absence of any other significant problems with the expression or understanding of language, and it is presumed that there is some essential connection with the motor control of the face, although the real origin of these deficits still remains something of a mystery.

THE PREFRONTAL CORTEX

A number of rather different functions are associated with the prefrontal cortex, and this is not surprising in view of its extensive area. Prominent among these functions are several linked with motor control, and which form the tertiary level of the motor control system.

The *tertiary level of motor control* exerts its influence by operating upon all lower levels of the motor system, both in the cortex and at subcortical levels. The control is therefore not of specific components of movement, but rather of the planning and programming of motor acts and their flexible adaptation to particular circumstances. Monitoring of movement patterns ensures that behaviour is appropriate and adaptive, and lesions of the prefrontal cortex therefore result in motor behaviour becoming inflexible and stereotyped.

An example of this inflexibility can be seen in the Wisconsin Card Sorting Test (Drewe, 1974; and, in a modified form, Nelson, 1976). A set of four cards are placed before the patient, as shown at the top of Fig. 3.3. The cards contain one, two, three or four shapes, each in one of four forms and in one of four colours. The patient is then asked to sort cards containing similar stimuli into piles below the initial set, but without being told the rule for sorting. The cards might thus be sorted according to the number of shapes, the type of form, or the colour. The examiner tells the patient whether he is correct after each card is sorted, so that the patient has to discover the correct rule by

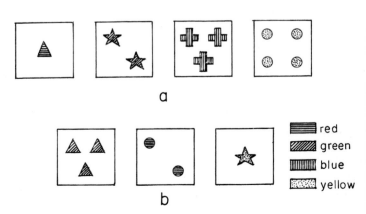

Figure 3.3. Wisconsin Card Sorting Test: (a) the four cards under which the test cards must be sorted and (b) examples of the test cards.

which to sort the cards. Normal subjects, and also patients with frontal injuries, are able to discover this initial rule. However, after the sorting rule has been learned, the examiner changes the rule without warning the patient. This initially causes puzzlement and frustration in most subjects, but normal subjects and patients with other than frontal lesions rapidly realize what has happened and search out the new rule, they readily adapt to subsequent changes of rule. However, frontal lobe patients are extremely slow to adapt to the new rule, and many do not manage it at all. They simply continue sorting according to the first rule, getting responses correct only by chance. This behaviour, continuing with a response once it is no longer appropriate, is known as *perseveration*. The general problem seems to be one of impaired response inhibition, that is, once certain responses have been brought to the fore they cannot be replaced by more appropriate responses. A similar example of perseveration is seen in the patient who, asked to subtract 7 serially from 100, responds with '93 . . 86 . . 76 . . 66 . . 56 . .' instead of '93 . . 86 . . 79 . . 72 . .'.

A final example may be shown with the Stroop phenomenon. Here, subjects are asked to follow a list of words which are the names of colours but which are printed in ink of different colours, and to name the colour of the ink. Normal subjects take longer to go down such a list than a list of comparable words which are not colour names because the colour names interfere with naming the ink colours. The interference is quite extreme in some frontal lobe patients, who find it impossible to inhibit reading the colour names (Perret, 1974). The failure to inhibit associated but incorrect responses may also be seen in the responses to vocabulary tests, where the patient's response is confused with that appropriate to a similar sounding word (Walsh, 1978).

Another aspect of motor control in prefrontal cortex is the *programming and planning* of sequences of behaviour. At the level of programming simple sequences, it is best demonstrated by the work of Kolb and Milner (1979). They asked patients to imitate certain facial gestures (see Fig. 3.4), and found that patients with prefrontal lesions were not impaired when imitating single gestures, but when asked to copy a series of three gestures, they showed significant impairment. A similar difficulty with planning is sometimes shown by patients who perform badly on paper and pencil mazes, such as the Porteus mazes (see Fig. 3.5), because they are not able to build up a sequence of moves which will get them to the goal.

Patients with difficulties of this kind may also have difficulties with

Figure. 3.4. Examples of the stimuli used by Kolb, showing gestures to be copied by the patients.

problem solving of a more general kind, including visuo-constructive problems. When asked to perform the Block Design task mentioned above, these patients may fail. Part of the difficulty may lie in the way in which the design to be reproduced is presented, for it does not clearly show how individual blocks will form parts of the design (see Fig. 3.6). If this information is given to the patient he may be able to perform normally (Barbizet, 1970). The patient's difficulty again seems to be in building up a plan of component moves to attain a complex goal. In a similar way, patients may be unable to reproduce a complex non-figurative drawing unless they are specifically taught to

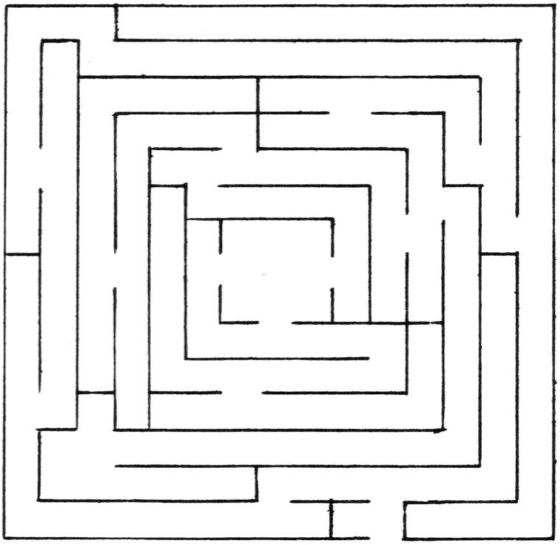

Figure 3.5. A maze similar to the Porteus Mazes at the adult level of difficulty.

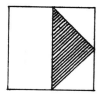

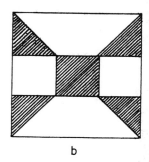

a   b

Figure 3.6. The type of pattern to be constructed in a Block Design task (a) using four blocks (b) using nine blocks.

build it up in a series of discrete steps (Lhermitte, Derouesné and Signoret, 1972). While patients with prefrontal lesions do not show difficulty with arithmetical computations (compare the effects of parietal lesions, p. 101), they may have difficulty with arithmetical problems, especially if these are couched in the form of sentences, such as 'There were 18 books on two shelves, and there were twice as many books on one as on the other. How many books were on each shelf?' The patient seems unable to abstract the elements of the problem, and then to arrange these into a plan for its solution (Christensen, 1975).

A final, and specialized, aspect of motor control is that of *voluntary eye movements*. Prefrontal cortex contains an area known as the *frontal eye fields* in which eye movements related to scanning of the environment and the inspection of visual objects are controlled. This can be illustrated by comparing the recordings of eye movements of patients with damage to this area with those of normal subjects when shown a complex picture (see Fig. 3.7). Normal subjects rapidly detect the picture's most significant and informative elements and follow a series of glance paths between these elements when asked to extract meaning from it. In marked contrast, those with frontal injuries show a disorganized series of movements which lack the adaptive articulation of normal subjects (Yarbus, 1967). This difficulty may underlie a number of more general problem solving deficits in frontal lobe patients, as well as the poor performance in visual search tasks (locating a target item in a larger array of similar items) which is sometimes apparent. Alternatively, all these difficulties, including the eye movement problem, may be manifestations of a basic deficit in generating and operating strategies for collecting and processing information needed for intellectual tasks.

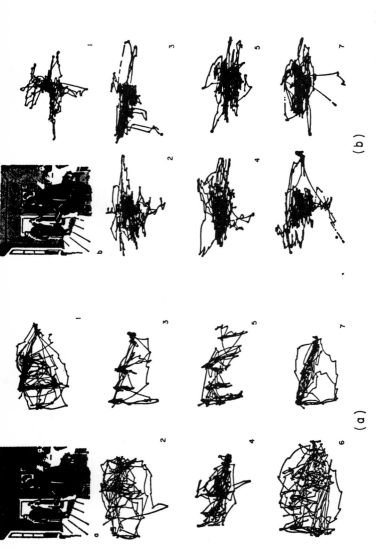

Figure 3.7. Eye movement patterns of (a) a normal subject and (b) a patient with massive frontal lobe lesion while examining the picture shown top left: free observation (1); after the questions, 'Is the family rich or poor?' (2); 'How old are the people in the picture?' (3); 'What were they doing before the man entered the room?' (4); 'Can you recall how the people were dressed?' (5); 'How were the people and furniture placed in the room?' (6); 'How long had the man been away from his family?' (7).

(Reproduced from A. R. Luria, *The Working Brain*, Penguin, 1973.)

The motor difficulties of damaged frontal lobe patients may also show in reduced spontaneous behaviour, and they may therefore be referred to as *pseudo-depressed*. Such patients sit around, have almost nothing to say, engage in little activity, and typically present a flat emotionless expression. The deficit in verbal fluency (by which patients with frontal lesions are unable to generate a normal number of different words beginning with a given letter in a set period of time) is considered to be associated with the overall reduction in response emission (Milner, 1964). Some writers, notably Luria (Luria, Pribram and Homskaya, 1964), have considered this and other frontal lobe motor deficits to be due to a failure in the verbal regulation of behaviour.

The idea which underlies this concept of *verbal regulation* is that we use covert language to control complex motor activity. For example, you may be aware when learning some new motor skill, say driving a car, of 'talking to yourself' to help sort out what to do, but with practice the skill becomes more automatic and the internal commentary is no longer necessary. It has certainly been shown by Luria that children can be helped to perform such tasks as a go/no-go problem (squeeze the bulb if the green light comes on, but do not squeeze if the red light comes on) at a younger age than would normally be possible if they are taught to use explicit verbal mediation (saying 'press' or 'don't press' to the green or red light). The idea is that as a skill becomes practised, the verbal mediation becomes covert and internalized, and the difficulties which frontal lobe patients have in motor control can thus be explained in terms of a deficit in the verbal regulation of behaviour. While this hypothesis is widely quoted, Drewe (1975) has tested frontal lobe patients with go – no-go learning tasks and failed to find clear support for it.

Some *perceptual deficits* are also associated with prefrontal cortex, one of which is perhaps unexpected and concerns making judgements about egocentric space. Semmes showed patients diagrams of the human figure from in front and behind with numbers indicating parts of the body: the palm of the left hand, the back of the right calf, and so on. The patient was given a number and asked to point to the appropriate part on his own body. Frontal patients did poorly on this task in comparison with patients with other lesions (Semmes, Weinstein, Ghent and Teuber, 1963). (If you think this is an easy task, try standing in front of a mirror with a child, and asking him to point to various parts of the body while looking in the mirror.)

Associated with this deficit is impaired performance in the Aubert task. In this task the patient is seated in a dark room in a chair which can be tilted to the left or right. In front he sees a luminous rod which he must try to set to the vertical. Normal subjects show an effect of head and body tilt, so that the rod is misaligned away from the horizontal in the opposite direction to that of the subject's tilt. Greater tilt produces greater error. The effect is much more pronounced in those with frontal lesions (Teuber and Mishkin, 1954). Teuber (1964) has proposed that both of these perceptual deficits may be explained by impaired *corollary discharge*. Here, the idea is that when movements are executed, information is sent out to other parts of the system so that the effects of the movement can be anticipated and accounted for. The obvious example is that when you move your eyes the world does not appear to move but remains apparently stable. If your eyes are passively moved (try gently pushing your half-open eye with a finger on the eyelid) then the world does apparently move about. When you make active eye movements, the systems interpreting information from the eye are forewarned and make all the necessary adjustments, but these cannot be made when unexpected passive movements are imposed upon the eye. A gymnast performing on parallel bars would come dramatically unstuck if the world did not appear to remain stable as the body moved through the exercises. The perceptual world is in fact whirling about, but knowledge of the muscle movements being made allows all the necessary compensation to be introduced.

In the Aubert task, it is assumed that damaged frontal lobe patients fail to generate appropriate corollary discharges for the compensation in muscular tonus which occurs during tilt, leading to a faulty perception of where the vertical should be. By extension, this can be applied to the judgement of egocentric space. The patient fails to keep proper track of where his body is in space, and cannot accurately relate the external world to his own body.

One specific aspect of *memory* which is affected by prefrontal lesions is that of recency. In other words, if a patient is shown a series of items one at a time, and then shown two items, he may be able to recognize them correctly as having been in the list, but may not be able to report correctly which of the items was presented more recently (Milner, 1971). This seems to be the only pure memory function to be affected by frontal lesions, although various aspects of learning may be affected in a secondary way by other frontal lobe deficits.

BROCA'S AREA

The third region of the frontal lobes is Broca's area, which is sited in the left frontal lobe and has the primary function of expressive speech. This, however, will be discussed with other elements of the language system in Chapter 7.

THE ORBITAL CORTEX

The final region of the frontal lobes subserves aspects of *personality* and *social behaviour*. The classic example of the effects of lesions of this area is that of Phineas Gage, a construction worker on the American railroads who in 1848 suffered an accident in which an iron bar, over 3½ feet long and 1¼ inches thick, was blown through the front of his head, entering at the lower cheek and exiting from the upper forehead (see Fig. 3.8). Gage survived, but underwent a marked change in personality. From being a capable foreman and efficient worker (Harlow, who attended Gage and reported the case, says he was

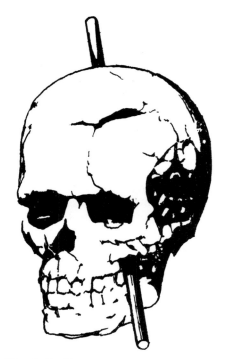

Figure 3.8. The skull of Phineas Gage, after a contemporary drawing.

'energetic and persistent in executing all his plans of operation'), he became impulsive, wilful, inconsiderate and obstinate. He took to swearing, which had not previously been his habit, and constantly changed his mind. Indeed, he was so dramatically altered that his 'friends and acquaintances said that he was no longer Gage'.

Although this type of personality change generally only follows large, and usually bilateral, frontal injuries (not uncommon as the result of road traffic accidents), it can quite often be seen. The changes may also be accompanied by what can only be described as silliness, and patients may constantly sing, whistle, and repeat rather poor jokes. In fact there is a term for this puerile kind of jocularity: *Witzelsucht*. An additional symptom may be a lack of social graces: these patients engage quite freely in belching, picking their noses, and even less savoury proscribed social activities in public, without any apparent concern. A similar effect can sometimes be seen in the maze performance of frontal lobe patients. They may simply go through the walls of the maze, failing to pay attention to the rules governing performance. Alternatively, asked to learn a maze pathway in which the correct path is not apparent (the stylus maze, Milner, 1965) but in which feedback is given at each point, the patients do badly because they fail to obey the rules or make appropriate use of the feedback information given to them. An alternative pattern of response may be that of indifference, lack of initiative and general loss of drive, part of the pseudo-depression already noted. These patients say very little and exhibit almost no emotional expression.

Finally there may be associated changes in *sexual behaviour*. These may be in terms of a loss of social inhibitions, resulting in exhibitionism and public masturbation, although the amount of sexual activity is not increased. However, they are more often in terms of a loss of libido (which may also be associated with prefrontal lesions). These patients do not lose the capacity for sexual activity but lose interest in it.

Orbital lesions may therefore result in personality and social behaviour changes which may loosely be characterized by impulsiveness, facetiousness and mild euphoria; by diminished anxiety and concern for the future; and by lack of initiative and spontaneity. It was these observations which led to this area being the site for the operation of prefrontal leucotomy, which will be discussed in Chapter 8.

LATERALIZATION IN THE FRONTAL LOBE

A theme that runs through almost all of this book is that of cerebral lateralization. It has been clear throughout the history of neuropsychology that there are differences between the functional specializations of the two hemispheres. In terms of clinical evidence, this means that some deficits are more frequently associated with right sided lesions and some with left, and some deficits only appear with bilateral lesions (in both hemispheres). It should be emphasized that this is rarely a firm distinction, but is one of *relative specialization*. The evidence relating to frontal lobe injuries makes this clear.

Benton (1968) constructed a study in which he gave six tests to a group of patients wih either left, right or bilateral frontal lobe damage. Two of the tests (Verbal Fluency and Verbal Learning) were expected to be associated with left sided lesions, and indeed in both tests the patients with left lesions more frequently showed a deficit than those with right lesions. Those with bilateral lesions had difficulty as frequently as those with left lesions for Verbal Fluency, and more often for Verbal Learning. The 'right hemisphere tasks' (Block Design and Design Copying) also produced the expected results: those with right lesions or bilateral lesions had a deficit more commonly than those with left lesions. Lastly, the final two tests (Time Orientation – to see if the patient knows the time, day and date and can locate himself in time – and the Gorham Proverbs Test, in which the patient must explain the meaning of some well known proverbs) showed that impaired performance was associated much more frequently with bilateral lesions than with unilateral lesions of either side.

These hemisphere specializations can loosely be divided into verbal and symbolic (left hemisphere) versus visuo-spatial (right hemisphere), although we shall question the validity of this distinction in Section III. In fact, evidence against such a simple dichotomy is already apparent in that failure in the Proverbs task only occurs commonly with bilateral lesions. Also, the test of identification of body parts in egocentric space which has already been mentioned is associated with lesions of the left frontal lobe, and not the right, as might have been expected. This information on lateralization is important, not only because it helps in locating lesions in patients under examination, but also for the construction of neuropsychological models of the organization of the brain.

Clinical Studies

CONCLUSION

Some of the most important specific functions associated with the frontal lobes have been discussed, and are summarized in Table 3.2.

TABLE 3.2. SOME SPECIFIC FUNCTIONS ASSOCIATED WITH REGIONS OF THE FRONTAL LOBE

Motor and premotor cortex:
    Primary and secondary levels of motor control
    Verbal fluency and design fluency
    Spelling

Prefrontal:
    Tertiary level of motor control
    Adaptability of response pattern
    Programming and planning of sequences of behaviour
    Level of response emission
    Verbal regulation
    Problem solving
    Voluntary eye movements
    Perceptual judgement
    Memory (recency)

Broca's area:
    Expressive speech

Orbital cortex:
    Personality
    Social behaviour

Although we have no space to deal with it here, there is very considerable research literature on the effects of frontal lobe lesions in animals. The evidence which this provides is extensive and complex, but given the difficulties of generalizing results even from apes to man, then the results are remarkably similar. Some deficits found in higher animals do not have clear parallels in man, but there are few fundamental disagreements. (See Further Reading for the various reviews that are available.) With reference to the suggestion that the frontal lobes are in some way special in man, neither the evidence from animal studies (when compared with human clinical data) nor that from brain damaged patients would support this conclusion. We may still regard the frontal lobes as undertaking some of the highest intellectual tasks in man, but there is no essential discontinuity between these abilities in man and those in the higher animals.

Is it possible to conceive of general neuropsychological systems which might account for the deficits found in the frontal lobes? The answer at present is 'no', which should hardly surprise us in view of the extent of frontal cortical tissue. Teuber's corollary discharge theory holds some, but not complete, explanatory power. Luria (1973) has suggested that the three special functions of the frontal lobes are: the regulation of activation processes; the execution of verbally programmed behaviour processes; and problem solving behaviour. This explanation is also incomplete, and cannot be supported in all its details by scientific evidence. A general theory that the frontal lobes operate by undertaking the temporal structuring of behaviour (Fuster, 1980) is no more satisfactory. The frontal lobes are involved in many such functions, but among a variety of other functions. We are not yet at the stage where neuropsychological systems can be so explicitly summarized. Nor are many neuropsychologists sure whether they are seeking a single theory of frontal lobe function, or whether the ideal model would relate general functions to more circumscribed areas within the frontal lobes.

We can conclude that the frontal lobes play a major role in the higher levels of motor control and in the planning and controlled execution of motor acts and skills. They contribute also to general problem solving behaviour, and the regulation of eye movements is an important aspect of this performance. Associated with these functions, in prefrontal cortex, are some specific verbal abilities, some perceptual functions, and some limited aspects of memory. Lesions, especially in the orbital cortex, may lead to changes in personality and social behaviour.

At about the turn of the century, Hughlings Jackson described the frontal lobes as the 'least organized' area of the cortex. It has always also been the least understood, and remains the most challenging to neuropsychologists.

FURTHER READING

First, there are some general texts which apply to all the chapters in Section III. The most general and systematic books approach the subject by anatomical region:

Kolb, B. and Whishaw, I. Q., *Fundamentals of Human Neuropsychology* (San Francisco, W. H. Freeman, 1980).

Walsh, K. W., *Neuropsychology: a Clinical Approach* (Edinburgh, Churchill Livingstone, 1978).

Alternatively, some books approach the subjects by functional topics. These are probably more useful as reference sources for students:

Dimond, S. J., *Neuropsychology* (London, Butterworth, 1980).
Hécaen, H. and Albert, M. L., *Human Neuropsychology* (New York, Wiley, 1978).
Heilman, K. M. and Valenstein, E., eds., *Clinical Neuropsychology* (New York, Oxford University Press, 1979).

And finally a text which covers all the tests used by clinical neuro-psychologists:

Lezak, M. D., *Neuropsychological Assessment* (New York, Oxford University Press, 1976).

With specific reference to the frontal lobes, see:

Damásio, A., 'The Frontal Lobes', in Heilman & Valenstein (op. cit.); for a good review of the anatomy of the frontal lobes.
Hécaen, H. and Albert, M. L., (op. cit.), Chapter 8; for a useful brief review of the research on animals.
Jouandet, M. and Gazzaniga, M. S., 'The Frontal Lobes', in M. S. Gazzaniga, ed., *Handbook of Behavioral Neurobiology: vol. 2, Neuropsychology* (New York, Plenum Press, 1979); for a stimulating theoretical discussion of animal and human research.

REFERENCES

Barbizet, J., *Human Memory and its Pathology* (San Francisco, W. H. Freeman, 1970).
Benton, A. L., 'Differential Effects of Frontal Lobe Disease', *Neuropsychologia*, 6 (1968), 53–60.
Black, F. W., 'Cognitive Deficits in Patients with Unilateral War-related Frontal Lobe Lesions', *Journal of Clinical Psychology*, 32 (1976), 366–372.
Christensen, A. L., *Luria's Neuropsychological Investigation* (Copenhagen, Munksgaard, 1975).
Drewe, E. A., 'The Effect of Type and Area of Lesion on Wisconsin Card Sorting Test Performance', *Cortex,* 10 (1974), 159–170.
Drewe, E. A., 'An Experimental Investigation of Luria's Theory on the Effects of Frontal Lobe Lesions in Man' *Neuropsychologia*, 13 (1975), 421–430.
Fuster, J. M., *The Prefrontal Cortex* (New York, Raven Press, 1980).
Kolb, B. and Milner, B., cited in B. Kolb and I. Q. Wishaw, eds., *Fundamentals of Human Neuropsychology* (San Francisco, W. H. Freeman, 1980).
Lhermitte, F., Derouesné, J. and Signoret, J. L., 'Analyse Neuropsychologi-que du Syndrome Frontal', *Revue Neurologique,* 127 (1972), 415–440.

Luria, A. R., *The Working Brain* (London, Penguin, 1973).

Luria, A. R., Pribram, K. H. and Homskaya, E. D., 'An Experimental Analysis of the Behavioural Disturbance Produced by a Left Frontal Arachnoidal Endothelioma (meningioma)', *Neuropsychologia.* 2 (1964), 257–280.

Milner, B., 'Some Effects of Frontal Lobectomy in Man', in J. M. Warren and K. Akert, eds., *The Frontal Granular Cortex and Behaviour* (New York, McGraw-Hill, 1964).

Milner, B., 'Visually-guided Maze Learning in Man: Effects of Bilateral Hippocampal, Bilateral Frontal, and Unilateral Cerebral Lesions', *Neuropsychologia*, 3 (1965), 317–338.

Milner, B. 'Interhemispheric Difference in the Localization of Psychological Processes in Man', *British Medical Bulletin*, 27 (1971), 272–277.

Nelson, H. E., 'A Modified Card Sorting Test Sensitive to Frontal Lobe Deficits'. *Cortex*, 12 (1976), 313–324.

Perret, E., 'The Left Frontal Lobe of Man and the Suppression of Habitual Responses in Verbal Categorical Behaviour', *Neuropsychologia*, 12 (1974), 323–330.

Pikas, A., *Abstraction and Concept Formation* (Cambridge, Mass., Harvard University Press, 1966).

Reitan, R. M. and Davison, L. A., *Clinical Neuropsychology* (New York, Wiley, 1974).

Semmes, J., Weinstein, S., Ghent, L. and Teuber, H-L., 'Impaired Orientation in Personal and Extrapersonal Space', *Brain*, 86 (1963), 747–772.

Taylor, L., 'Psychological Assessment of Neurological Patients', in T. Rasmussen and R. Marino, eds., *Functional Neurosurgery* (New York, Raven Press, 1979).

Teuber, H-L., (1964). 'The Riddle of Frontal Lobe Function in Man', in J. M. Warren and K. Akert, eds., *The Frontal Granular Cortex and Behaviour* (New York, McGraw-Hill, 1964).

Teuber, H-L. and Mishkin, M., 'Judgment of Visual and Postural Vertical after Brain Injury', *Journal of Psychology*, 38 (1954), 161–175.

Walsh, K. W., *Neuropsychology: a Clinical Approach* (Edinburgh, Churchill-Livingstone, 1978).

Yarbus, A. L., *Eye Movements and Vision* (New York, Plenum Press, 1967).

CHAPTER 4

The Temporal Lobes

The temporal lobes are rather better understood than the frontal lobes, although there are mysteries yet to be unravelled. However, it is clear that the temporal lobes play the major role in dealing with all aspects of auditory perception, with certain higher aspects of visual perception, and in the receptive aspects of language. In addition, they are of central importance, and contribute to affective, emotional and personal experience.

The temporal lobes on each side of the brain are easily identified, and each forms a separate, forward pointing protrusion rather like the folded wing of a bird. If the anterior pole of the temporal lobe is gently drawn away from the rest of the brain, then it is possible to see the cortex running right round the inner (*mesial*) surface of the lobe, and also an underlying cortical surface facing it which is part of the *insula*. The location of this inner surface of the temporal lobe is shown in Fig. 4.1(b).

The lateral surface of the lobe, the part which is normally visible, is usually divided into three horizontal strips, separated by two clearly visible fissures (see Fig. 4.1(a)). These strips are termed the *superior, middle* and *inferior temporal gyri*. If we were to continue the sequence of strips underneath the temporal lobe and up the mesial surface behind, we should next encounter the *fusiform* and *parahippocampal gyri*, and at the superior border, the *uncus*. These mesial areas of the temporal lobe have intimate connections with the limbic system (hence 'parahippocampal' – close to the hippocampus), and because they belong to an older evolutionary system, they are sometimes referred to as *palaeocortex*. The only other terminology which needs to be noted is that for the region within the superior temporal gyrus, at its superior and posterior end, and folding over into the lateral fissure, which is known as *Heschl's gyrus*.

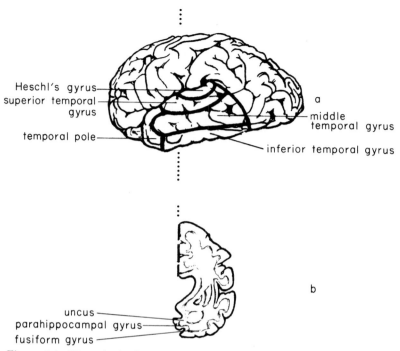

Heschl's gyrus
superior temporal gyrus
temporal pole
a
middle temporal gyrus
inferior temporal gyrus
b
uncus
parahippocampal gyrus
fusiform gyrus

Figure 4.1. The principal areas of the cortex of the temporal lobe; (a) lateral view; (b) coronal section of the left temporal lobe showing medial divisions.

AUDITION

Just as the frontal lobes include three levels of cortical organization for motor control, the temporal cortex includes three levels for audition.

The *primary auditory cortex*, which deals with the initial sensory reception of auditory stimulation, is located in the region of Heschl's gyrus extending into the insula. The projection of the auditory pathways up from the auditory nerve (the cranial nerve connected to the ear) contains both crossed and uncrossed pathways (see Fig. 4.2), that is, stimulation received at one ear is conveyed to the auditory cortex of both temporal lobes. Within this system, however, the crossed (contralateral) pathway is dominant. It is both anatomically thicker and preferred if competing information is being fed into the system from the left and right ears. The use of competing stimulation to study the organization of the brain is known as *dichotic listening*, which will be discussed at some length in Chapter 11. The evidence from such studies, with both clinical patients and normal subjects, points to the greater importance of the crossed pathway, although in normal hearing both pathways are almost certainly being used.

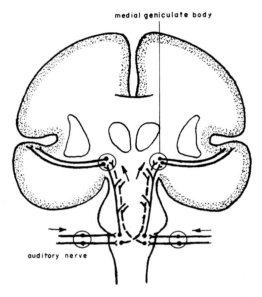

Figure 4.2. The auditory pathways to the temporal cortex.

Because of the bilateral projection of auditory sensation, lesions in one of the pathways do not result in deafness (except in some specialized cases of brain stem lesions) because one of the pathways may carry information from both ears by one crossed and one uncrossed pathway. Damage to primary auditory cortex does, however, result in change in auditory detection thresholds in the contralateral ear, again illustrating the primacy of the crossed pathway. The evidence from lesion studies suggests that auditory sensation is represented in primary cortex according to the pitch of the sound, and to some extent according to the sound's location and the harmonics present.

This conclusion about the elements of auditory sensation is supported by the evidence from *stimulation* studies. Because the brain contains no sensory receptors, once the skull has been opened for surgery under general anaesthesia, it is possible to maintain the patient under local anaesthetic, conscious, alert and able to report the experiences which follow mild electrical stimulation of the cortex (see Fig. 4.3). This enables the surgeon to gain some direct evidence of cortical localization, assisting his decisions about the likely effects of removing a given area of tissue. The name most associated with this procedure is Penfield (see his 1975 review), and the mapping of the primary motor and somatosensory cortex (shown in Fig. 2.9) was established by this method. If the primary auditory cortex is stimulated in this way, then the patient reports hearing tones of a certain pitch, perhaps seeming to come from a particular direction, and associated with certain harmonics.

The *secondary auditory cortex* is principally located in the superior temporal gyrus, including the part known as Heschl's gyrus. Stimulation studies of this region produce reports of fully formed auditory

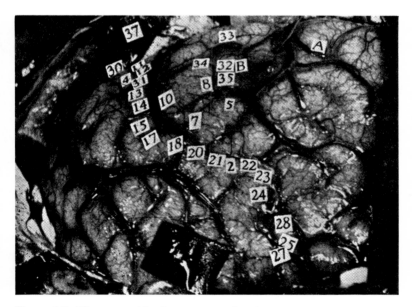

Figure 4.3. The exposed brain at surgery, showing the points where stimulation elicited a response. The line of tickets from 27 up to 11 follows the right Rolandic fissure from just above its junction with the lateral fissure. A tumour lies between points A and B.

(Reproduced from *The Cerebral Cortex of Man* by Wilder Penfield and Theodore Rasmussen, copyright 1950 by Macmillan Publishing Co., Inc., renewed 1978 by Theodore Rasmussen)

percepts, that is, patients report sound that are meaningful to them. They may hear a very specific sound, such as part of a song, or an identifiable voice, which is associated with the memory of a specific auditory event, or they may hear more general sounds, such as a tap running, but which nevertheless carry meaning for them.

At this level we find evidence for laterality in auditory processing. Lesions of the left temporal lobe, especially if towards the posterior part, may be associated with deficits in phonemic hearing, so that the patient may have difficulty in discriminating between similar phonemes such as 'ba' and 'pa', or 'da' and 'ta'. This difficulty is often associated with other language problems. Lesions of the left temporal lobe are, for example, also associated with changes in the report of dichotic digits (digits simultaneously presented to both ears). The patient's ability to report digits presented in this way, may be affected although he may be able to report other dichotic stimuli. If in addition primary auditory cortex is affected, then these changes may be in the order of report of the digits, indicating changes in normal superiority of the crossed pathways (see Chapter 11, and Berlin, 1977; Oscar-Berman, Zurif and Blumstein, 1975).

The right temporal lobe has, by contrast, been clearly associated with musical perception. The classic tests for musical abilities are the Seashore Tests, which involve presenting varying musical stimuli from gramophone recordings for matching or identification. Two of these tests show clear deficits resulting from right, but not left, lesions: the tests of tonal memory and timbre (which involves the perception of harmonics) (Milner, 1962). This handicap may extend to difficulty with the location of sources of sound in space. These data clearly indicate that lateral specialization is a feature of cerebral organization at this level of auditory analysis.

It is a little difficult to separate the secondary and tertiary auditory cortices since *tertiary auditory cortex* is also situated around the superior temporal gyrus, but it is more anterior, and extends into the middle division of the temporal lobe. The deficits which follow lesions to this region are known as the *auditory agnosias* – 'agnosia' means loss of knowledge – and such loss may affect a single modality, so that a bell might be recognized by sight or touch but not by its sound, or may affect several modalities together. It is generally, but not universally, accepted that this term should be reserved for non-speech sounds and not applied to difficulties in the perception of speech stimuli, although both deficits are associated with these regions of the temporal lobe. (Speech sounds will be discussed with language functions in Chapter 7.)

Auditory (or 'acoustic') agnosia may be evident in the inability to interpret the meaning of non-speech sounds, so that the patient can neither name the sound, nor signify anything meaningful about it. He cannot, for example, name the sound of running water or indicate that it might imply drinking or washing or swimming. The agnosia may alternatively be evident in lack of musical abilities, producing *amusia*, so that the patient is tone or melody 'deaf', or unable to recognize or discriminate particular rhythms, tempos or musical measures (Critchley and Henson, 1977). There is again evidence of lateralization from studies by Vignolo (1969). He showed that there was a dissociation between performance on a Meaningful Sounds Identification Test, impaired by left temporal lesions, and a Meaningless Sounds Discrimination Test, impaired by right temporal lobe lesions. On the basis of an analysis of the errors made by auditory agnosic patients, he also proposed two types of auditory agnosia: one concerned with the perception and discrimination of sounds, and one concerned with the associations generated by sounds. All of these deficits are of course intimately bound up with difficulties in the reception of spoken language, which will be discussed later.

VISION

Although the temporal lobes are more important for hearing than for vision, two aspects of visual function should be noted.

The first is that as the visual pathways pass back towards the occipital cortex, they run underneath the temporal lobes. Lesions of the temporal cortex, if they extend down below the cortex into the tissue below, may interrupt the visual fibres (here forming the *optic radiation*). The result is a loss of vision in the upper homonymous quadrants; that is, a loss in the upper half of vision on one side (the opposite side of vision to the side of injury), for both of the eyes. This emphasizes the importance of remembering that most lesions do not simply affect the cortex, but extend more or less radically into subcortical tissue. Lesions are three-dimensional.

The second aspect of visual function is that the *tertiary visual cortex*, located principally in the occipital lobes, extends into the middle and inferior gyri of the temporal lobes. It is more convenient to discuss these regions in the context of the complete system for vision in Chapter 6, but it should be noted that visual agnosia for objects (affecting the naming, recognition and appropriate use of objects) or for drawings (affecting recognition may be associated with temporal lesions. Indeed one visual deficit, *prosopagnosia*, which means the loss of the ability to recognize faces, is produced principally by such lesions, although it is more commonly seen following lesions of the right temporal lobe. This difficulty seems to affect not the perception and recognition of the component elements in faces, but the way in which associative meaning is attached to the face, and the problem may well lie in memory components of facial recognition. Although the full form of prosopagnosia is fairly rare, it may be so extreme that the patient fails to recognize close relatives, and may even have difficulty recognizing his own face in a mirror.

LANGUAGE

Functions connected with language are discussed in Chapter 7, but it should be noted here that the temporal lobes make a major contribution to the reception and comprehension of language. In particular, systems in the superior temporal gyrus and in the region at the junction of the temporal, parietal and occipital lobes (Wernicke's area and the angular gyrus) supply the essential elements for understanding speech and written language. These systems are highly lateralized, to the left temporal lobe in most individuals.

ATTENTION

As the highest levels of analysis of both auditory and visual stimulation occur in the temporal lobes, it is not surprising that lesions of many parts of the lateral surface of the lobe can result in deficits in selective attention to visual or auditory input, that is, there is an inability to attend deliberately to one source or type of stimulation while filtering out others, or there is a generally reduced awareness of some particular form of stimulus. In the auditory modality this is shown by the changes in dichotic listening performance already mentioned. There is a parallel finding in the visual modality, so that the ability to report stimuli presented in the lateral visual fields (see Chapter 10) may be affected. Left hemisphere lesions may affect the report of items in the right visual field, while right lesions affect the report from both visual fields (Dorff, Mirsky and Mishkin, 1965; Moore and Weidner, 1974). Perhaps the deficits in peformance shown by the McGill Picture Anomalies Test (Fig. 4.4) may be associated with these problems. In this test, fairly detailed pictures which contain some incongruous element are shown to the patient, who must spot which is the unexpected feature (Milner, 1958; Shalman, 1961). It is not clear whether the difficulty experienced by temporal lobe patients, especially those with right sided lesions, results from a problem with the higher levels of visual perception, or from a problem with attention.

Figure 4.4. The type of stimulus presented in the McGill Picture Anomalies Test.

The integration of stimuli perceived in different sensory modalities is also considered a function of the temporal lobes. The primary evidence for this is clinical, coming from the abnormal experiences reported by patients with temporal lobe epilepsy (see pp. 80 and 152), where there seem to be errors in the way in which sensory data obtained in one modality are transposed into sensory experiences in another. Although the frontal lobes are concerned with controlling the overall alerting system which maintains attentional tone in the cortex (shown principally by studies of the electrical activity of the brain), the temporal lobes also contribute to the cognitive control of attention, dependent upon aspects of the stimulation which relate to higher levels of meaning. There has, however, not yet been an extensive study of this area of function.

MEMORY

Besides its major roles in auditory perception and language comprehension, the temporal lobe is known to be involved in memory. Patients with memory dysfunction show a rather different picture depending on whether their lesion is bilateral or unilateral.

Bilateral Lesions — the Amnesic Syndrome

Bilateral temporal lobe lesions may lead to one of the most remarkable states seen by neuropsychologists. A famous example is that of HM, an intensively studied patient, who in 1953, when in his mid-twenties, underwent an operation for severe epilepsy in which the mesial part of the temporal lobes, with parts of the hippocampus, amygdala and uncus, were removed on both sides of the brain. The operation dramatically improved HM's epilepsy, but left him with severe *anterograde amnesia* — a loss of memory for all events forward in time. HM literally remembers nothing that has happened since 1953, although his memory for events before that time is at least as good as one might expect. Although of normal intelligence (in fact his intelligence increased by thirteen IQ points following the operation, presumably in part because of the reduction in his anti-convulsant medication), he needs continual care and protection. At his reassessment in 1967, he was able to draw a sketch plan of the bungalow in which he had been living for eight years, but was unable to describe anything about the routine work which he had been doing regularly for the previous six months, or the place in which he did the work (Milner, Corkin and Teuber, 1968). In hospital at the time of this reassessment, he is reported to have rung repeatedly for the nurse during the night to ask where he was and why he was there. He has described his experience as 'like waking from a dream', aware of events but only half able to make sense of them because they are out of the context of whatever went before.

On formal testing, HM's span of attention is normal. He has the normal digit span of about seven items, and shows the normal decay of primary memory. However, in any task in which there is an interval between presentation and recall, that is, any learning task, HM fails completely. Extensive series of test trials have been conducted, with no evidence of learning or memory whatsoever. This result applies to words, prose, digits, faces, shapes or pictures. In fact early studies concluded that there was no learning of any kind in HM. It is now clear that there are two very limited exceptions to this conclusion. Asked to learn the visually guided stylus maze (see p. 62), HM failed completely. However, with a much simplified form of the maze, in which the number of choice points was within his immediate memory span, he learned the solution in 155 trials, showed clear savings (a reduced time to relearn) after a week, and some savings even after two years. Secondly, HM shows remarkably good motor learning. An example of a motor learning test is the mirror drawing task (see Fig. 4.5), where the subject repeatedly traces the outline of a star, but is only able to visually guide his pencil by watching it in a mirror. The rate of improvement, in speed and errors, can be recorded as an index of learning. HM shows almost normal learning on this task, and also shows an effect of learning which carries over days, even though he is unable to recall having performed the task before.

Figure 4.5. The mirror drawing task.

It is clear from other clinical evidence that the crucial element in producing HM's dramatic amnesia is the bilateral loss of the hippo-campus. However, another form of the *amnesic syndrome*, known as *Korsakoff's psychosis*, suggests that other structures may be of impor-tance, including the amygdala, mammillary bodies and anterior thalamus. Korsakoff's psychosis is usually a consequence of chronic alcoholism, and is also characterized by a severe anterograde amnesia. Not all the patients show an amnesia as dense as that of HM, but many are similarly handicapped. They fail to learn their way about hospital wards, can continually reread the newspaper as if they had never seen it, and have no recall for people, places or events. It is a curious experience to spend considerable time with such a patient, to leave the room for a short period, and return to be greeted as an entirely unfamiliar person. These patients may also deny their disability and may confabulate, that is, invent details to fill the gaps created by their absent memories. Like HM, these patients show some limited savings on certain tasks. On the Gollin Incomplete Figures, where a highly incomplete drawing is shown to the patient, followed by increasingly complete versions until the drawing is recognized (Fig. 4.6), normal subjects show rapid learning, identifying the item earlier and earlier in the sequence on repeated trials. Amnesic patients show some very slight savings on this task (although their performance is still well below normal), as well as on a parallel task with sets of fragmented words which become successively less fragmented (Warrington and Weiskrantz, 1968).

These patients have been an important source of research data, although there is currently a very hotly argued debate over the precise explanation for the difficulties which they show. If we adopt a model of memory involving the stages of encoding, storage and retrieval, then one possibility is that the patients encode memories normally, but are unable to retrieve them. Supporters of this position have argued that by providing certain types of cue at the time recall is demanded, the performance of these patients may be improved. The alternative view is that there is a failure of encoding, perhaps as a result of increased sensitivity to interference, so that memories are not laid down normally in the first instance. The evidence here is that deliberately aiding patients in the use of strategies which should improve encoding also improves later recall (Iversen, 1977; Butters and Cermak, 1980). The argument is a technical one, with many of the experimental results disputed, especially as it is difficult to distinguish experimentally between, for instance, a failure of storage and a failure of retrieval – if the item is stored, but inaccessible, then how do you find out if it is stored? This debate is not entirely academic, in that the techniques which should be taught to patients to help them overcome their handicap depend upon which theory is accepted. What is not in doubt is that the hippocampus, the associated areas of mesial temporal cortex, and some other limbic structures are of central importance in the laying down and retrieval of long-term memory.

Figure 4.6. Examples of the Gollin figures.
(Redrawn after E. S. Gollin, *Perceptual and Motor Skills*, 11 (1960), 290).

Unilateral Lesions – Temporal Lobectomy

Unilateral lesions of the hippocampus and its associated cortex may also produce effects upon memory, and these effects depend upon the side of the lesion. Lesions on the right side may, as well as affecting the learning of mazes whether performed under visual or tactual guidance, affect memory for spatial information. This has been shown experimentally using the Corsi block tapping task, in which the patient must learn to tap a sequence of locations on an array of irregularly arranged blocks (Fig. 4.7). The number of blocks to be tapped just exceeds the span of the patient's immediate memory, but the sequence of trials includes a particular sequence every third trial. Normal subjects learn this repeating sequence fairly easily, but not the patients. An associated deficit may also appear in memory for pure spatial position when patients are asked to reproduce the location of a point placed along a line. In contrast, left hippocampal lesions affect the recall of nonsense syllables (like 'zot' or 'pel') or the digit span tested under conditions similar to the block tapping task (Corsi, 1972).

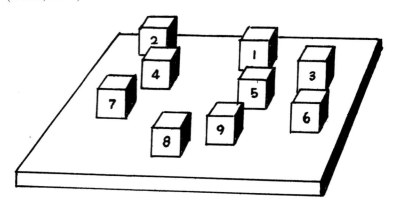

Figure 4.7. The Coris block tapping task. This is the examiner's view; the subject does not see the numbers indicating the sequence of the blocks.
(After B. Milner, *British Medical Bulletin*, 27 (1971), 275)

More general unilateral temporal lesions may also have effects upon memory, although not of so dramatic a nature as in the amnesic syndrome. The most complete experimental evidence comes from studies of patients who have undergone temporal lobectomy, studies principally carried out by Milner (1972). *Anterior temporal lobectomy* is a neurosurgical procedure carried out for certain types of epilepsy in which the epileptogenic focus is in the anterior temporal lobe, of which the surgeon removes the entire anterior portion (see p. 152). By studying these patients before and after surgery, it is possible to gain a very clear idea of the functions undertaken by this region of the brain, but it should be remembered that even before surgery these patients have abnormal brains, and we must be cautious about generalizing from them to normal individuals.

An associated procedure, that of testing by *intracarotid sodium amytal*, sometimes known as the *Wada technique*, may also be mentioned here.

In most individuals verbal memory functions are associated with the left temporal lobe, and non-verbal memory functions with the right. Since deficits in verbal memory are very much more disabling in everyday life than non-verbal, a surgeon performing a temporal lobectomy operation is particularly anxious to limit the amount of tissue removed from the 'verbal' side. The Wada technique provides a way of checking which is the patient's 'verbal' side. Sodium amytal, which depresses the activity of nervous tissue, is injected into the internal carotid artery of one side of the head, and is carried to the anterior and central parts of the brain on that side, where it temporarily suppresses all activity in that hemisphere. The drug has no harmful effects, but the risks attached to the injection only justify the use of the technique in cases being assessed for surgery. The procedure can be carried out on the two sides on separate occasions, but when the drug is injected on the 'verbal' side, the patient loses the ability to speak or understand language. We shall return to this in later chapters. For the present, it should be emphasized that although the procedure seems to be neat and well-controlled the period of time during which testing is possible is very brief, and it is carried out under adverse conditions with patients who are anxious and possibly confused or distressed, and upon brains which are not normal.

As mentioned previously the effects of temporal lobectomy on memory are lateralized and in most subjects left lesions affect verbal memory, while right lesions affect spatial memory; in both cases there is a delay between presentation and recall. It can be shown that information is initially encoded, because it may be reproduced in immediate recall. The evidence from focal traumatic lesions, and from the Wada test, supports these conclusions. Verbal memory, and the effect of left lesions, are usually tested by the Logical Memory subtest of the Wechsler Memory Scale. In this test the patient is read a short prose passage, rather like a brief newspaper article, and asked to reproduce it immediately following presentation. The patient is scored not for precise reproduction but for recall of the semantic elements in the passage, and he may therefore substitute words of similar meaning, rephrase parts of the story, or revise the order. At this stage temporal lobe patients perform normally. After an interval, usually one hour, the subject is asked again to reproduce the passage, without having expected to do so. Scoring on this occasion is calculated as a percentage of immediate recall. Patients with left temporal lesions are handicapped at this task: post-operative scores were only about 33 per cent of immediate recall, while right temporal lobectomy patients averaged a fairly normal 68 per cent.

There is a parallel deficit shown by patients with right sided lesions when tested on memory for the Rey-Osterreith Figure (see Fig. 4.8). In this case the patient copies the figure (and all patients do as well as normal subjects, so they perceive the figure, have attended to it, and can draw it), and after an hour are asked, unexpectedly, to draw it again. Scoring is calculated by expressing delayed recall as a percentage of immediate copying, and normal subjects, generally to their own surprise, can reproduce the figure quite well. Right temporal lobectomy patients, however, show a deficit which is not seen in left temporal lobectomy cases.

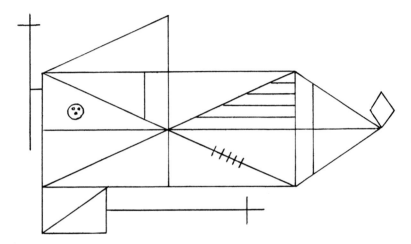

Figure 4.8. A figure similar to the Rey-Osterreith Figure.

Another facet of this memory deficit is in *novelty tasks*, in which the subject, after being shown a list of items, is then presented with two items, one of which has occurred in the list and one of which is novel, and is asked to indicate which is the novel item. Again there is a lateralized dissociation, with left lesions resulting in difficulty when the stimuli are words, and right lesions when the stimuli are abstract paintings.

Effects of temporal lobectomy can also be seen in *paired associate learning*, where the patient must learn a series of associated pairs of items and, on being given one member of the pair, be able to respond with the other. Patients who have undergone left temporal lobectomy show marked impairment in learning verbal material, whether the paired associates are presented in the visual or the auditory modality.

Difficulty with this task may persist for over a year after operation, although improvement may continue, although slowly, for up to six years afterwards. Studies have also shown that slowing the rate of presentation may produce an improvement in the performance of this task by handicapped patients. This may be because it is helpful to use verbal mediators (perhaps by making up a sentence linking the two paired elements), and a slower rate of presentation provides more opportunity for these to be generated (Blakemore, 1969; Jones-Gotman and Milner, 1978).

Finally, although there is very clear evidence for lateralization of memory abilities, we should beware of too simple a view of their localization. Studies using the Wada technique have shown that when the injection of sodium amytal is on the same side as the lesion, recognition for *both* verbal and non-verbal material is relatively intact (although recall may be affected), and only when the injection is on the opposite side to the lesion are there substantial effects on recognition (Milner, 1975).

PERSONALITY

Temporal lobe epilepsy is associated with certain changes in personality and with altered states of experience. These changes do not invariably occur, and are more or less limited to this particular form of epilepsy, but the link is sufficiently clear for us to conclude that the temporal lobes are involved.

Those who suffer from epilepsy stemming from a focus in the temporal lobes, which may not produce the full-blown 'grand mal' seizures but perhaps merely short 'absences', blackouts or periods of automatic behaviour, are often described as having a particular sort of personality. These patients seem to talk about themselves a great deal, especially about their personal problems. They may be peculiarly pedantic in their speech, a little paranoid in their ideas, and the sort of person it is difficult to get away from in social encounters (hence 'sticky'). There may be a tendency for aggressive outbursts, and it is reported that among this group of patients sudden religious conversion occurs more frequently than would be expected. Not all these traits occur in any one patient, but one or more is likely to be present.

Sufferers from temporal lobe epilepsy may also experience *illusions, hallucinations* and other abnormal states, in association with their fits. The hallucinations may be very like those which are reported by schizophrenics, but may be visual or olfactory as well as auditory. The illusions are usually distortions of perception so that things appear larger or smaller or sounds louder or softer, than they should. The patient is usually aware of the distortion, which may apply to specific objects, or may in some way apply to the whole environment. Normal individuals sometimes report similar experiences when they are very tired, perhaps after periods when a lot of sleep has been lost. The illusions and hallucinations are not always pleasant, and the olfactory hallucinations in particular are usually reported as offensive.

Linked with these disorders of perception are more general disorders of consciousness. The patients often report out-of-the-body experiences, or *depersonalization*, in which they seem to be able to watch themselves from 'outside', often at a distance and at a height above themselves. Alternatively they may suffer *déjà vu*, in which novel places, objects or sounds have a familiar feeling about them, or *jamais vu*, where familiar situations suddenly seem as though they are entirely novel. Again, most people have experienced the feeling that they recognize a place which they cannot have visited before. Such experiences seem particularly powerful and compelling for patients suffering from temporal lobe epilepsy, although paradoxically they may at the same time be aware that their experiences are false. These phenomena lead us to regard the temporal lobe as playing some role in governing correct perception of the self located within an experiential framework.

There are also changes in sexual activity associated with temporal lobe epilepsy. As with most brain disorders the change is towards reduced sexual activity and interest, although very occasionally changes in sexual orientation, perhaps linked with an increase in activity, are reported. The number of such cases is small and may not be of great significance. However, it is known that dramatic changes in sexual activity can follow extensive bilateral temporal lesions. Such lesions occur rarely in humans, but there are a number of well documented cases, and research on monkeys supports the evidence. The result of such lesions is known as the *Klüver-Bucy syndrome*, in which, together with deficits in language and memory, there is grossly aberrant sexual behaviour. Sexual activity increases dramatically and is quite indiscriminate in its orientation: homosexual activity is as prevalent as heterosexual activity, and sexual acts may also be directed towards inanimate objects. This occurs in a context of relatively flat emotions. In addition, there may be a tendency for patients to explore objects by putting them into their mouths, and an insatiable appetite, even for inappropriate objects. As in the case of memory, it is the association between temporal cortex and the underlying limbic structures which leads to cortical lesions having such radical effects upon behaviour.

CONCLUSION

The temporal lobes provide the apparatus for the reception of auditory stimulation, its interpretation into perceptual elements, and the subsequent extraction of meaning. They also include elements for the

TABLE 4.1. SOME SPECIFIC FUNCTIONS ASSOCIATED WITH THE TEMPORAL LOBES

AUDITION

> Reception of auditory stimulation (Heschl's gyrus)
> Perception of auditory stimuli (superior temporal gyrus)
> Cognitions relating to auditory events (anterior superior and middle temporal gyrus)
> Musical abilities (right temporal lobe).

VISION

> Tertiary visual function (middle inferior temporal gyrus)
> Perception of faces (right inferior temporal gyrus)

LANGUAGE

> Reception and comprehension of speech and writing (left superior temporal gyrus and temporal-parietal-occipital junction)

ATTENTION

CROSS-MODAL INTEGRATION

MEMORY

> Amnesic syndrome (bilateral mesial temporal lobe)
> Verbal long-term memory (left temporal lobe)
> Spatial long-term memory (right temporal lobe)
> Paired associate learning (anterior temporal lobe)

PERSONALITY

> Experiential perception (anterior temporal lobe)
> Sexual behaviour (anterior, especially bilateral)

higher level interpretation of visual stimulation, and the syntheses which must be attained between these two sensory modalities. A specialized aspect of these perceptual systems is the reception of language stimuli.

Bilateral temporal lobe lesions may, in association with limbic structures, produce severe anterograde amnesia in which almost all capacity for long-term memory and learning is lost. Unilateral temporal lobe lesions may also affect memory for material which must be stored over significant intervals of time. The effects may be specific to the type of material (verbal or spatial), although not the modality, and while the effects may be lateralized, it is important to distinguish recall from recognition tasks.

There are also non-cognitive functions which may be associated with the temporal lobes. Temporal lobe abnormality may produce personality changes, abnormal states of experience, and changes in sexual behaviour. A summary of the functions associated with the temporal lobes appears in Table 4.1.

FURTHER READING

The general texts for this section, given at the end of Chapter 3, provide the main source of further reading for this chapter, but three additional texts may be of interest. The first deals with problems of memory. The second is an invaluable reference for all the psychiatric effects of disorders of the brain, including temporal lobe epilepsy. Finally, there is a useful text on sexual disorders.

Whitty, C. W. M. and Zangwill, O. L., eds., *Amnesia*, 2nd edition (London, Butterworth, 1977).

Lishman, W. A., *Organic Psychiatry* (Oxford, Blackwell Scientific Publications, 1978).

Boller, F., and Frank, E. *Sexual Dysfunction in Neurological Disorders: Diagnosis, Management and Rehabilitation* (New York, Raven Press, 1982).

REFERENCES

Berlin, C. I., 'Hemispheric Asymmetry in Auditory Tasks', in S. Harnad, R. W. Doty, L. Goldstein, J. Jaynes and G. Krauthamer, eds, *Lateralization in the Nervous System* (New York, Academic Press, 1977).

Blakemore, C. B., 'Psychological Effects of Temporal Lobe Lesions in Man', in R. N. Herrington, ed., *Current Problems in Neuropsychiatry: Schizophrenia, Epilepsy, the Temporal Lobe*, British Journal of Psychiatry Special Publication No. 4 (London, Royal Medico-Psychological Association, 1969).

Butters, N. and Cermak, L. C., *Alcoholic Korsakoff's Syndrome* (New York, Academic Press, 1980).

Corsi, P. M., 'Human Memory and the Medial Temporal Region of the Brain', unpublished Ph.D. thesis, McGill Univeristy, (1972) cited in B. Kolb and I. Q. Whishaw, *Fundamentals of Human Neuropsychology* (San Francisco, W. H. Freeman, 1980), 339.

Critchley, M. and Henson, R. A., eds, *Music and the Brain: Studies in the Neurology of Music* (London, Heineman Medical Books, 1977).

Dorff, J. E., Mirsky, A. F. and Mishkin, M., 'Effects of Unilateral Temporal Lobe Removals on Tachistoscopic Recognition in the Left and Right Visual Fields', *Neuropsychologia*, 3 (1965), 39–51.

Iversen, S. D., 'Temporal Lobe Amnesia', in C. W. M. Whitty and O. L. Zangwill, eds. *Amnesia*, 2nd edition, (London, Butterworth, 1977).

Jones-Gotman, M. and Milner, B., 'Right Temporal Lobe Contribution to Image-mediated Verbal Learning', *Neuropsychologia*, 16 (1978), 61–71.

Milner, B., 'Psychological Defects Produced by Temporal Lobe Excision', *Research Publications, Association for Research in Nervous and Mental Disease*, 36 (1958), 244–257.

Milner, B., 'Laterality Effects in Audition', in V. B. Mountcastle, ed., *Interhemispheric Relations and Cerebral Dominance* (Baltimore, The Johns Hopkins Press, 1962).

Milner, B., 'Disorders of Learning and Memory after Temporal Lobe Lesions in Man', *Clinical Neurosurgery*, 19 (1972), 421–446.

Milner, B., (1975). 'Psychological Aspects of Focal Epilepsy and its Neurosurgical Management', *Advances in Neurology*, 8 (1975), 299–321.

Milner, B., Corkin, S. and Teuber, H.-L., 'Further Analysis of the Hippocampal Amnesic Syndrome: 14-year Follow-up of HM', *Neuropsychologia*, 6 (1968), 215–234.

Moore, W. H. and Weidner, W. E., 'Bilateral Tachistoscopic Word Perception in Aphasic and Normal Subjects', *Perceptual and Motor Skills*, 39 (1974), 1003–1011.

Oscar-Berman, M., Zurif, E. B. and Blumstein, S., 'Effects of Unilateral Brain Damage on the Processing of Speech Sounds', *Brain and Language*, 2 (1975), 345–353.

Penfield, W., *The Mystery of the Mind* (Princeton, N. J., Princeton University Press, 1975).

Shalman, D. C., The Diagnostic Use of the McGill Picture Anomalies Test in Temporal Lobe Epilepsy', *Journal of Neurology, Neurosurgery and Psychiatry*, 24 (1961), 220–222.

Vignolo, L. A., 'Auditory Agnosia: a Review and Report of Recent Evidence', in A. L. Benton, ed., *Contributions to Clinical Neuropsychology* (Chicago, Aldine, 1969).

Warrington, E. K. and Weiskrantz, L., 'A Study of Learning and Retention in Amnesic Patients', *Neuropsychologia*, 6 (1968), 283–292.

CHAPTER 5

The Parietal Lobes

Any difficulty in describing the functions of the parietal lobes comes not from the complexity of ideas about their function, but from the quite bewildering range of symptoms which may be shown by those with parietal lesions. In fact, the parietal lobes seem simply to deal with the perception of somatosensory events, and then to undertake functions with some spatial element which combine the somatosensory information with information in other modalities. There is a very broad range of functions which meet this description, and which may therefore be affected by damage to the parietal lobes.

The area which we call the parietal lobe is delimited in a rather arbitrary way, and we should not pretend that its posterior boundary is exact. Some of the complex subdivisions found in textbooks have little functional significance, and for our purposes we can simply divide the parietal lobe into an anterior and posterior section, as in Fig. 5.1. The anterior region, the *postcentral gyrus*, lies posterior to the Rolandic fissure and is sometimes referred to as the *sensory strip*. Behind this region and its associated secondary cortex, the posterior

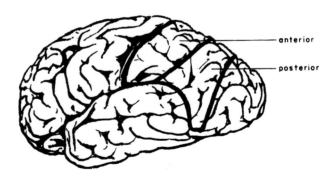

Figure 5.1. The principal divisions of the parietal lobe.

region is composed almost entirely of tertiary cortex. Some other landmarks, the superior and inferior parietal lobules, the angular gyrus and the supramarginal gyrus are sometimes referred to in research reports. Precise localization of function to these specific areas is, however, not yet possible.

We shall take the anterior region first, and its major functions of somatosensory perception, tactile perception and body sense. In the posterior region we will consider language, spatial orientation and neglect, symbolic syntheses, apraxias, cross-modal matching, and memory.

SOMATOSENSORY PERCEPTION

As already mentioned in Chapter 2, there is a clear point-to-point localization in the post-Rolandic sensory strip, which has been demonstrated by stimulation studies (see Fig. 2.9). As with motor representation, the amount of cortex devoted to any particular body area seems to be more or less proportional to the sensory acuity of that area. Regions where we have very acute somatosensory perception, such as the tips of the fingers or the lips, are associated with large amounts of cortex, while insensitive areas like the back have little cortex devoted to them. The sensory acuity of a region of the skin can be tested with an instrument with two sharp points (try a pair of dividers – carefully!). Either one or two points are placed on to the skin, out of the subject's sight, and the distance between the points is varied until the smallest distance at which the number of points can be reliably discriminated is found. This is the *two-point threshold*.

The representation in this area of *primary somatosensory* cortex is mainly contralateral, although there are both contralateral and ipsilateral (uncrossed) sensory projections. In fact there is good evidence that there are two independent sensory systems, operating by different anatomical pathways, one (the *lemniscal*) dealing with touch sensation, and the other (*extralemniscal*) dealing with temperature and pain. However, stimulation of the secondary somatosensory cortex, which is behind the primary cortex and in an area at the inferior end of the sensory strip (just above the Sylvian fissure), results in simultaneous bilateral reports of sensory perceptions.

Lesions of both the primary and secondary somatosensory cortex result in changes in normal *sensation from the body*. These changes are more the interest of the neurologist, and they include loss or alteration of sensation (anaesthesia) for parts of the body, which may be total or confined to certain types of sensation (touch, pressure, temperature, and so on). Not only sensation from the skin, but also kinaesthetic information about the position of limbs and their movement may be affected. In turn this may lead to primary errors in spatial perception because the patient has impaired position sense and may be mis-informed about the position of his own limbs. There may also be changes in sensory acuity not only in terms of the two-point threshold, but also in terms of the threshold for the intensity which can be perceived. The study of changes of this kind, a full account of which can be found in most textbooks on neurology, may sometimes seem a little dull to the psychologist. They are important, however, firstly because they can be the basis of more complex disorders seen in higher functions, and secondly because in considering cognitive models of higher dysfunction, it is often important to rule out the effects of primary somatosensory loss. For instance, if we were to postulate a specific function for dressing movements (see p. 102), it would be important to show that difficulties in dressing could not be explained entirely by impaired position sense, although there is likely to be some contribution from the more basic function.

An interesting debate exists about whether there is an asymmetry in the form of representation of these functions in the left and right hemispheres. In an extensive study of soldiers with missile wounds, Semmes, Weinstein, Ghent and Teuber (1960) found that, when the lesion was in the left hemisphere, only lesions of the postcentral gyrus produced somatosensory deficits. On the other hand, lesions in the right hemisphere over a much wider area could produce such deficits. This conclusion was not supported by another major study by Corkin, Milner and Rasmussen (1970), who found changes in position sense, intensity and two-point threshold, pressure sensitivity and point localization to be affected only by the contralateral postcentral gyrus. Effects were seen most clearly in the hand contralateral to the lesion. The disagreement between these studies is difficult to resolve, but an important factor is the difference in the patients studied: surgical cases as against the war-injured. The size and specificity of the lesions involved, the premorbid state of the patients, and the degree of trauma undoubtedly differed between the studies and this may well account for the different conclusions.

Because sensory feedback is important in motor control, some motor functions are also affected by lesions of primary and secondary somatosensory cortex. The loss of normal sensory feedback can result in clumsy movements, particularly of the fingers, and if the sensory face area of the left hemisphere is involved, there may be difficulty in speaking resulting from problems in articulatory control.

TACTILE PERCEPTION AND BODY SENSE

The deficits of tactile perception and body sense are known as somatosensory *agnosias* (literally a 'loss of knowing'). These deficits result from damage to the secondary somatosensory cortex, and may or may not be associated with primary sensory deficits. It is convenient to divide these agnosias into those which relate to external objects, and those which relate to the patient's own body.

Loss of the ability to recognize objects by touch is known as *astereognosis*. The patient is unable by touch alone to name objects, describe them or demonstrate their use or significance. When the loss is specifically in recognizing the nature of the object from the somatosensory information alone, then the term *asymbolia* is sometimes used. This may occur in the presence or absence of a primary sensory deficit. When the sensory deficit is absent, it is usually the ability to recognize shape, rather than other attributes of the object, which is affected (Semmes, 1965). Apart from the difficulties which a patient may show in informal clinical testing, it may be possible to demonstrate this deficit by impaired performance on the tactile version of the Seguin-Goddard formboard. This formboard consists of a series of simple geometrical shapes cut from a wooden sheet which must be fitted back into their appropriate holes as rapidly as possible. When required to do this blindfold using touch alone, patients with parietal injuries may find the task difficult or impossible.

Demonstrating just how complex is the interrelationship of deficits of cognitive ability, there is a link between astereognosis and *visual object agnosia*, which is an impairment of visual object recognition. This may initially seem a little strange when we have so far concentrated upon the somatosensory modality in discussing the parietal lobes. However, if the difficulty in astereognosis arises from some fundamental difficulty in forming and manipulating spatial-shape representations of objects, then the same kind of process may be required in some aspects of visual object recognition, and may be performed by related structures. This view of how these associated symptoms are integrated is reinforced by the tests which are often used to demonstrate visual object agnosia: the Gollin Figures, the Mooney Closure Faces Test and the Unconventional Views of Objects Test. The Gollin Figures were described in the last chapter (see Fig. 4.6), and the Mooney Closure Faces Test is similar in that it requires that a whole percept be formed from a series of cues which do not make a normal partial form of the figure (see Fig. 5.2). The

Figure 5.2. Mooney Closure Faces Test.
(After C. M. Mooney. *Canadian Journal of Psychology*, 2 (1957), 219–226)

Unconventional Views Test (see Fig. 5.3) was devised by Warrington and Taylor (1973) and consists of photographs of common objects taken from an unusual viewpoint. Again the task requires that a set of cues not normally experienced for an object be integrated and turned into a representation from which meaning can be extracted. The

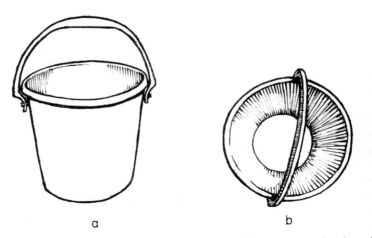

a   b

Figure 5.3. Unconventional Views of Objects Test: an everyday item is presented in (a) conventional and (b) unconventional representations.

parietal lobe patient, especially if the injury is to the right parietal lobe, may find particular difficulty with this task.

When the somatosensory agnosia is not for external objects, but relates to the patient's own body, then it is termed *asomatognosia*. There are two principal forms of asomatognosia: anosognosia and autotopagnosia (although, as is so often the case in clinical neurology, there are a host of other less commonly used terms).

Anosognosia is one of the most remarkable symptoms seen in neurological patients, and more frequently occurs with right sided lesions, which therefore usually affect the left side of the body. The patient becomes unaware of the disposition of his limbs, and when these limbs are affected by sensory or motor losses, he may deny the handicaps which these limbs suffer. In the most striking cases, the patient will disown a limb as belonging to him, and cases are recorded in which the patient has repeatedly called the nursing staff to complain of the strange arm or leg which is in his bed. The affected arm or leg is quite commonly allowed to hang out of the bed without concern for its comfort or safety, exactly as if it did not belong to the patient and was none of his concern. Like so many neuropsychological deficits, this is a powerful reminder of the great range of functions we continually perform automatically and without any conscious awareness, for our own biological survival.

Linked to anosognosia is a particularly troublesome handicap, which is *asymbolia for pain*. Patients with this dysfunction fail to correctly interpret pain sensations from areas of the body, and are usually indifferent to pain. As a result, considerable damage can occur to some limb or body part because the perception of pain does not lead to remedial action. If linked to a more general anosognosia, then it may mean that an arm, for example, might be left on a hot stove or a hot radiator until the smell of burning flesh alerts either the patient or someone else to what is happening.

The second form of asomatognosia, this time more commonly seen following left sided injuries, is *autotopagnosia*. This is an impairment in the localization or naming of parts of the patient's own body. The patient is unable to point to parts of the body named by the examiner, or to move them, and may not be able to identify them on the examiner's body, or on a diagram. That the problem may be extended to moving a body part a short time after the examiner has touched it shows that the deficit is not fundamentally related to the verbal aspects of the task.

A particular form of autotopagnosia, to which much significance is often attached, is *finger agnosia* (Kinsbourne and Warrington, 1962).

Although the disorder is the specific difficulty of naming and identifying the fingers, it is often tested in two particular ways. In one, (the In-between Test) two fingers are touched simultaneously, and the patient is asked to report the number of fingers which lie in between the two which have been touched. The other is the Two-point Finger Test, where two touches are made upon the fingers, and the patient must decide whether they are on the same finger or not. However, tests for finger agnosia may also extend to naming the fingers, moving particular fingers on command, or in some other way indicating that the fingers can be identified and that their spatial arrangement is known and understood.

LANGUAGE

The whole subject of language function will be discussed in Chapter 7, but it should be noted here that the more posterior areas of the parietal lobes play an important role in language function, as do the frontal and temporal lobes. Particularly, the left parietal lobe in right handed subjects is concerned with aspects of the reception of spoken language, and also with reading.

SPATIAL ORIENTATION

Underlying many of the functions of the parietal lobe is spatial representation. We have seen this in the somatosensory agnosias, and it is even more clear in *visuospatial agnosia*. This is an impairment of spatial location and orientation. The orientation may be of objects with respect to the observer, or of the relative orientations between objects. It is not difficult to imagine the kind of problems which a patient with this dysfunction experiences, but the tests which have been used to demonstrate visuospatial agnosia make it completely clear. A sample item (Fig. 5.4) is shown from the Pool Reflections Test. In this test, the patient is shown a sample pattern and is asked to select from a multiple choice array the pattern which is a reflection of the sample rotated on its horizontal axis (Butters, Barton and Brody, 1970). A similar test, but which requires some constructional ability (see below) is the Stick Test (Benson and Barton, 1970; Butters and Barton, 1970). Here, the patient is asked to reproduce a simple pattern made from matches which the examiner has demonstrated forming. The patient must first perform the test sitting alongside, and

then again opposite, the examiner so that some translation of the
spatial elements of the construction is necessary. A more complex
spatial task has also been used in which the subject sees the model of a
village and is asked to judge which of a set of photographs is of the
model, rejecting photographs of the same elements but in different
positions.

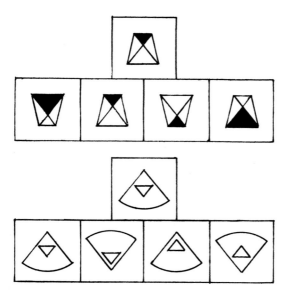

Figure 5.4. Pool Reflections Test. In these two sample items the subject
selects from the four alternatives in the bottom row the one identical to the
standard figure rotated 180 degrees in its fronto-parallel plane.
(After Butters, Barton and Brody, 1970)

There are aspects of memory for spatial position which are also
sometimes impaired together with these functions. The task which
may be set the patient is essentially the same, but will involve some of
the spatial information being retained in memory. The Tactual
Performance Test, which forms part of the Reitan Battery, may be
used to assess this aspect of spatial function. It is in fact an extension
of the Seguin-Goddard formboard, in which, after the blindfold test,
the patient is asked, unexpectedly, to draw the shapes and their
locations. The Benton Visual Retention Test (see Fig. 5.5) which
demands the memory retention of relatively complex, abstract, spatial figures, is an alternative way of testing impairments of this kind.

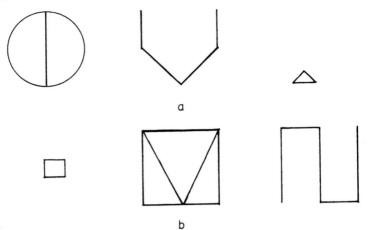

a

b

Figure 5.5. Two items similar to those found in the Benton Visual Retention Test.

Disturbances of spatial location and orientation can also be shown on less abstract tasks, more like the situations encountered in everyday life. Just as the patient's report of familiar surroundings may be inaccurate or abnormally lacking in spatial detail, and he may experience particular difficulties in following a route, then it is possible to see deficits on formal tests of route following ability. The most widely used form of assessment of this ability is the Locomotor Map Following Task (also known as the Semmes Maps, or Weinstein Maps; see Semmes, Weinstein, Ghent and Teuber, 1955). Nine large dots are placed upon the floor, and the patient is handed a 'map' showing a simple route between these points (see Fig. 5.6). The patient must

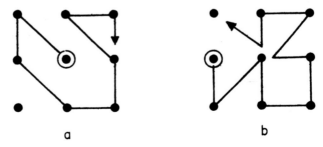

a   b

Figure 5.6. Weinstein Maps. The subject must follow the routes indicated around the nine points laid out on the floor.

follow the route by walking between the dots, but keeping the map in the same orientation to his own body throughout. Turning the map to preserve its orientation with respect to the points on the floor is not allowed, so that translation of spatial relationships between the map and the points in space is required for correct performance on the task. Difficulties on this and related tasks are associated with parietal lesions on the right side of the head.

The final aspect of this collection of spatial functions is left-right discrimination. Although many normal adults show a marked degree of left-right confusion, patients with right parietal lesions may show an even more pronounced dysfunction. It may be demonstrated by informal clinical evaluation or by more formal assessments (Benton, 1959), which might include the Money Road Map Test. This test demands that the patient decide at each turn of a route which is marked on a schematic street plan whether the route turns to the left or to the right, with respect to its previous direction, (see Fig. 5.7).

We have to be careful about the aspects of lateral differentiation which are affected in a particular patient, because, as we have already noted, the left frontal lobe plays some role in orientation to egocentric space. The right parietal injuries are, by contrast, more likely to affect extrapersonal space. (If you are uncertain about the variety of abilities involved in spatial orientation, try sitting down and drawing a rough map of your daily route to work or college, or draw a plan of your home, trying to observe the mental activities which you must engage in.)

It is interesting that when normal subjects show directional confusion (you must have had the experience of being directed by someone who tells you to turn to the right, while pointing away to the left), then it is usually the verbal label which they get wrong. They rarely point in the wrong spatial direction. The parietal lobe case will, however, show much grosser confusion about which side is which in space, and the fact that he cannot relate the two sides to the lateral verbal labels stems from a fundamental spatial deficit. When the difficulty is in relating points in extrapersonal space, this strongly suggests a right parietal lesion.

SPATIAL NEGLECT

Strongly associated with difficulties of spatial orientation are difficulties of *spatial neglect*. This is a complex topic in which the presence of associated sensory impairment, language difficulties and

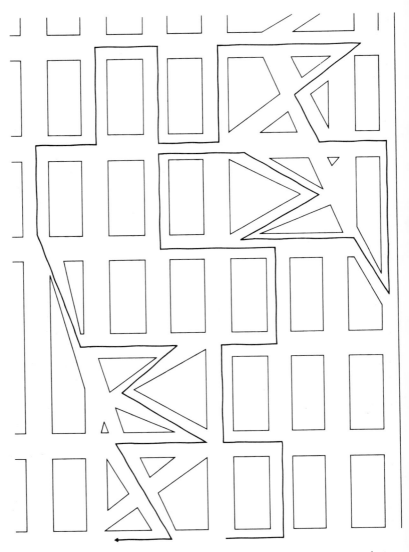

Figure. 5.7. The Road Map Test. The subject, having seen a route drawn similar to that indicated by the heavy line, must indicate whether each turn, in sequence, is to the left or the right.

general changes of intellectual ability may affect the functional impairments which are seen. However, as the name suggests, the problem is essentially that patients do not pay attention to a particular area of space, usually the half of space opposite to the side of the lesion. As this is more commonly the right side, it is more usual to see left sided neglect or *hemi-inattention* (see Weinstein and Friedland, 1977, for an excellent review of this whole topic). The disorder is, however, also seen in isolation from sensory or other deficits, which indicates that it can exist as a purely attentional disorder. The patients suffering from this impairment will often appear with bruising and scratching down one side of the body, because they constantly bump into objects and scrape along walls and hedges on the unattended side. Given tasks to perform they will neglect information which would normally appear to the one side of space, and may, characteristically, write or draw neglecting one side of the paper or the figure being copied (see Fig. 5.8). They may shave only on one side of the face and may forget to complete dressing on one side of the body. It is as if these patients simply do not consider one half of space to exist at all, although once their attention is explicitly drawn to that side, they can see what has been neglected and perform the necessary adjustments (McFie and Zangwill, 1960).

Since the symptoms of neglect clear following treatment, the impairment has been described as passing through two phases. The first is *allesthesia* where attention is paid to the spatial elements on the previously neglected side, but they are treated as if they were on the unaffected side. The patient consequently completely misdirects his responses to the unaffected side of the body. This may be followed by the second stage, in which only *simultaneous extinction* is to be observed, that is, the patient responds normally and attends effectively to both sides of space until there is simultaneous competing stimulation of both the sides. Then neglect of one of the two stimuli will reappear and only one will be attended and responded to.

It is interesting to consider whether spatial neglect is normally a purely attentional condition, or whether spatial orientational factors are inevitably linked with the disorder. In one case a bus driver was referred for investigation after he repeatedly, when drawing to a halt at a bus stop, drove up on to the pavement, to the consternation of those waiting to board the bus. Here, elements of both errors of spatial perception on the left of the body, and attentional neglect to this side, resulting from a right parietal tumour, contributed to his alarming behaviour. Defective spatial perception may be a feature of many cases, and it is important to rule out primary visual field defects. Just

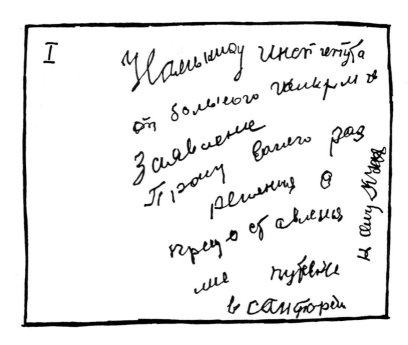

specimen   specimen

performance   performance

Figure 5.8. The writing and drawing performance of a patient showing left
sided neglect.
(Reprinted from A. R. Luria, *The Working Brain*, Penguin 1973)

as with the temporal lobes, the visual projection passes behind the inferior parts of the parietal lobes, and lesions extending below the cortex can interfere with this pathway to produce loss in the lower half of vision on the contralateral side (lower quadrant homonymous hemianopia). The relation of all these factors to spatial neglect is an issue which cannot be resolved at the present time, and illustrates how complex and fascinating it can be to attempt to unravel the basis of such cognitive impairments. In most patients it is almost certainly the case that a number of factors contribute to a deficit of a high level function like hemi-spatial attention.

SYMBOLIC SYNTHESES

Symbolic (quasi-spatial) syntheses is the rather grand term some-times given to certain difficulties which at first appear to be purely symbolic, but which are considered to stem from a basic spatial dysfunction. One of the clearest of these is *acalculia*, or loss of the ability to perform arithmetical calculations. The reason that this may be considered to involve spatial elements is that analysis of the errors made by patients doing arithmetic indicates that many people use spatial representations to solve such problems. It is as if they write the problem down, as they were originally taught in primary school, and then proceed to solve it by working on an internal representation of the numbers involved. The errors arise because patients muddle up the order of the digits representing a number, or fail to 'carry one', or forget that the lower item is being subtracted from the upper item within their mental representation. This is not to say that this is how all subjects tackle arithmetic, but many certainly do adopt this strategy. This is not the only reason for arithmetic errors – simple failure to read numbers, or neglect of one side of the problem may be others – but it is one illustration of how pervading spatial representa-tions are in our thinking, and how they may be disturbed by parietal lesions. A similar failure of symbolic synthesis may underlie some difficulties in reading, where regular spatial scanning of a text is important.

APRAXIA

Certain *apraxias* (the loss of intentional movements) may arise from parietal lesions. These may occur in the absence of paralysis, or of any impairment of sensory or motor function. They may relate to almost any kind of purposeful movement, although gross proximal movements of the body and limbs are more commonly affected. However, imitational movements of the hands and face, tapping and complex manual sequences do not escape impairment (Kimura, 1977). The patient is unable to organize some motor task if he must start from the most abstract description of that task. In other words, he may be perfectly able to carry out some movement automatically, or in the context of everyday life, such as drinking from a cup, or striking a match, but asked to demonstrate *how* to drink from a cup, or strike a match, the patient is quite unable to do so. Sometimes he may find it possible if he has the relevant object to act as a cue, but he will fail if asked to perform the action without a cup or a match to act as a trigger. Certain forms of this apraxia are given terms such as *ideomotor* or *ideational apraxia*, but these terms are not used consistently, and the existence of some of the specific forms is hotly contested. It is clear that precise testing is crucial in determining exactly what deficits are seen, and the whole question awaits more thorough scientific investigation.

One theory about apraxia, promoted by Geschwind (1974), but originally derived from Liepmann, is that there is a system which links the left posterior parietal region with the left frontal lobe (through a tract called the arcuate fasciculus) where speech mechanisms may be involved in verbal regulation (see p. 59). Motor control then proceeds by the left motor cortex for the right hand, and via the corpus callosum and the right motor cortex for the left hand. This would neatly explain the reported bilateral apraxias following left lesions, but unilateral left hand apraxia following right lesions, as well as making anatomical sense. However, these observations are not generally accepted, and the theory is the subject of considerable debate.

There are two special forms of apraxia which ought to be mentioned. The first is *dressing apraxia*, which is a particular deficit in putting on clothes. Patients may become entirely confused about the sequence of dressing, or how a particular garment should be put on, often with bizarre results. Why this can apparently occur as an isolated form has never been satisfactorily explained.

The second, and more important, form is *constructional apraxia*. This can be a difficult concept to grasp, but it involves the idea of an activity in which the relationships between component elements must be clearly understood so that they can be brought together and properly synthesized. It is most commonly demonstrated by drawing or by simple constructional tasks, although it is sometimes also demonstrated by route finding tasks of the kind already mentioned. The four tasks used in a study by Benton (1969) probably represent the core functions involved in constructional apraxia. These tasks were the Benton Visual Retention Test (see Fig. 5.5), the Stick Construction Test, the Kohs block design task (Fig. 3.6), and the test of Three Dimensional Constructional Praxis. In this last test, a variety of increasingly complex arrangements must be made of a collection of wooden blocks (see Fig. 5.9). The aim of Benton's study

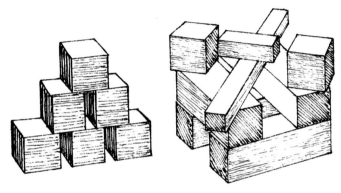

Figure 5.9. Three Dimensional Constructional Praxis: a simple, and a more complex, model to be copied by the patient.
(After A. L. Benton and M. L. Fogel, *Archives of Neurology*, 7 (1962), 349)

was in fact to see if there was a unitary constructional apraxia which affected all four tasks. He did not find uniformity in performance across the tasks, but he did find a reasonable degree of association between the last three tests, and concluded that there may be separate syndromes which affect graphical and constructional ability. More severe constructional apraxia was more usually found to follow right lesions, and this has been supported by subsequent studies (Benson and Barton, 1970).

A final word should be added about difficulties in drawing. There are characteristic drawing errors which may be linked with the parietal lobe and are unlike those seen with occipital lesions. With parietal injury, it is the arrangement and interrelation of the elements of the drawing, rather than more basic visuoperceptual production, which are affected (see Fig. 5.10). Even within parietal drawing deficits, it has been suggested that there are qualitative differences

Copies   Spontaneous

(a)

Copies   Spontaneous

(b)

Left hemisphere cases   **Right hemisphere cases.**

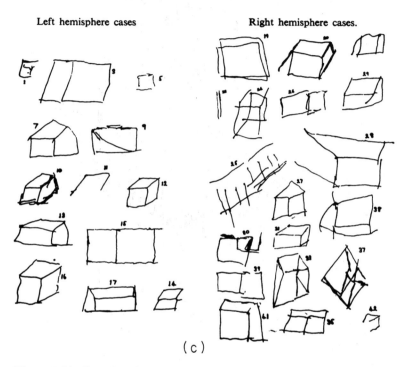

(c)

Figure 5.10. Drawings by patients with parietal lobe lesions: drawings of a house by left hemisphere cases (a) and by right hemisphere cases (b); (c) copies of a cube.

(Reproduced from M. Piercy, H. Hécaen and J. De Ajuriaguerra, *Brain*, 83 (1960), 234, 236)

which follow the laterality of the lesion (Warrington, 1969). The drawings of right parietal cases are often fragmented, with component parts put in the wrong place and orientation, and with a variety of lines subsequently added in an attempt to correct the drawing. Left lesion patients, by contrast, often simplify their drawings, probably because they cannot formulate plans to execute them effectively, so that the result is a correct but laborious drawing, notably lacking in detail. These qualitative differences are difficult to quantify, but make sense in terms of our overall view of the functions of the parietal lobes.

INTERSENSORY ASSOCIATION

A difficulty in intersensory association, or cross-modal matching, may well contribute to certain of the deficits shown by patients with posterior parietal lesions, such as those which have been described above. Lesions of the parieto-temporal junction in particular may result in difficulties with integration of this kind, which is really an extension of the kind of function seen in neighbouring temporal zones as visual-auditory association. In the parietal lobe, the deficit is more likely to be in tactile-visual cross-modal integration. If an object is palpated by the patient, he may then have difficulty in selecting that object from an array of visually presented objects (Butters and Brody, 1968; Butters, Barton and Brody, 1970). The difficulty may, however, be shown between any or all combinations of auditory, visual and tactile stimuli. There may be some asymmetry in that the left hemisphere deals more particularly with the *what*, while the right deals more with the *where*, but the division is not absolute. Undoubtedly, these difficulties may contribute to higher level impairments, such as constructional apraxia.

SHORT-TERM MEMORY

There is little evidence for the localization of short-term memory in the cerebral cortex, except that a small number of patients have been described with difficulties in short-term auditory memory following parietal lesions (Shallice and Warrington, 1974). These patients, in particular a patient called Kenneth ('KF'), showed abnormally rapid forgetting of auditorily presented verbal information (spoken lists of words or numbers), and were especially susceptible to the effects of distractor items. This forgetting could not be accounted for by problems in either speech or hearing. Whether this functional impairment is really restricted in all cases to the auditory modality is in dispute, as is whether it should be considered an aspect of more general language disturbances.

THE GERSTMANN SYNDROME

The Gerstmann syndrome must be mentioned because of the amount of attention it has attracted, although current opinion rejects it as a unitary syndrome. Gerstmann proposed that four symptoms were associated in a single syndrome: agraphia (loss of the ability to write), acalculia, right-left confusion and finger agnosia. He also proposed that this collection of symptoms indicated a specific lesion of the angular gyrus in the left parietal lobe. A considerable amount of investigation points to the conclusion that these four symptoms do not occur together as a unitary syndrome, although large lesions of the posterior parietal lobe may well produce all four symptoms (Benton, 1961; Heimberger, Demeyer and Reitan, 1964). These large lesions also, however, tend to produce general language difficulties which make it difficult to decide whether the symptoms are present in 'pure' form, and although patients can be found with one, two, three or all of the symptoms, their presence is not strong evidence for specific lesions of the angular gyrus rather than of the surrounding region.

CONCLUSION

The variety of symptoms which may be produced by parietal lesions can be confusing, especially as many are referred to by terms which do not immediately convey the nature of the impairment. The laterality of functional specialization may also seem rather more complex than in the frontal and temporal lobes, particularly if we try to account for left as well as right handed patients (see Critchley, 1953). Some effects are only seen with bilateral lesions, some with unilateral lesions of either side, and some with only left or right sided lesions. In each case there is rarely a firm division but only a relative frequency of association, perhaps because the high level functions which are normally examined involve such a range of more basic cognitive processes.

The classic study of McFie and Zangwill (1960) is a useful example of the asymmetries which may be found. They gave a set of seven tasks to a number of patients with parietal injuries and found only three tasks to be completely lateralized. The cube counting and paper cutting tasks were affected only by right sided lesions, and the test of right-left discrimination only by left sided lesions. Three further tests, of unilateral neglect, of dressing ability and of topographical perception, were seen more commonly in patients with right injuries, but were also seen in those with left lesions. The final task, the Weigl Sorting Test, showed impairment much more often with left lesions. In general, however, tasks with purely spatial elements tend to be affected by right sided lesions, but when verbal processes are involved (perhaps as a strategy for solving spatial problems), the function is more likely to be represented upon the left. Some of the confusion about lateralization may result from the adoption of different cognitive strategies by different patients as their preferred cognitive mode.

The specific functions associated with the parietal lobes are summarized in Table 5.1. In general the parietal lobes in the anterior regions are concerned with somatosensory sensation and perception, and are associated with a number of visual and tactile agnosias in which spatial representations are involved. In the posterior regions of

TABLE 5.1. SOME SPECIFIC
FUNCTIONS ASSOCIATED WITH
THE PARIETAL LOBES

ANTERIOR
> Somatosensory perceptions
> Tactile perception
> Body sense
> Visual object recognition

POSTERIOR
> Language
>> Reception of spoken language
>> Reading
> Spatial orientation and attention
>> Route following
>> Left-right discrimination
> Symbolic syntheses
>> Calculation
> Intentional movement
> Constructional ability
>> Drawing
> Cross-modal tactile-visual matching
> Short-term auditory memory

---

the parietal lobe, there is further integration of this kind of information with information from other modalities to perform spatial and spatially related functions. These include certain forms of intentional movement, including complex skilled constructions, understanding and manipulation of the spatial environment with respect to both the patient's own body and the extrapersonal world, and certain tasks in which spatial representations may be more symbolically involved, including calculation and a variety of language functions (to be discussed later). This range of spatial processes also involves the integration of somatosensory information and spatial operations with visual and auditory processes (again especially with respect to language). It is the pervasive nature of so many of these functions in our general cognitive abilities which leads to the variety and complexity of the handicaps which may follow from lesions of the parietal lobe.

FURTHER READING

The general references for this section (at the end of Chapter 3) again form the main texts for further study. The books by Hécaen and Albert, and Heilman and Valenstein mentioned there provide particularly useful coverage of apraxias and agnosias. In addition it may be worth consulting a textbook of neurology to learn more about primary somatosensory impairments. Classic reference texts of this kind include:

Brain, Lord, *Clinical Neurology*, 5th edition, revised R. Bannister, (Oxford, Oxford Medical Publications, 1978).
Vinken, P. J. and Bruyn, G. W., eds, *Handbook of Clinical Neurology*, (Amsterdam, New Holland, 1969).

Two other texts deserve a minor mention:

Critchley, M., *The Parietal Lobes* (London, Arnold, 1953). This text is now rather dated, but it still contains much of value, especially for those interested in handedness and cerebral dysfunction.
Milner, B. and Teuber, H.-L., 'Alteration of Perception and Memory in Man: Reflections on Methods', in L. Weiskrantz, ed., *Analysis of Behavioural Change* (New York, Harper and Row, 1968). Again, this is now dated, but it forms a useful and extensive review of the classic work done on somatosensory perception following the Second World War.

REFERENCES

Benson, D. F. and Barton, M. I., 'Disturbances in constructional ability', *Cortex*, 6 (1970), 19–46.
Benton, A. L., *Right-Left Discrimination and Finger Localization* (New York, Harper and Row, 1959).

Benton, A. L., 'The Fiction of the "Gerstmann Syndrome" ', *Journal of Neurology, Neurosurgery and Psychiatry*, 24 (1961), 176–181.

Benton, A. L., 'Constructional Apraxia: Some Unanswered Questions', in A. L. Benton, ed., *Contributions to Clinical Neuropsychology* (Chicago, Aldine, 1969).

Butters, N. and Barton, M., 'Effect of Parietal Lobe Damage on the Performance of Reversible Operations in Space', *Neuropsychologia*, 8 (1970), 205–214.

Butters, N., Barton, M. and Brody, B. A., 'Role of the Right Parietal Lobe in the Mediation of Cross-modal Associations and Reversible Operations in Space', *Cortex*, 6 (1970), 174–190.

Butters, N. and Brody, B. A., 'The Role of the Left Parietal Lobe in the Mediation of Intra- and Cross-modal Associations', *Cortex*, 4 (1968), 328–343.

Corkin, S., Milner, B. and Rasmussen, T., 'Somatosensory Thresholds', *Archives of Neurology*, 23 (1970), 41–58.

Critchley, M., *The Parietal Lobes* (London, Arnold, 1953).

Geschwind, N., *Selected Papers on Language and the Brain* (Boston, Mass., D. Reidel, 1974).

Heimberger, R. F., Demeyer, W. and Reitan, R. M., 'Implications of Gerstmann's Syndrome', *Journal of Neurology, Neurosurgery and Psychiatry*, 27 (1964), 52–57.

Kimura, D., 'Acquisition of a Motor Skill after Left Hemisphere Damage', *Brain*, 100 (1977), 527–542.

Kinsbourne, M. and Warrington, E. K., 'A Study of Finger Agnosia', *Brain*, 85 (1962), 47–66.

McFie, J. and Zangwill, O. L., 'Visual-constructive Disabilities Associated with Lesions of the Left Cerebral Hemisphere', *Brain*, 83 (1960), 243–260.

Semmes, J., 'A Non-tactual Factor in Astereognosis', *Neuropsychologia*, 3 (1965), 295–315.

Semmes, J., Weinstein, S., Ghent, L. and Teuber, H.-L., 'Spatial Orientation in Man after Cerebral Injury. I: Analysis by Locus of Lesion', *Journal of Psychology*, 39 (1955), 227–244.

Semmes, J., Weinstein, S., Ghent, L. and Teuber, H.-L., *Somatosensory Changes after Penetrating Brain Wounds in Man* (Cambridge, Mass., Harvard University Press, 1960).

Shallice, T. and Warrington, E. K., 'The Dissociation between Short-term Retention of Meaningful Sounds and Verbal Material', *Neuropsychologia*, 12 (1974), 553–555.

Warrington, E. K., 'Constructional Apraxia', in P. J. Vinken and G. W. Bruyn, eds, *Handbook of Clinical Neurology*, vol. 4 (Amsterdam, New Holland, 1969).

Warrington, E. K. and Taylor, A. M., 'The Contribution of the Right Parietal Lobe to Object Recognition', *Cortex*, 9 (1973), 152–164.

Weinstein, E. A. and Friedland, R. P., eds, *Hemi-Inattention and Hemisphere Specialization. Advances in Neurology*, vol. 18 (New York, Raven Press, 1977).

CHAPTER 6

The Occipital Lobes

Because the occipital lobes contain only primary and secondary cortex subserving vision, they are almost exclusively concerned with elementary aspects of visual sensation and perception. As a result, in recent years they have seemed to be of less interest to many neuropsychologists, who have been attracted by the study of higher cortical functions. However, at least two recent developments, the study of 'blindsight' and the research into visual prostheses, have revived interest in this region of the cortex, and we can probably expect to see an increase in research into the functions of the occipital lobes.

ANATOMICAL DIVISIONS

The occipital lobes are much less clearly demarcated by anatomical landmarks than the other three pairs of lobes, but they are usually considered to be formed of three regions, which may be characterized by the type of cell contained in each. These cytoarchitectonic regions are Brodmann's areas 17, 18 and 19, and these numbers are often used to refer to the three occipital regions. More common, perhaps, is the use of the terms *striate* (because of its striped appearance when sectioned), *parastriate* and *peristriate*, for regions 17, 18 and 19 respectively (see Fig. 6.1).

The delineation of these regions by the type of cortical cell which they contain is particularly valuable in this lobe because it allows some generalization to be made from studies of the visual cortex in animals to the visual cortex in humans. There is no good reason to doubt that fundamental mechanisms differ between the cat or the monkey and man, and we can therefore assume that regions made up of similar cells will perform the same elementary functions in man as in the animals studied. A great deal of highly sophisticated physiological work has been done on the functions of the visual cortex of higher

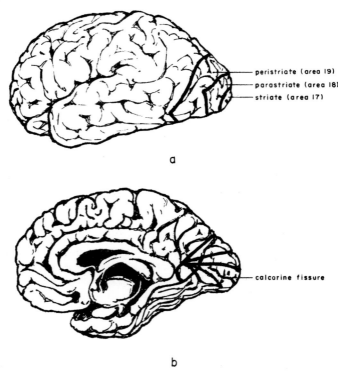

peristriate (area 19)
parastriate (area 18)
striate (area 17)

a

calcarine fissure

b

Figure 6.1. Anatomical divisions of the occipital lobe in (a) lateral and (b) medial views.

mammals, of which that of Hubel and Wiesel (1979) is a particularly successful example, and this has enabled a remarkably clear picture of the basic mechanisms involved in vision to be built up.

At each level in the visual system, there is a clear spatial mapping of the visual world. It is possible to identify cells at each level which respond to stimuli at a certain point in space, and these cells are arranged in a way which corresponds to the relationships of the points in external space, although with some minor distortions. This principle should not be extended too far, because it is not a simple representation of the visual world which is being copied up towards the brain, and within the spatial mapping of the system, a variety of forms of analysis is operating to extract different features and dimensions of the visual stimulation before the information reaches the cortex of the brain. Nevertheless, within these subsystems, which operate at various levels within the visual pathways, a certain amount of spatial information is preserved by spatial mapping of the anatomical cell arrangements.

The spatial mapping of visual stimulation extends right up to *primary visual cortex*, which is the striate region or area 17. This is principally on the medial surfaces of the hemispheres around the *occipital pole* and extending up and around the *calcarine fissure* (see Fig. 6.1). Because this region is so well tucked up inside the medial surface of the hemispheres, it is relatively well protected from damage, and the most common cause of large lesions of the area is a failure of blood supply, usually as a result of *cerebral ischaemia*, or a narrowing and blockage, leading to a 'stroke', of the posterior cerebral artery, which provides the entire blood supply to this area.

From the striate cortex, the visual information is passed out, by a reflection of the spatial map, to the parastriate region, area 18, which surrounds it. This forms the secondary visual cortex, and also has rich interhemispheric connections through the posterior part of the corpus callosum, known as the *splenium*. From area 18, the information may pass on to the peristriate region, area 19, as well as forward into the inferior and middle temporal gyri.

An important qualification should be made to what has been said so far about the visual system. It is now clear that there are two systems involved in mammalian vision: the *geniculostriate* and the *tectopulvinar* systems (Dick, 1976; Masterton, 1978). These systems are sometimes referred to as the *primary* and *secondary visual systems* (and the secondary as the 'subcortical' visual system). What we have discussed so far is the primary geniculostriate system, which runs through the lateral geniculate nucleus of the thalamus back to the occipital cortex, and can be considered roughly to subserve the perception of forms, patterns and colour. By contrast the tectopulvinar system runs by the superior colliculus to the pulvinar and the lateral posterior regions of the thalamus before projecting out to the inferior and middle gyri of the temporal lobes. This system, which may in some ways be more primitive than the primary system, probably deals with visual location and to some extent movement, although the division of function between the two systems is not entirely clear. What is clear, as we shall see, is that this system is increasingly considered to play a significant role in human vision. For the present, however, we shall continue to discuss the primary geniculostriate system, which certainly plays the more important part in visual perception.

BASIC VISUAL FUNCTIONS

In line with the three level model of cortical functions we have followed so far, lesions of the primary visual cortex result in loss of visual sensation, while lesions of the secondary cortex result in perceptual impairment.

Damage to the striate cortex simply results in loss of vision. If the lesion is extensive, this may extend over the whole of the visual field, and if confined to a single hemisphere, it will affect vision in the contralateral visual field, that is, on the opposite side of space to the side of the lesion. Smaller areas of damage will result in gaps in vision known as *scotomas*, which may be surrounded by regions of partial deficit which are described as *amblyopic*. Even if the whole visual field is affected, then there may be sparing of the very central, *macular*, region of vision, which leaves the patient with a small central region in which some vision is preserved. This macular sparing may come about because this region, which is normally that of highest visual acuity, has a double blood supply from the middle and posterior cerebral arteries, or because it receives bilateral projections from the left and right visual half-field systems.

By contrast, stimulation of the primary visual cortex in patients whose visual system may be damaged but whose cortex is intact results in reports of points or flashes of light, and sometimes of simple shapes, such as triangles, squares or circles. These images are usually small, discrete and have a specific spatial location, so that the patient can point to where they seem to appear. They can be regarded as elementary visual sensations, and when resulting from artificial stimulation are termed *photisms* or *phosphenes*. It is possible that you have experienced these following a sharp blow to the head, particularly from behind, and 'seeing stars' is the apt common phrase often used to denote such after-effects. What probably happens is that the blow results in the brain coming up rather sharply against the inside of the skull, with the result that abnormal mechanical stimulation follows, producing phosphenes. A blow to the front rather than the back of the head may have the same result, because it may lead to a kind of 'whiplash' effect inside the head, so that the major contact of the brain with the skull is at the occipital pole. In severe cases, this kind of blow may lead to serious damage of the cortex opposite to the site of the blow, and is known as a *contre-coup* injury.

An interesting and rather surprising aspect of many cases of loss of vision following occipital injury is the patient's lack of awareness of

the deficit. It is not uncommon to see patients who may have effectively lost half of their vision – all vision to one side of their central
midline – and yet be apparently unaware that they have any disability. This is more likely to be the case if the loss results from a slowly
developing lesion so that the loss is progressive, perhaps from the
periphery inwards.

This lack of awareness can be attributed to two factors. The first is
that of *completion* (King, 1967). This is a very powerful mechanism
which operates in normal vision to fill in gaps in the visual information available. It no doubt results from the systems which work so
effectively to provide us with a stable, rich and complete visual
perception of the world from the series of jerky glimpses which our
constantly moving and dithering eyes provide. Visual perception is
essentially a reconstruction of the visual world 'out there' from the
information at our disposal, and completion is just one part of that
process. Its clearest demonstration is in the way it fills in the normal
'blind spot' in vision which results from the gap in the retina of the eye
through which blood vessels and neural wiring pass. (If you have
never located your own blind spot, close one eye and hold a finger up
at arm's length, facing a fairly plain background. Now fix your gaze
on the background and, keeping your eyes still, move your finger out
to the same side as the open eye, about six inches and perhaps a little
down. You should easily locate the point where the tip of the finger
apparently just disappears.) We are never normally aware of the
blind spot because completion compensates for the missing portion,
just as it may for the scotoma (blind region) of the brain injured
patient. Completion can compensate for remarkably large areas of
scotoma, and there seems no difficulty in its operation across the
visual midline.

The second factor which may result in lack of awareness of the
deficit is that associated with *denial* of the disability. This can sometimes be part of Anton's syndrome, of which denial of blindness (often
with unconvincing confabulation – 'There's no light in here.') is a
central element. It is probably a mistake to think of this simply as the
patient trying to cover up his difficulty, especially as there are studies
which show that patients with visual loss and hemiplegia may deny
the loss of vision, but not the loss of motor abilities. It is better to
consider that the visual functions have become disconnected from the
rest of the cognitive systems, so that these patients do not see the gaps
in their vision because they are not seeing at all. This is the same
problem, conceptually, for most of us as conceiving the experience of
the congenitally blind. It may be therefore that some of these patients

do not report their visual handicap because they have stopped seeing altogether in certain regions of space.

A final point about basic visual processes which cannot be over-stressed is the difficulty of accurately delimiting visual field deficits (see Milner and Teuber, 1968, for an excellent discussion). This is firstly because the extent of vision depends crucially on the type of stimulation. Whether the stimulus is stationary or moving, neutral or brightly coloured, large or small, contrasting or blending with the background, will all determine whether the patient can see it or not. Secondly, the functional state of many patients is highly unstable, and the extent of any visual disability may vary from day to day, with fatigue and perhaps with psychological state. It is therefore a grave mistake to think of visual field defects as being simple, easily delineated and represented on a chart of the visual fields. Certainly, there will be common regions where the defect is relatively dense and constant, but around these regions there will be a great deal of variability. This raises considerable problems for research studies, where we may simply need to know 'Does this patient see the stimulus material, or not?', and may be unable to obtain an entirely satisfactory answer. Whether considering research studies or indi-vidual clinical cases, descriptions of visual field defects, especially if based on simple confrontational testing or perimetry, should be treated with great caution.

VISUAL PERCEPTUAL FUNCTIONS

The job of *secondary visual cortex* is to translate the assembled visual sensations from primary cortex into meaningful percepts, and to pass this perceptual information on to the tertiary association cortex where it can be integrated with information from other modalities and other cognitive data. Area 18 of the occipital lobe performs the secondary elaboration and synthesis of visual percepts, while area 19, in associa-tion with regions of the temporal cortex, performs intersensory inte-gration and higher level processing.

Lesions of the occipital secondary visual cortex therefore tend to result in deficits in simple perceptual functions. The classic work in this area was performed on brain injured combatants of the Second World War by Teuber's group (Teuber, Battersby and Bender, 1960), and has been little extended in recent years. Patients have difficulty in discriminating objects which differ in shape, size, orienta-tion or colour, and in addition may be poor at bisecting lines or judging their length or orientation (Benton, Hannay and Varney, 1975). This may be evident in patients' drawings (see Fig. 6.2), in which the deficit is qualitatively different from that seen with parietal lesions (compare Fig. 5.10). Here it is not simply the articulation of the elements which results in defective performance, but the elementary processes of judging the relationships and distances between elements, forming straight lines, angles and curves, and relating drawing movements to the elements already put down on the paper.

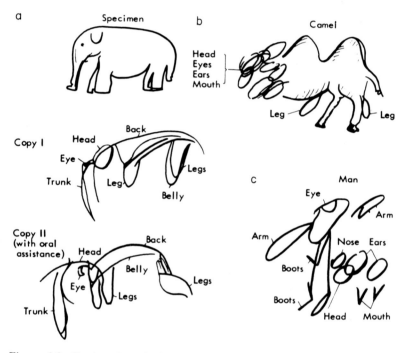

Figure 6.2. Copies of an elephant and drawings of a camel and a man by a patient with an occipital lesion.
(Reprinted from A. R. Luria, *The Working Brain*, Penguin Press, 1973)

Patients with occipital lesions may also show gross distortions of perception, seeing things as too small (micropsia), too large (macropsia), at a great distance (teleopsia) or repeated (polyopsia). Boundaries of objects may become distorted or displaced, and there may be fluctuations in the intensity or clarity of vision. These *metamorphopsias* by which the shape of things becomes changed are difficult to imagine and clearly have radical implications for all kinds of psychological skills. In addition, visual events may curiously perseverate (palinopsia) and remain longer than they should or, even more bizarrely, be repeated after a short interval, for example, the sight of someone walking past the bed may be 'replayed' over again after a brief interval, and even repeated a number of times. Some of these more dramatic symptoms are relatively rare, but their varied and extensive nature shows just how disturbing and disabling can be the malfunction of the normally powerful systems which govern visual perceptual processes. Lesions of secondary visual cortex therefore result in widespread disturbances in temporal and spatial accuracy and stability of visual perception.

Some interesting work has been carried out on the recovery of function which may follow certain vascular accidents which affect the occipital cortex (Gloning, Gloning and Hoff, 1968). There seems to be a fairly clear functional sequence in the recovery process, with initial darkness being relieved first by photisms, and then by undifferentiated light. Primitive movement detection follows, at first without clear perception of direction or speed, followed by contours of increasing stability, and finally with the addition of colour. It may be wrong to think of this as a hierarchy of visual functions, but there is some reason to believe it reflects functional levels of the visual perceptual system.

Beyond the elementary perceptual processes, there are of course higher cognitive functions, impairments of which result in *visual agnosia* (a term introduced by Sigmund Freud during his early career). Most of these, including visual object agnosia, and agnosia for drawings and facial recognition, involve regions of the temporal lobe together with the occipital lobes, and have already been discussed (see p. 73). Some other functions rely more heavily on the occipital contribution, although not without some involvement of temporal and parietal cortex.

One group of these functions involves colour perception. In *colour agnosia* the patient may be able to discriminate colour accurately by simple matching, but may be unable to link appropriate colours to objects or to sort colours into groups. The patient may also be unable to operate symbolic colour-based codes or to extract meaningful associations from colours. Whether there is also a deficit in naming colours (*colour anomia*) will depend on whether certain language systems around the temporo-parieto-occipital junction are affected (Damásio, McKee and Damásio, 1979). Whether colour anomia is an independent deficit from colour agnosia is still a matter of debate. Linked to these deficits is *achromatopsia*, in which the patient perceives the world as colourless, so that it appears in shades of grey or occasionally shades of a single colour.

Visual spatial agnosias may also result from occipital lesions, particularly if they involve stereoscopic vision. As might be expected, the deficit results in a perceptual world which seems limited to two dimensions, or where sensible interpretations cannot be made of depth relationships. This no doubt arises from interference with the important interhemispheric splenial connections which link areas 18 and 19 in the two hemispheres and which serve to tie together the two halves of visual space, integrating information about the two visual fields with information about images from the two eyes. Spatial agnosias which involve topographical concepts or the neglect of visual space are more likely to have significant parietal involvement.

Associative visual agnosia is sometimes distinguished as an independent entity (Albert, Reches and Silverberg, 1975; Mack and Boller, 1977). Here the patient may copy and draw objects quite accurately, either from the original or a model drawing, but still be unable to name or indicate their proper use or associations (although the object may automatically be taken up and used as part of an habitual sequence). Deep lesions of the occipital lobes have been found to produce this deficit, although temporal lesions may also do so.

The final important form of visual agnosia that should be mentioned is *simultanagnosia*. This dysfunction results in the patient being unable to formulate simultaneously more than one percept. It is usually demonstrated on tasks which involve hidden or embedded figures (see Fig. 6.3), of which there are a number of popularly used sets for testing. The true simultanagnosic patient will pick one percept from among the overlaid outlines of such a stimulus and then be unable to determine any others. On subsequent occasions of

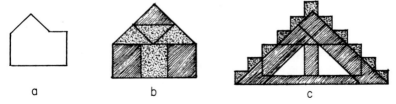

a   b   c

Figure 6.3. Embedded figures. The patient must find the form (a) hidden in figures (b) and (c).

testing, the same single percept is likely to be elicited, with no additional responses. As a similar deficit, the ability to find figures embedded in complex perceptual displays may also be affected, although there is some dispute as to whether these problems occur in the absence of significant primary visual field defects (Bisiach, Capitani, Nichelli and Spinnler, 1976). There is considerable difficulty in completely dissociating most of these agnosic deficits from primary perceptual disorders on the one hand, and language mediated mechanisms on the other (Spinnler, 1971).

A passing reference should also be made to a rare but significant condition known as *alexia without agraphia, agnosic alexia* or *pure word blindness*. In this condition the patient cannot read, although he may write spontaneously and to dictation, and may speak normally. Such patients may also be unable to read their own writing once its content has been forgotten. There is some dispute about the existence of this condition in a 'pure' form, but it is argued to result from lesions of the occipital lobe and the splenium of the corpus callosum, which effectively disconnect the visual perceptual mechanisms of reading from other functional language systems (Geschwind, 1965; Benson, 1976).

BLINDSIGHT

One dramatic development which has served to enliven research into the neuropsychological functions of the occipital lobes has been the studies of 'blindsight'. This phenomenon was reported in the early part of this century but then largely neglected until the last decade. It was noted that patients, although reporting themselves entirely blind, did possess some aspects of visual responsiveness. They could make certain visual judgements but without having any perceptual experience.

In the modern studies, these abilities have been found to be quite extensive, whether following damage from trauma, from stroke, or from surgical lesions introduced either early or later in life. The abilities preserved in the 'blind' areas of these patients have of course varied but they include: orientation of the eyes towards the source of some flashed stimulus (Pöppel, Held and Frost, 1973), accurate pointing and reaching responses to some point source of light, differentiation of the orientation of lines, differentiation between large 'X's and 'O's, and an acuity (established by the discrimination of fine gratings) only a little poorer than regions of preserved normal vision (Perenin and Jeannerod, 1978; Weiskrantz, Warrington, Sanders and

Marshall, 1974). Even more extensive stimulus identification and discrimination have been reported by Torjussen (1978). Although these patients have constantly to be encouraged to perform, because they have no conscious awareness of the stimuli, and no idea of whether they are performing accurately or not, they can still show quite considerable ability.

The explanation for these preserved abilities is in the operation of the secondary tectopulvinar visual system mentioned above. These functions are precisely those which from animal studies we might expect to be undertaken by such a system. It may continue to operate once the primary system has been damaged, and provide visual perception, to a limited degree, but without the conscious visual experience which is a feature of the primary system.

It is hoped that these discoveries may lead to rehabilitative strategies for some of the patients who suffer cortical blindness, and although the opportunities must naturally be somewhat limited, they nevertheless provide some hope that retraining and the use of new behavioural strategies may ameliorate the handicap.

VISUAL PROSTHESES

An even more dramatic development, as yet still in the initial tentative research stage, is the possibility of prostheses for those who are blind following damage to the eyes or to the visual tract, but whose visual cortex is intact. The idea, which is artificially to stimulate the visual cortex so as to give the appropriate sensations of vision, has been tried in at least two centres (Dobelle, Quest, Antunes, Roberts and Girvin, 1979; Rushton and Brindley, 1977). In each patient, an array of tiny electrodes was placed over the visual cortex with connections out through the skull so that patterns of stimulation could be delivered directly to the cortex. The aim is to work towards some device which would perhaps incorporate a camera mounted on top of the head that would then transmit to a large array of very closely spaced stimulators over the cortex, giving a useful degree of artificial vision.

The results seem at least encouraging. Following stimulation, these patients experience phosphenes which are spatially relatively stable and which enable them to recognize simple patterns, including letters, transmitted to them. One patient has even been able to read 'visual braille' at a rate that was faster than was possible by touch, which is a remarkable achievement.

There are bound to be limits to what can be accomplished by such methods. There are bioengineering problems in constructing stimulation arrays of sufficient density to form a long-term implanted prosthesis, although current developments in microelectronics are making many of the associated computing requirements seem entirely feasible. And there are biological problems, too, in the response of the system to repeated and prolonged stimulation, and in the amount of useful cognitive information that can be derived from such a crude input without all the associated links with eye and head movement systems, general postural and orientational senses, and intersensory integration circuits. Nevertheless, if any useful vision can be reconstructed for these patients, and it seems not impossible that this could be the result, then the research is clearly worth pursuing.

CONCLUSION

The occipital lobes subserve the functions of primary visual sensation and visual perception based upon these sensations. These functions are summarized in Table 6.1. They cooperate with neighbouring regions in the high level cognitive functions which involve vision, for

TABLE 6.1. SOME FUNCTIONS OF
THE OCCIPITAL LOBES

Primary visual sensation (points of light, simple forms)
    Completion

Visual perception
    Contours
    Magnitude
    Orientation
    Depth
    Stereopsis
    Brightness
    Colour
    Movement

Semantic connotation of visual objects

Reading

---

the interpretation and semantic processing of visual objects and representations. Many of the deficits associated with the occipital lobes are variable, complex and unstable in character, and visual field defects are difficult to delineate. The contribution of primary perceptual dysfunctions, and the role of language systems in determining the presence of visual agnosias, is as yet unclear.

INTEGRATION OF CORTICAL FUNCTIONS

Now that we have looked at the functions of the four cerebral lobes, although we have yet to discuss the language system, this seems an appropriate point to introduce some comments about the complexity and integration of functional cortical systems. While in order to understand the organization of the cerebral cortex we have to try to dissociate the functions which may be linked with particular areas from other functions in other areas, and this information is in turn useful to the clinician in diagnosing lesions and planning the rehabilitation of patients, this should not lead us to lose sight of the complexity of cognitive functions in everyday life. It is easy to adopt a model of the cortex in which some area does a particular task, and then another area takes over to do something else, and so on, but the reality is clearly different. Most of the brain is involved, most of the time, in contributing to everyday intelligent behaviour.

As I sit at this microcomputer typing the text you are reading, I am using verbal systems to generate the symbolic form of the semantic content I wish to convey. At the same time I keep reading my notes, looking at the screen to see what has been typed, and planning how I must move my fingers to type the words, introducing little routines for capitals, new paragraphs, and so on. I have to maintain a map of where the keyboard, the screen, my notes and my limbs are all placed relative to each other, and all the while I am listening out for the telephone, trying to ignore that I feel thirsty, and carrying on a separate debate in my head about how much nicer it would be out walking somewhere. Periodically I mutter things to myself, scratch my head and notice that one of my teeth is aching a little. Not many of the functional elements mentioned in our tour of the lobes are not implicated somewhere in this sample of a few seconds of my behaviour.

Take an even simpler sample of behaviour: a tennis player about to hit the ball. A motor program is certainly being executed for that stroke, but many other operations are also being simultaneously performed. The body has to be moved to the right place on the court, and balance and control maintained. The ball is being watched, as is the opponent's position. A map is being maintained of spatial positions within the court, and constantly updated. The sound of the ball striking the racket will be attended to in order to check that the stroke was well executed, and feedback will be obtained through the arm at all stages of the stroke. At the same time future strategy is being planned, previous positions and plays are being remembered, the score is being maintained and calculations being made about points won and lost. Motivational systems are at work, feelings about the present position are being monitored, and an inner verbal dialogue (if not explicit speech) is being conducted.

This is perhaps labouring a point which is obvious. In everyday life most complex intelligent activities involve a great variety of cognitive skills and processes, all of which are interrelated and integrated within the overall operation of the brain. It is unreasonable to expect any of us to be able to grasp the actual complexity of this system, but at least in principle it is important to be aware of it, and not to allow the functional dissection which neuropsychological localization involves to blind us to how elaborate the operation of the brain actually is. No neuropsychologist can specialize in the study of only one area of the brain. The regions of the brain are not like 'bolt on parts', although the way that much of the research has been conducted might encourage you to think so. The brain, and not even only the cerebral cortex, *must* be seen as a whole, and considered as acting within the framework of a single comprehensive system of behavioural control.

FURTHER READING

As in Chapters 4 and 5, the principal texts for further reading are given at the end of Chapter 3. Among these, it is worth noting the extensive treatment given to metamorphopsias and to the visual agnosias in Chapter 4 of Hécaen and Albert (1978).

REFERENCES

Albert, M. L., Reches, A. and Silverberg, R., 'Associative Visual Agnosia without Alexia', *Neurology*, 25 (1975), 322–326.
Benson, D. F., 'Alexia', in J. T. Guthrie, ed., *Aspects of Reading Acquisition* (Baltimore, Maryland, The Johns Hopkins University Press, 1976).
Benton, A. L., Hannay, H. J. and Varney, N. R., 'Visual Perception of Line

Direction in Patients with Unilateral Brain Disease', *Neurology*, 25 (1975), 907–910.

Bisiach, E., Capitani, E., Nichelli, P. and Spinnler, H., 'Recognition of Overlapping Patterns and Focal Hemisphere Damage', *Neuropsychologia*, 14 (1976), 375–379.

Damásio, A. R., McKee, J. and Damásio, H., 'Determinants of Performance in Color Anomia', *Brain and Language*, 7 (1979), 74–85.

Dick, A. O., 'Spatial Abilities', in H. Whitaker and H. A. Whitaker, eds., *Studies in Neurolinguistics*, vol. 2. (New York, Academic Press, 1976).

Dobelle, W. H., Quest, D. O., Antunes, J. L., Roberts, T. S. and Girvin, J. P., 'Artificial Vision for the Blind by Electrical Stimulation of the Visual Cortex', *Neurosurgery*, 5 (1979), 521–527.

Geschwind, N., 'Alexia and Color-naming Disturbance', in G. Ettlinger, ed., *Functions of the Corpus Callosum* (London, Churchill, 1965).

Gloning, I., Gloning, K. and Hoff, H., *Neuropsychological Symptoms in Lesions of the Occipital Lobe and Adjacent Areas* (Paris, Gauthier-Villars, 1968).

Hubel, D. H. and Wiesel, T. N., 'Brain Mechanisms of Vision', in *Scientific American: The Brain* (San Francisco, W. H. Freeman, 1979).

King, E., 'The Nature of Visual Field Defects', *Brain*, 90 (1967), 647–668.

Mack, J. L. and Boller, F., 'Associative Visual Agnosia and its Related Deficits: the Role of the Minor Hemisphere in Assigning Meaning to Visual Perceptions', *Neuropsychologia*, 15 (1977), 345–350.

Masterton, R. B., ed., *Handbook of Behavioural Neurology: vol. 1, Sensory Integration* (New York, Plenum Press, 1978).

Milner, B. and Teuber, H.-L., 'Alteration of Perception and Memory in Man: Reflections on Methods', in L. Weiskrantz, ed., *Analysis of Behavioural Change* (New York, Harper and Row, 1968).

Perenin, M. T. and Jeannerod, M., 'Visual Function within the Hemianopic Field following Early Cerebral Hemidecortication in Man. I. Spatial localisation', *Neuropsychologia*, 16 (1978), 1–13.

Pöppel, E., Held, R. and Frost, D., 'Residual Visual Function after Brain Wounds involving the Central Visual Pathways in Man', *Nature*, 243 (1973), 295–296.

Rushton, D. N. and Brindley, G. S., 'Short- and Long-term Stability of Cortical Electrical Phosphenes', in F. C. Rose, ed., *Physiological Aspects of Clinical Neurology* (Oxford, Blackwell Scientific Publications, 1977).

Spinnler, H., 'Deficit in Associating Figures and Colours in Brain Damaged Patients', *Brain Research*, 31 (1971), 370–371.

Teuber, H.-L., Battersby, W. H. and Bender, M. B., *Visual Field Defects after Penetrating Missile Wounds of the Brain* (Cambridge, Mass., Harvard University Press, 1960).

Torjussen, T., 'Visual Processing in Cortically Blind Hemifields', *Neuropsychologia*, 16 (1978), 15–21.

Weiskrantz, L., Warrington, E. K., Sanders, M. D. and Marshall, J. (1974). 'Visual Capacity in the Hemianopic Field following a Restricted Occipital Ablation', *Brain*, 97 (1974), 709–728.

CHAPTER 7

Language

The discussion of language functions has been deferred until now because, while it is reasonable to assign most functions to one of the four central lobes (although it inevitably involves some distortion by oversimplification), the language system involves sites spread across a large part of the cortex. We will now examine that system and its disorders, which are known as *aphasias*.

THE LATERALIZATION OF LANGUAGE

When lateralization of function has been mentioned in previous chapters, it has been qualified as relating to right handed subjects. The reason is that it has long been clear that individuals differ in their cerebral organization, and that one of the variables most clearly associated with this is handedness. This is a complex topic which will be treated in more detail in Chapter 13, but it is of particular relevance to studies of language.

An early piece of evidence for differing speech organization in right and left handed people came from the observation that right sided focal lesions rarely produce disorders of speech in the right handed, but frequently do so in the left handed. A number of studies have collected data on the relative frequency of aphasia in right and left handed patients, and there has been considerable debate over their significance. It became rapidly clear that only a few, if any, left handers have a 'reversed' pattern of organization from right handers. Many have left sided speech representation, which is the typical pattern in right handers, while others seem to have more bilateral representation. Left handers thus have a less clear lateralization of speech, with both cerebral hemispheres contributing to the processing of language. The relative frequency of these different patterns of organization, and how they can be identified, is the subject of the debate.

Evidence from a number of techniques of investigation is pertinent to this question (see Section III), but taking here only the data on the frequency of aphasia, a fairly clear conclusion has emerged from the work of Paul Satz (1980). He has reviewed the studies between 1935 and 1973 in some detail and mathematically fitted some of the models which have been proposed for left handed speech organization. The results of the most recent analyses (Carter, Hohenegger and Satz, 1980; Satz, 1979, which is more recent than the fuller account published in 1980), clearly support a model in which many left handers have speech in both hemispheres. The best fitting model was that in which 76 per cent of left handers had bilateral speech representation, 25 per cent left lateralized and none right lateralized. For right handers the best model was: 95 per cent left lateralized, none bilateral and 5 per cent right lateralized.

Another clear piece of evidence that right and left handers differ in the way in which language is organized in their brains comes from the Wada test, in which intracarotid sodium amytal is injected to depress temporarily the function of one of the two hemispheres (see p. 80), a technique developed to provide surgeons with information on speech lateralization. The most recent report of the accumulated data from patients in Montreal who were tested by this method was published by Rasmussen and Milner (1975), and is shown in Table 7.1.

Of the patients without early left hemisphere brain damage, the vast majority of right handers had left sided speech representation, as did 70 per cent of the left handers, and the remaining 30 per cent of left handers were divided equally between right and bilateral speech. The

TABLE 7.1. SPEECH REPRESENTATION IN PATIENTS OF DIFFERENT HANDEDNESS ON THE WADA TEST (DATA FROM RASMUSSEN AND MILNER, 1975)

	N	Left	Bilateral	Right
		SPEECH REPRESENTATION (%)		
Without early left sided damage				
RIGHT HANDERS	140	96	0	4
LEFT/MIXED HANDERS	122	70	15	15
With early left sided damage				
RIGHT HANDERS	31	81	6	13
LEFT/MIXED HANDERS	78	30	19	51

proportions were different for those with early left hemisphere damage, where it is believed that the young brain's plasticity allows some relocation of language function, and where a higher proportion of patients with right or bilateral speech is therefore to be expected. However, the proportions here differed quite dramatically from those inferred by Satz. This is partly accounted for by differences in the methods used to infer speech representation, partly by differences in criteria for 'bilateral' representation, and partly by different ways of classifying handedness, but none of these considerations convincingly accounts for the difference. Resolution of this debate must await further evidence and further development of analytical techniques and theoretical models.

There are, of course, practical problems in finding out about the brain lateralization of individual patients. Knowing the handedness of a patient does not allow us to infer his speech lateralization. If the Wada evidence is correct, then we should expect nearly everyone to have left speech representation, and if we accept Satz's analysis of the aphasia data, then we should expect most left handers to have bilateral speech representation. The fact is that neither study has allowed the construction of a satisfactory model of the relation of the lateralization of speech to handedness and associated variables. We will, however, return to models of handedness in Chapter 13. It should also be noted here that other methods of determining individual speech lateralization, based upon dichotic listening, seem to hold some promise in clinical applications (see Chapter 11).

A final point about left handers and aphasia is that left handers are considered to suffer more severely in the initial stages of the illness from lesions which affect speech, but then make more rapid and complete recovery from aphasia than right handers. It is presumed that this is due to the relative bilateralization of their language representation, so that an undamaged hemisphere is more likely to be able to take over the functions previously performed by its damaged partner.

With this qualification about the language lateralization of left handers, we can return to consider the forms of aphasia, and will again assume the typical right handed pattern of left hemisphere speech lateralization.

VARIETIES OF APHASIA

The classification of aphasias has been one of the most hotly contested issues in the history of neuropsychology, and there is as yet no firm agreement. Not only has the terminology differed markedly from scheme to scheme, but the level of complexity of different systems has also varied greatly. Among those who have been willing to subdivide aphasias – and there has not been complete agreement that they differ in anything other than severity – some have considered there to be only two forms, which might be termed as *receptive* and *expressive* (Weisenberg and McBride, 1935); *fluent* and *nonfluent* (Howes and Geschwind, 1964); or *anterior* and *posterior* (Benson, 1967). At the other extreme there are very detailed classifications, often associated with esoteric and unhelpful terminology, which are more commonly found in neurology textbooks. Each scheme of classification has its particular strengths and weaknesses, and useful tabulations of the various common classifications appear in Benson (1979), Kertesz (1979) and Lesser (1978).

The scheme used here is the one which seems to be most widely accepted at present, and is known as the Boston classification. It has developed from the work of Geschwind (1965) and Goodglass and Kaplan (1972), and while a number of variants of the classification are used, it forms perhaps the best basis for students of aphasia. This classification divides aphasias into the following six categories (with some roughly equivalent terms given in parentheses):

1. Broca's (motor, nonfluent) aphasia
2. Wernicke's (sensory) aphasia
3. conduction (central) aphasia
4. anomic (amnesic) aphasia
5. transcortical motor aphasia
6. transcortical sensory aphasia (isolation syndrome).

To these forms must be added *global* aphasia, in which there is massive and severe disturbance of language functions across a number of these categories. *Alexia* and *agraphia*, specific disorders of reading and writing respectively, are also included within the classification by some. (Note that while 'a-' should imply total loss and 'dys-' partial loss, these prefixes are used rather imprecisely in many of these terms.) It should also be recognized that there are other more peripheral forms of speech pathology, which affect articulation for example, but which are not of primary interest to the neuropsychologist (see Crystal, 1980).

There are a number of reasons for accepting the Boston classification, in particular that there is some agreement that it is clinically valuable and allows sensible distinctions to be made between patients. One aspect of this is that it can be related, at least in broad terms, to lesions at particular sites on the cerebral cortex, and it therefore has some diagnostic validity. It has also proved possible to relate it to the results of various aphasia test batteries, so that the results of these tests can be expressed in terms of the classification. In fact, one of the strongest arguments in its support is that a taxonomic analysis of the results of one of these batteries (the Western Aphasia Battery) on a large group of patients produced a classification which maps very neatly on to the Boston scheme (Kertesz, 1979). This is impressive support, but it should be remembered that the battery was constructed in a milieu in which the Boston scheme was the accepted model of the aphasias, and the result is therefore a little less surprising than at first appears.

One disadvantage of the Boston scheme is that it does not formally recognize the neurolinguistic analyses of aphasias which have become of increasing importance in recent years. Rather than classifying aphasias in terms of performance on various tasks in various modalities, studies have been based upon a linguistic analysis of dysfunction, concentrating on the linguistic structures which have been affected, on distinguishing syntactic and semantic processes, and the parts of speech and characteristics of the language elements which are abnormally processed (Lesser, 1978). Many neuropsychologists are relatively inexpert at linguistic analysis, and neurologists even more so, but the development of aphasiology to include linguistic parameters is logical, and may be of considerable value.

Although aphasias will be described here in terms of the Boston classification, there are other valuable ways to subdivide them. One example is the scheme proposed by Luria and Hutton (1977), which is much more in the tradition of the Russian work, and another attractive system has been suggested by Brown (1976, 1979). Brown divides aphasias firstly into anterior and posterior disorders, and then into various levels of linguistic involvement. The anterior series progresses from complete mutism through selective mutism to agrammatism and finally anarthric aphasia (in which the difficulty is making the movements to produce speech), thus moving from global action to more discrete faciovocal activity and finally to speech articulation. The posterior series moves from semantic through nominal to phonemic disorders, being a progression towards increasing specificity in the selection of particular words. Each of these series reflects a structural progression from limbic transitional cortex through generalized neocortex to focal neocortex. Brown's theory is not easy to grasp when stated so starkly, but the nature of some of the functions mentioned should become clearer as the different forms of aphasia are discussed in more detail below. An advantage of his scheme is that it does make explicit reference to linguistic parameters, while still being directly linked to anatomical structures. An added attraction of the scheme is that it treats the cortex as a three-dimensional stucture and considers the depth of lesions in subcortical tissue. This aspect of cerebral lesions is too often ignored, and the cortex treated as if it had only two dimensions, relatively divorced from what lies beneath. Brown's scheme has yet, however, to gain wide acceptance.

ANATOMICAL STRUCTURES

Before proceeding to describe the various forms of aphasia, it may be helpful to look again at some of the anatomical locations thought to be involved in the language system (shown in Fig. 7.1). Beginning

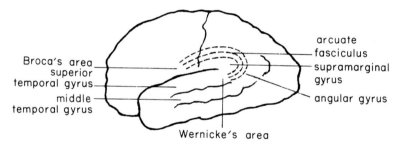

Figure 7.1. The principal structures in the left hemisphere associated with language functions.

anteriorly, the most important structure is *Broca's area* in the inferior posterior frontal cortex (of the left hemisphere, of course). This was the first location to be clearly associated with language function, in Broca's report of 1861 (although Dax may have some claim to have established it earlier; see Critchley, 1979) supported by post mortem findings. Also in the frontal lobe, although separate from Broca's area, is a region of *anterior mesial cortex* which, as we shall see, is associated with transcortical motor aphasia.

Posteriorly, there is a more complex group of structures. *Wernicke's area* is in the superior middle and posterior regions of the temporal lobe, not far away from Heschl's gyrus, which is involved in auditory reception (see p. 69). Wrapped around the posterior end of the

Sylvian fissure is an area of association cortex (*peri-Sylvian association cortex*), and moving posteriorly there are also the areas known as the *angular gyrus* and the *supramarginal gyrus*. The region referred to as the angular gyrus may extend rather beyond its strict topographical bounds into the middle posterior temporal region. The only other structure that we must denote is the *arcuate fasciculus*, which is an important tract of corticocortical (connecting two regions of cortex) fibres running approximately from the region around the posterior end of the Sylvian fissure forward to the posterior regions of the frontal lobe, and thereby serving as a direct link, so it is inferred, between the posterior and anterior language zones.

Before describing how all these different structures contribute to the language system, it should be pointed out that there is some danger of overlooking the considerable variability in the system by abstracting information from it which allows us to make sense of localization. The system should not ideally be described in such neat terms, with apparently accurate cortical localization. Figures presented by Kertesz, Lesk and McCabe (1977) are derived from isotope scans of lesions producing various forms of aphasia and show that the lesions do no more than centre on a particular region. In Fig. 7.2, for example, the lesions producing anomic aphasia involve the angular

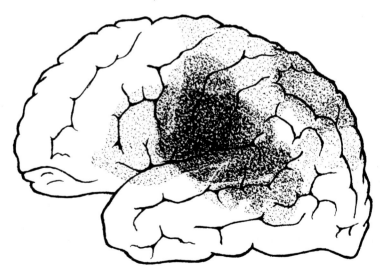

Figure 7.2. The regions of the brain associated with anomic aphasia.
(Redrawn after Kertesz, Lesk and McCabe, 1977)

gyrus and middle posterior temporal lobe, and it is clear from the figure that they may commonly involve a variety of other regions.

Not only the isotope scans, but also studies of stimulation of the exposed cortex at surgery have raised considerable doubts about the precise localization of language functions (Ojemann and Whitaker, 1978; Ojemann and Mateer, 1979). Others have more generally questioned the localization of structures involved in language, even to questioning the identification of such well-established landmarks as Wernicke's area (Bogen and Bogen, 1976; Whitaker and Selnes, 1976; Zangwill, 1975). Care should therefore be taken to recognize both the variation between individuals and the degree of imprecision which may in reality characterize apparently precise accounts of the language system.

THE FORMS OF APHASIA

Broca's Aphasia

This is associated with lesions of Broca's area in the inferior posterior frontal lobe. It is the most generally recognized form of aphasia, and is the classical nonfluent form. The principal sign is that the patient's speech output is severely impaired. Most likely to be affected are articles, adverbs, adjectives and other function words, so that speech tends to be reduced to nouns and verbs only. In the most extreme cases there is muteness, and in severe cases nouns may be restricted to their singular form, and verbs to the infinitive or a participle. This kind of speech is sometimes described as 'telegraphic'. The meaning is often evident, and words tend to be in the correct order, but it is as if speech has been reduced to its essential elements by agrammatic deletions. Short automatic phrases, of the kind common in 'small talk', may well be inserted, and in fact used excessively and inappropriately.

There may also be errors in the actual production of words. *Paraphasias*, as these are known, are relatively common, but are of the phonemic variety where the target word is usually identifiable. Some error in the selection or production of sound elements seems to occur, but as the word produced usually approximates to the target word, and as the context may also provide some clues, it is generally possible to tell what the patient is intending to say.

There is, in addition, some difficulty with repetition and with naming, although prompting by sounds or context can be of significant help with the latter. However, it is probably best to see these particular difficulties as secondary to the problems with speech output, limiting the performance which might otherwise be attained. This is probably not a complete explanation, because written output may well be affected in the same way as speech, presumably by sharing certain output mechanisms, and the difficulty therefore seems to lie in language production generally rather than specifically with speech.

All these problems occur, however, with language comprehension intact. Patients understand perfectly what is said to them, and read as well as they comprehend speech. They often show extreme frustration at their own inability to communicate by speech, while understanding what they read and hear, although not all of them are aware of their speech limitation.

Wernicke's Aphasia

The lesion causing this dysfunction is to be found in Wernicke's area, as originally described in 1874 but, as has already been noted, there is some dispute about how precisely this area may be identified. This form of aphasia is, in contrast with Broca's, fluent and is characterized by a severe deficit in auditory comprehension. Patients may be able to tell speech from nonspeech, but they are able to extract little if any meaning from it. There is usually some related impairment in both reading and writing, parallel with auditory comprehension and speech output respectively. Naming is often also impaired to some degree, and repetition is always affected.

Fluent does not mean that speech is normal, and the most striking feature of patients suffering from this type of aphasia is their verbal behaviour. Although they produce normal, and sometimes excessive, amounts of speech, they are generally quite unintelligible. The speech is filled by paraphasias which are in this case of a semantic nature. The patient substitutes different words for the ones which he presumably intends to utter. These may be semantically related to the target words ('red' for 'green', 'table' for 'chair'), but they may also be neologisms, resulting in *jargon aphasia*. This jargon is usually meaningless, as for example in this response of a patient asked what a pen was used for: 'This is a tape of brouse to make buke deproed in the auria.' (Kertesz and Benson, 1970). The form and often the intonation makes such speech sound like sensible English, even though it is nonsense. Again, short phrases, particularly if relatively 'automatic' or well used, may be preserved. In the following example, from Kertesz (1981), a patient was asked by the examiner to describe a picture: 'Dahnay. Enambalsay. Fack-anadee. Whynowneea. Oldeea.

Eggerferma gerfriend.' Examiner: 'What's he doing?' Patient: 'Goin' tagowi. She's got a rabliun. I think I wanta . . . Oh he . . .' Examiner: 'Do you know what this is over here?' Patient: 'No. Balky. I-isetinga.'

One way to understand this problem in speech is to see it as caused partly by the comprehension deficit. It may be that the mechanisms for monitoring speech output are common with those for interpreting incoming language, so that the patient loses control of his language expression by being unable to check on what is being produced. The result is often 'word salad'.

Conduction Aphasia

There is less agreement about this form of aphasia than the previous two, but it is also an aphasia where repetition is disordered and this provides the central characteristic. Patients with conduction aphasia comprehend both speech and writing normally. They will also produce more or less normal speech: it is at least reasonably fluent, the meaning is clear and appropriate, and the syntax is usually correct. Occasionally phonemic paraphasias may be introduced, but these are relatively minor and the target word is generally clear both from the context and from the form of the actual word produced. Naming may be mildly affected, but again the impairment tends to be connected with phonemic paraphasias.

However, although these patients can understand language normally, and generally produce acceptable speech, they are severely impaired if asked to repeat material which is spoken to them. The same problem may be evident if they attempt to read aloud, even though they comprehend the written material. This remarkable behaviour probably arises from some disconnection between the posterior systems for language reception and the anterior systems for language production, and there are a number of models of how this might occur, although none is widely accepted.

Reflecting this disconnection, the critical lesion site producing conduction aphasia is often considered to be in deeper tissue and affecting the arcuate fasciculus, which connects anterior and posterior language centres. This makes for a neat model of how the 'conduction' from reception to expression might be interrupted, but it is by no means universally accepted. Further, the role of short-term memory dysfunction in association with this aphasia has never been properly clarified.

Anomic Aphasia

This form of aphasia is generally considered to be produced by lesions

TABLE 7.2. A CLASSIFICATION OF THE APHASIAS
WITH THEIR ASSOCIATED SYMPTOMS, AS PRESENTED
IN THE TEXT

Aphasias	LESION	FLUENCY	SPEECH OUTPUT	REPETITION
BROCA'S (Motor, Nonfluent)	Inferior posterior frontal	Mild to severe impairment	Phonemic paraphasias; agrammatic deletions; Word order + meaning normal	Limited
WERNICKE'S (sensory)	Superior, Middle + Posterior Temporal	Normal to hyperfluent	Normal to jargon; word order normal to impaired; meaning irrelevant, vague	Impaired
CONDUCTION (central)	Arcuate fasciculus and deep	Mild to moderate impairment	Some phonemic paraphasias; word order normal; meaning appropriate	Severely impaired
ANOMIC (amnesic)	Angular gyrus, Posterior middle temporal	Normal (except noun blocking)	Normal except nouns may be omitted, substituted or paraphrased	Normal
TRANSCORTICAL MOTOR	Anterior mesial frontal	Normal when repeating	Normal when repeating	Normal
TRANSCORTICAL SENSORY (isolation syndrome)	Peri-Sylvian association cortex	Normal	Normal to jargon as Wernicke's	Normal
GLOBAL	Impaired	Impaired	Impaired	Impaired
Other language disorders				
ALEXIA, AGRAPHIA	Supramarginal gyrus Angular gyrus	Normal	Normal	Normal

of the angular gyrus, and of the middle posterior temporal lobe. It is perhaps the most common of the aphasias, and may exist as a residual form following recovery from one of the other types. Both comprehension and expression are essentially intact, and repetition is normal. There is a specific difficulty, nevertheless, with finding the names for objects (as 'anomic' implies).

This specific deficit in word finding, particularly prominent for nouns, has a limited effect in speech output, although it may not be immediately apparent. There is often some blocking or hesitation in speech as a noun is being searched for, and careful testing often shows that words are substituted to avoid the problems raised by a word which cannot be found. This formally constitutes a semantic paraphasia, but as the substitutions are often appropriate and acceptable, it may go undetected in spontaneous speech. However, the kind of circumlocution which some patients employ to evade their handicap is more marked, and in severe cases the speech may be described as 'empty' because the content lacks principal noun elements.

Although common, this form of aphasia is poorly understood.

	NAMING	AUDITORY COMPREHENSION	WRITTEN OUTPUT	READING
	Limited	Normal (function to words limited)	As speech	As comprehension
	Impaired	Mild to severe impairment. Can tell if speech	As speech	As comprehension
	Impaired	Normal	As speech	Normal to mild impairment
	Impaired	Normal	May be as speech	As comprehension
	Limited	Normal	Impaired	Normal to mild impairment
	Impaired	Severely impaired. Can tell syntactic errors	Impaired	Impaired
	Impaired	Impaired	Impaired	Impaired

	Normal	Normal	Severely impaired	Severely impaired

Word finding is clearly a complex process. To name an object, its essential characteristics must first be abstracted for identification, and then the semantically correct word retrieved and translated into a form which can be produced in speech. At precisely which stage the difficulty occurs is not clear, and indeed it may differ among cases.

Prompting is often not of great assistance to the anomic patient, and neither is giving him the context in which the word occurs, nor its initial sound, nor a rhyming word. Curiously, these patients can often use a related verb, which may be the same word, to explain how they cannot find the correct noun. For example, unable to get the word 'comb', a patient might suddenly say, 'I know, you use it when you want to comb your hair', and still be unable to say that it was a comb. Perhaps the classic example is the patient who says, 'No, doctor, I just can't say "no"!'

Transcortical Motor Aphasia

The lesion associated with this disorder is generally to be found in the frontal association cortex, which is anterior or superior to Broca's area and is assumed to be linked to it. In both transcortical motor and sensory aphasias a very curious phenomenon appears. In the most extreme form, which combines both motor and sensory elements, and is relatively rare, the patient does not understand speech and cannot read. He is also totally nonfluent, speaks only if spoken to, and usually cannot write. Nevertheless, the patient can repeat what he hears with almost no impairment. This ability to repeat language, in the presence of an otherwise dense aphasia, has more descriptively been called *echolalic* aphasia. The only other preserved language ability reported in these patients is to complete proverbs, well-known sayings or simple sentences. Singing, the production of automatic phrases, and swearing are also preserved, as in almost all of the aphasias.

In transcortical motor aphasia the impairment in speech output predominates. The patient therefore preserves some auditory comprehension and understands what he reads, but his speech is normally fluent only when he is repeating what he hears, and his writing is impaired along with spontaneous speech. Giving cues to assist with naming or to promote more fluent speech helps most of these patients.

Transcortical Sensory Aphasia

The lesion associated with this is usually found in peri-Sylvian association cortex, around the junction of the parietal and temporal lobes. In this type of transcortical aphasia, language reception is usually severely affected, but the ability to repeat is preserved. It is sometimes known as the *isolation syndrome*, implying that the speech cortex has been isolated from other elements of the language system, but beware because this term is not used consistently and is sometimes applied only to complete transcortical aphasia, and sometimes only to the motor form. All these aphasias are called 'transcortical' because it is thought that the lesion allows transmission across the cortex of information between language reception and production, but links with mechanisms which subserve comprehension, or links between the formulation of language and speech output, are not available.

In the sensory form of transcortical aphasia, the patient can repeat what is said to him, but understands little of either what he repeats or what he reads. He nevertheless produces fluent speech output, although it is often little more intelligible than that produced by the Wernicke's aphasic. Because, however, the response to a question may involve the direct repetition of elements which were in the question, some patients may produce slightly more recognizable and meaningful answers. In general however, the speech of these aphasics is filled with jargon and paraphasias.

ALEXIA AND AGRAPHIA

Both reading and writing disorders, alexia and agraphia, may occur as relatively isolated syndromes in which there is relatively little loss in the comprehension of spoken language or in speech production, although there is often some evidence for subtle linguistic deficits in other modalities than written language. Both may be associated with lesions in the region of the angular and supramarginal gyri.

In discussing alexia or dyslexia, we must be careful to distinguish between *developmental dyslexia*, in which there is a failure to develop the ability to read, and *acquired dyslexia* which is the loss of the ability already acquired, usually as the result of cerebral lesions. The same applies to dysgraphia, although developmental dysgraphia without an associated dyslexia is extremely rare. As this section is concerned with the effects of lesions on the abilities of adults, developmental dyslexia will not be discussed here, even though a great deal of research is being conducted into the disorder in a neuropsychological context. Good introductions to this work are to be found in Beaumont and Rugg, 1978; Benton and Pearl, 1978; Farnham-Diggory, 1979; and Knights and Bakker, 1976.

The study of acquired dyslexias is one area where there has been a fruitful interchange between neuropsychologists and cognitive psychologists interested in theoretical models of the process of reading. Not only has the study of clinical cases allowed some of the models to be tested, but it has also stimulated the development of improved models of how reading is normally carried out. In return, there is now a better understanding of the deficits shown by clinical patients, with the prospect that this may result in more effective approaches to rehabilitation. Patterson's 1981 review, which incidentally sets the dysfunction firmly in the context of theories of normal reading, provides a clear illustration of this exchange. She classifies the acquired dyslexias into four forms: deep dyslexia, phonological dyslexia, letter-by-letter reading and surface dyslexia.

Deep dyslexia is a condition in which relatively severe difficulty in reading is characterized by semantic errors ('lawn' for 'grass', 'lift' for 'elevator'), visual errors ('wine' for 'wire', 'space' for 'pace'), function word substitution ('up' for 'down', 'with' for 'or') and derivational errors ('clothing' for 'clothes', 'teacher' for 'teach'). The reading of 'non-words' (such as 'brod' or 'pake') is impossible, there is an effect of the parts of speech and how imageable is the word, and a greater difficulty with function words than content words. There has been a great deal of research on this condition (which is also sometimes called *phonemic* dyslexia), despite its relative rarity, and an extensive review has been published by Coltheart, Patterson and Marshall (1980) which illustrates the breadth of the debate about it. One leading theory holds that it is the semantic error which is the primary symptom, and this is then interpreted in terms of possible points of breakdown in a logogen model of reading.

Phonological dyslexia appears rather more straightforward (perhaps because it has received less attention). These patients read words remarkably well, but do very poorly when asked to read non-words. In this difficulty with non-words they are rather similar to deep dyslexics, although the difference between the effects of words and non-words is much greater in phonological dyslexics. However, they also have difficulties in reading generally, from content words, which they find the easiest, to function words, which cause the greatest difficulty, and they also may misread word endings. It is not certain how clearly this dyslexia may be dissociated from deep dyslexia, although the reading of content words by phonological dyslexics is markedly better than the (relatively good) performance of the deep dyslexics. No effect of the imageability of the word has been reported for phonological dyslexic errors. However, it seems that the phonological route in reading is implicated in both disorders.

Letter-by-letter reading is a form of dyslexia which may be seen in alexia without agraphia, or 'pure' alexia. Such reading is relatively accurate, but slow, and it seems that the patient must spell out the individual letters, and often does this overtly, before he is able to read the word. The actual linguistic characteristics of the word seem to have little effect on reading speed or accuracy. Whether errors occur largely depends on whether the patient accurately identifies each letter and then remembers it long enough to integrate the series of letters into a word.

Surface dyslexia, also termed 'semantic' dyslexia, is much more like the reading that one expects from a developmental dyslexic, or a child in the early stages of learning to read. Errors are more likely with longer than with shorter words, and there is particular difficulty with words which are irregularly spelt. It is as if the patient breaks the word down into phonemic elements, then does the grapheme to phoneme conversion to assemble the word. Errors occur either in integrating the elements, or in not applying the many complex modifications to the conversion rules demanded by everyday English. Short words may be managed as single elements and read as a whole, but longer words have to be broken down, thus allowing errors to enter into the reading process.

Agraphia has been much less well studied than alexia, and is generally regarded as combining features which are seen in speech output performance with processes related to graphemic translation (and hence its association with alexia). Hécaen and co-workers (Marcie and Hécaen, 1979) have worked almost alone in this area which, together with the study of spelling, deserves more attention.

APHASIA ASSESSMENT

Aphasia is generally assessed by means of a battery of subtests which are designed to cover comprehensively the major aspects of language function. These would typically include conversational speech; oral and written expression with tests of repetition, naming and fluency; and auditory comprehension and reading. A number of such batteries have been produced – a recent review (Kertesz, 1979) discusses thirteen of them – although not all are in common use. The value of a particular battery depends upon how well it covers language performance, how long and difficult it is to administer, how reliable are the results derived from its application and how valid are the conclusions which may be drawn from these results. It will also depend on the kind of sample for which normative data is available, and ultimately on how useful it is in acurately assisting in diagnosis, management and treatment.

Three batteries seem to be in relatively common use: the Schuell Short Examination for Aphasia (SSEA), the Porch Index of Communicative Abilities (PICA) and the Boston Diagnostic Aphasia Examination (BDAE). The SSEA is itself the short form of a larger battery, taking the most useful elements from the Minnesota Test for Differential Diagnosis of Aphasia, but still providing a relatively broad assessment of language abilities. The PICA is a more modern battery which includes eighteen subtests, even extending to the gestural modality. It provides quite a useful amount of diagnostic information, but does not include any assessment of conversational speech, and only three common types of aphasia are differentiated.

At least as widely used is the BDAE, which is specifically related to the scheme of aphasia classification used in this chapter. This test has an even larger number of subtests than the PICA, providing even greater analytic detail of the patient's performance, but at the expense of quite lengthy administration. A useful feature is the provision of supplementary tests which allow certain areas to be explored in greater detail.

A battery known as the Western Aphasia Battery has recently appeared (Kertesz, 1979) and aims to improve on others currently available. It concentrates on fluency, comprehension, repetition and naming, but takes account of recent psycholinguistic research. From early reports, it appears as though this may be a useful battery, and it will be interesting to see how widely it is taken up.

Apart from the formal batteries, there are some other tests which deserve mention. The Halstead-Wepman Aphasia Screening Test is still widely used as a relatively brief test instrument to check for the presence of aphasia, and the Token Test, and associated Reporter's Test, are also widely used (Boller and Dennis, 1980; Boller, Kim and Mack, 1978; DeRenzi and Ferrari, 1978). The Token Test examines speech comprehension by requiring the subject to perform simple operations with a number of elementary tokens. The tasks are of graded difficulty running from 'Touch the red circle' up to such problems as 'Pick up the rectangles, except the yellow one' or 'After picking up the green rectangle, touch the white circle'. The Reporter's Test requires the converse activity, so that the patient must describe the operation which is being carried out upon the tokens by the examiner. Both of the tests are quick and easy to administer, and the Token Test in particular has gained considerable popularity.

THE REHABILITATION OF APHASICS

Aphasia most commonly results from either traumatic injuries or strokes, the latter being more frequent. The extent of recovery depends on a number of factors, but the most important are probably the cause of the dysfunction and the severity of the handicap. The outcome is generally much better following trauma than following stroke, with more than half of the patients fully recovering their premorbid level of function. This difference is, however, confounded with age, since strokes occur more commonly among the elderly, and this probably accounts for the poorer prognosis. The greatest spontaneous recovery happens within the first three months following the damage, with further significant improvement up to six months. After that, progress tends to slow down, and there are few gains beyond a year after the damage has occurred.

Despite there being few well-controlled studies of aphasia therapy, there is some evidence that it is effective in aiding recovery. Most importantly, there is evidence that therapy is more effective if it is begun as early as possible after the injury. A wide variety of approaches to treatment are used by speech therapists with aphasic patients, but most have developed from Wepman's idea that the patient should be systematically stimulated by appropriate materials and environments (Wepman, 1951). This approach was developed by both Schuell (Schuell, Jenkins and Jimenez-Pabon, 1964) and Taylor (1964), but typical therapy sessions will involve the acting out of everyday situations, working with classes of objects such as food or clothing, or with similar sounding groups of words. There is a continual attempt to elicit words and stimulate responses, and extensive use is made of repetition and auditory stimulation.

Recently, therapy which aims to re-establish language by specific teaching programmes has become more popular. This approach allows a more systematic structure for the programme of therapy, which may be based on an explicitly linguistic approach, and may also employ behavioural learning techniques such as operant reinforcement. An example of this kind of approach is to be found in Weniger, Huber, Stachowiak and Poeck (1980). Specific information about the patient's linguistic deficits is translated into a training programme designed to teach these deficient aspects of language, with progress at each stage carefully monitored and the programme adapted accordingly. In some programmes, specific rewards will be given for success in producing particular responses, according to a formal and explicit system.

There are a variety of other, less popular, forms of therapy. Among these are Deblocking Therapy (Weigl, 1968), which aims to use the intact aspects of language function to assist in the redevelopment of the damaged areas, and Compensation Therapy (Holland, 1977), which teaches the patient strategies to enable him to circumvent his difficulties by using the intact areas of function. Melodic Intonation Therapy (Sparks, Helm and Albert, 1974) capitalizes on the fact that many aphasics maintain the ability to sing when they cannot speak, and so can learn to 'intone' the speech they wish to generate. Finally, Visual Communication Therapy (Gardner, Zurif, Berry and Baker, 1976) has translated some of the methods used to teach language to chimpanzees, based upon simple figural and geometric symbols, into a method which seems of particular value with severe globally aphasic patients.

Therapy can be of considerable value to many patients, and aphasics often regain a significant degree of language function. There are, however, a large number of patients whose handicap persists, and who form a major rehabilitational challenge. What are needed are more extensive and better designed studies of the value of particular therapies so that treatment can be applied more effectively and economically to those with language dysfunction.

CONCLUSION

The study of aphasia is currently a fruitful area of interchange between academic psychologists and clinical neuropsychologists, resulting in a better understanding of both normal and abnormal language processes. There are problems in classifying aphasias, but there is now a widely accepted scheme, based upon the Boston classification, which divides aphasias into six types (see Table 7.2). Each of these forms of aphasia may be associated with a particular region of the cortex, although this correspondence is not as clear as is sometimes supposed. The cortical areas serving language are lateralized, being in the left hemisphere of almost all right handers and the majority of left handers, although left handers typically have a more bilateral representation. Disorders of reading and writing are naturally associated with major disorders of comprehension and expression of speech. There are a variety of forms of therapy currently practised with aphasics, most of which appear effective, although there are few comparative and controlled studies of treatment.

FURTHER READING

Among the titles for further reading to be found at the end of Chapter 3 and which apply generally to this section, both Hécaen and Albert (1978) and Heilman and Valenstein (1979) have extensive discussions of aphasia, and the latter has useful chapters on alexia (by Albert) and agraphia (by Marcie and Hécaen). In addition the following books may be useful:

Crystal, D., *Introduction to Language Pathology* (London, Edward Arnold, 1980). This book is a useful introduction to all aspects of communication disorder, not only the aphasias.

Kertesz, A., *Aphasia and Associated Disorders* (New York, Grune and Stratton, 1979). A useful review with strengths in the coverage of classification, assessment and treatment.

Lesser, R., (1978). *Linguistic Investigations of Aphasia* (London, Edward Arnold, 1978). Perhaps the best introduction to aphasia for psychologists, a clear and well written text which sets language disorder in the context of psycholinguistics.

Language 145

Chapters concentrating on the linguistic analysis of aphasic deficits are found in the following:

Blumstein, S., 'Neurolinguistic Disorders; Language-Brain Relationships', in S. B. Filskov and T. J. Boll, eds., *Handbook of Clinical Neuropsychology* (New York, Wiley, 1981).
Bub, D. and Whitaker, H. A., 'Language and Verbal Processes', in M. C. Wittrock, ed., *The Brain and Psychology* (New York, Academic Press, 1980).

Finally, the best source on treatment is probably:

Sarno, M. T. and Höök, O., eds., *Aphasia: Assessment and Treatment* (Stockholm, Almqvist and Wiksell, 1980).

REFERENCES

Beaumont, J. G. and Rugg, M. D. 'Neuropsychological Laterality of Function and Dyslexia: a New Hypothesis', *Dyslexia Review*, 1 (1978), 18–21.
Benson, D. F. 'Fluency in Aphasia: Correlation with Radioactive Scan Localisation', *Cortex*, 3 (1967), 373–394.
Benson, D. F., 'Aphasia', in K. M. Heilman and E. Valenstein, eds., *Clinical Neuropsychology* (New York, Oxford University Press, 1979).
Benton, A. L. and Pearl, D., eds., *Dyslexia: An Appraisal of Current Knowledge* (New York, Oxford University Press, 1978).
Bogen, J. E. and Bogen, G. M., 'Wernicke's Region – Where Is it?', *Annals of the New York Academy of Sciences*, 280 (1976), 834–843.
Boller, F. and Dennis, M., eds., *Auditory Communication: Clinical and Experimental Studies with the Token Test* (New York, Academic Press, 1980).
Boller, F., Kim, Y. and Mack, J. L., 'Auditory Comprehension in Aphasia', in H. Whitaker and H. A. Whitaker, eds., *Studies in Neurolinguistics*, vol. 3 (New York, Academic Press, 1978).
Brown, J. W., 'The Neural Organization of Language: Aphasia and Lateralization', *Brain and Language*, 3 (1976), 482–494.
Brown, J. W., 'Language Representation in the Brain', in H. D. Steklis and M. J. Raleigh, eds., *Neurobiology of Social Communication in Primates* (New York, Academic Press, 1979).
Carter, R. L., Hohenegger, M. and Satz, P., 'Handedness and Aphasia: an Inferential Method for Determining the Mode of Cerebral Speech Specialization', *Neuropsychologia*, 18 (1980), 569–574.
Coltheart, M., Patterson, K. E. and Marshall, J. C., eds., *Deep Dyslexia* (London, Routledge and Kegan Paul, 1980).
Critchley, M., *The Divine Banquet of the Brain* (New York, Raven Press, 1979).
Crystal, D., *Introduction to Language Pathology* (London, Edward Arnold, 1980).
De Renzi, E. and Ferrari, C., 'The Reporter's Test: a Sensitive Test to Detect Expressive Disturbances in Aphasics', *Cortex*, 14 (1978), 279–293.
Farnham-Diggory, S., *Learning Disabilities* (London, Fontana, Open Books, 1979).

Gardner, H., Zurif, E. B., Berry, T. and Baker, E., 'Visual Communication in Aphasia', *Neuropsychologia*, 14 (1976), 275–292.

Geschwind, N., 'Disconnexion Syndrome in Animals and Man', *Brain*, 88 (1965), 237–294, 585–644.

Goodglass, H. and Kaplan, E., *The Assessment of Aphasias and Related Disorders* (Philadelphia, Lea and Febiger, 1972).

Holland, A. L., 'Some Practical Considerations for Aphasia Rehabilitation', in M. Sullivan and M. S. Kommers, eds., *Rationale for Adult Aphasia Therapy* (University of Nebraska Medical Center, 1977).

Howes, D. and Geschwind, N., 'Quantitative Studies of Aphasic Language', *Association for Research in Nervous and Mental Disease*, 42 (1964), 229–244.

Kertesz, A., *Aphasia and Associated Disorders* (New York, Grune and Stratton, 1979).

Kertesz, A., 'The Anatomy of Jargon', in J. W. Brown, ed., *Jargonaphasia* (New York, Academic Press, 1981).

Kertesz, A. and Benson, D. F., 'Neologistic Jargon: a Clinicopathological Study', *Cortex*, 6 (1970), 362–386.

Kertesz, A., Lesk, D. and McCabe, P., 'Isotope Localization of Infarcts in Aphasia', *Archives of Neurology*, 34 (1977), 590–601.

Knights, R. M. and Bakker, D. J., eds., (1976). *The Neuropsychology of Learning Disorders* (Baltimore, Maryland, University Park Press, 1976).

Lesser, R., *Linguistic Investigations of Aphasia* (London, Edward Arnold, 1978).

Luria, A. R. and Hutton, J. T., 'A Modern Assessment of the Basic Forms of Aphasia', *Brain and Language*, 4 (1977), 129–151.

Marcie, P. and Hécaen, H., 'Agraphia: Writing Disorders Associated with Unilateral Cortical Lesions', in K. M. Heilman and E. Valenstein, eds., *Clinical Neuropsychology* (New York, Oxford University Press, 1979).

Ojemann, G. A. and Mateer, C., 'Human Language Cortex: Localization of Memory, Syntax and Sequential Motor-phoneme Identification Syndromes', *Science*, 205 (1979), 1401–1403.

Ojemann, G. A. and Whitaker, H. A., 'Language Localization and Variability', *Brain and Language*, 6 (1978), 239–260.

Patterson, K. E., 'Neuropsychological Approaches to the Study of Reading', *British Journal of Psychology*, 72 (1981), 151–174.

Rasmussen, T. and Milner, B., 'Clinical and Surgical Studies of the Cerebral Speech Areas in Man', in K. J. Zülch, O. Creutzfeldt and G. C. Galbraith, eds., *Cerebral Localization* (Berlin, Springer-Verlag, 1975).

Satz, P., 'A Test of Some Models of Hemispheric Speech Organisation in the Left and Right Handed', *Science*, 203 (1979), 1131–1133.

Satz, P., 'Incidence of Aphasia in Left-handers: a Test of Some Hypothetical Models of Cerebral Speech Organisation', in J. Herron, ed., *Neuropsychology of Left-Handedness* (New York, Academic Press, 1980).

Schuell, H., Jenkins, J. and Jimenez-Pabon, E., *Aphasia in Adults*, (New York, Harper and Row, 1964).

Sparks, R., Helm, N. and Albert, M., 'Aphasia Rehabilitation Resulting from Melodic Intonation Therapy', *Cortex*, 10 (1974), 303–316.

Taylor, M. L., 'Language Therapy', in H. Burr, ed., *The Aphasic Adult: Evaluation and Rehabilitation* (Charlottesville, University of Virginia, Wayside, 1964).

Weigl, E., 'On the Problem of Cortical Syndromes', in M. L. Simmel, ed., *The Reach of Mind* (New York, Springer, 1968).

Weisenberg, T. and McBride, K., *Aphasia* (New York, Commonwealth Fund, 1935).

Weniger, D., Huber, W., Stachowiak, F.-J. and Poeck, K., 'Treatment of Aphasia on a Linguistic Basis', in M. T. Sarno and O. Höök, eds., *Aphasia: Assessment and Treatment* (Stockholm, Almqvist and Wiksell, 1980).

Wepman, J. M., *Recovery from Aphasia* (New York, Ronald, 1951).

Whitaker, H. A. and Selnes, O. A., 'Anatomic Variations in the Cortex: Individual Differences and the Problem of the Localization of Language Functions', *Annals of the New York Academy of Sciences*, 280 (1976), 844–854.

Zangwill, O. L., 'Excision of Broca's Area without Persistent Aphasia', in K. J. Zülch, O. Creutzfeldt and G. C. Galbraith, eds., *Cerebral Localization* (Berlin, Springer-Verlag, 1975).

CHAPTER 8

The Subcortex and Psychosurgery

It is easy to forget when reading texts on human neuropsychology that most cerebral lesions extend more or less radically into the subcortical tissue. However, lesions of the subcortex alone are relatively rare in humans, except in the case of certain neoplasms (tumours) when surgery often involves disturbance of the cortex. As damage to subcortical tissue is likely to have fatal consequences, or to have such radical effects on behaviour that study of the higher aspects of human abilities is precluded, there has been relatively little study of such damage in man, and much of our knowledge about the functions of subcortical structures comes from animal experiments. However, what clinical evidence is available suggests that generalizations from animals to man with respect to lower functions of the subcortex are not likely to be grossly inaccurate. Information about these functions is to be found in most textbooks on physiological psychology, and therefore only a general summary is given here.

Firstly, subcortical lesions may interfere with general activating systems, for example the ARAS in the brain stem (see p. 30), and thereby affect the level of consciousness, attention and awareness. Such changes may well be reflected in the responsiveness of bodily reflexes, and this is one reason why reflexes are carefully tested by the neurologist. Lesions in the lower brain stem may lead to sudden attacks of deep unconsciousness, and to changes in the pulse and the pattern of breathing. Cheyne-Stokes breathing, in which the pattern is slow, deep and perhaps periodic, is characteristic of some coma states. By contrast, lesions of the upper brain stem and around the thalamus produce states more like sleep. Sleep may also be short and fitful.

Subcortical lesions can also interrupt the afferent and efferent pathways as they pass to and from the cerebral cortex, so that lesions which involve the internal capsule or the pyramidal tracts may have primary effects on somatosensory and motor performance, even though the cortex is not itself involved.

Midbrain lesions in the area of the thalamus, besides leading to disturbances of consciousness, can result in motor disabilities, such as resting tremor, choreiform movements and the uncontrolled movements of dystonia, as noted in Chapter 2. Parkinsonian symptoms are also typical of lesions in this area, although the extent of any associated cognitive dysfunction is unclear. There is some evidence that thalamic lesions may also result in changes in verbal performance, particularly verbal fluency, and in face recognition and face matching, and that these deficits may vary with the laterality of the lesion (Vilkki, 1978). Stimulation of the region of the pulvinar through chronically implanted electrodes may produce transient dysphasia, memory loss, and poor visual discrimination and recognition (Fedio and Van Buren, 1975). It has even been suggested that the absence of the massa intermedia, which joins the two thalami in some but not all individuals, may be associated with higher intelligence in males (Lansdell and Clayton-Davies, 1972). Not all these functional relationships can, however, be regarded as well established.

Hypothalamic lesions have effects (which animal studies would lead one to expect) on basic drives, such as eating and drinking, sleeping and wakefulness. There are often, in addition, signs of dysfunction of the autonomic nervous system. Changes in sexual behaviour may also be seen, and the impotence which sometimes afflicts those who have pursued a long career in boxing is sometimes attributed to damage to the hypothalamic region resulting from repeated blows to the head.

Lesions of the basal ganglia, as noted in Chapter 4, are closely linked with the cortical functions of the temporal lobe, including memory, aggression and the appropriate direction of sexual behaviour. Finally, cerebellar lesions produce the effects which might be expected on motor coordination, and on balance and position sense. Patients with damage to the cerebellum show tremor and jerkiness when executing intentional movements, and may walk in a rather drunken fashion with a very broad-based gait. It has been argued that there are also significant non-motor functions of the cerebellum which should not be neglected (Watson, 1978), but these are far less prominent than the classical motor functions in the deficits shown by patients.

These more basic subcortical functions are generally of less interest to human neuropsychologists, although they are naturally of considerable importance in assessing the overall neurological and psychological status of a brain-damaged patient, and the rest of this chapter is devoted to the current debate about 'surgery on the mind': the procedures and outcome of neurosurgery and psychosurgery. In so far as is possible, a balanced summary of the scientific arguments for and against these treatments will be introduced.

NEUROSURGERY

A clear distinction is usually made between *neurosurgery* and *psychosurgery*. Neurosurgery is regarded as uncontroversial and acceptable, while psychosurgery is the subject of intense debate on scientific, ethical and legal grounds. When closely examined, however, the distinction between the two is not so clear. It is sometimes suggested that the basis of the distinction is that in neurosurgery pathological diseased tissue is being removed or some gross physiological abnormality is being corrected, while in psychosurgery tissue which is not grossly abnormal (and is therefore 'healthy' and 'normal') is being destroyed. This is not strictly accurate, because some neurosurgical procedures, for the relief of intractible pain or the correction of spastic limbs, for example, involve the destruction of healthy tissue. An alternative basis for the distinction is that neurosurgery is for physical conditions, while psychosurgery attempts to change mental symptoms. However, begging the question of how we might distinguish 'mental' from 'physical' conditions, the symptoms of some tumours may only be apparent in cognitive, and therefore mental, changes. Pain exists in no form other than as a mental phenomenon.

The distinction in reality is probably a false one, based upon what is generally accepted against what is controversial. It may be helpful not to regard psychosurgery as in any way fundamentally different from routine neurosurgery, and indeed some writers (proponents of psychosurgery) have suggested the substitution of the term 'psychiatric surgery'.

Whatever view you reach on psychosurgery, there are a large number of routine surgical procedures, mostly interventions in clearly pathological states, which are not in question. Surgery for the removal of neoplasms, to repair cerebrovascular accidents, to ameliorate spasticity and other movement disorders, to correct hydrocephalus, to relieve chronic pain, to correct neuroendocrine disorders, or remove the irritant cause of focal epilepsy, is widely practised. Many of these conditions are life threatening, all cause significant distress and suffering, and there is almost no prospect of spontaneous recovery or alternative effective treatment. The ability of the patient to consent to treatment is usually not in doubt. Many of the procedures are technically difficult and hazardous, but their justification is rarely in question, and in considering psychosurgery we should not neglect the significant, and in some ways more important, area of general functional neurosurgery, as the examples given below may illustrate.

It should also be pointed out here that the frequent assumption that drug treatment is a less powerful treatment than surgery, because of the more dramatic nature of the latter, is in some ways a misconception. Many psychotropic drugs are extremely powerful and yet not very selective in their effects, and many bring unpleasant and unwanted effects which have to be corrected by further medication. It is therefore inaccurate to contrast drugs with surgery on the assumption that the former are inherently safe, gentle and reversible, while the latter is crude, dangerous and irreversible. It often surprises students to hear that in cases where there is a history of coronary disease, and in old people, it is often considered safer to give electroconvulsive therapy than to administer certain anti-depressant drugs. Surgery *is* relatively hazardous, and irreversible, but the drugs are also extremely potent, and may also have irreversible effects.

Parkinson's Disease

One particular application of the development of stereotactic surgery has been in the treatment of Parkinson's disease. Stereotactic surgery involves the insertion of probes under general anaesthetic by reference to landmarks on the skull, brain maps, and radiographic images of the patient's brain. The insertion can be guided by further X-ray studies. Once inserted, the patient can be brought back to consciousness and the probes used to study the functional nature of the probe site before irreversible lesions are deliberately created by high frequency coagulation, freezing or radiation.

As Parkinson's disease involves the dysfunction of sites in the region of the thalamus, stereotactic lesions may be placed in this area, including the ventrolateral nucleus of the thalamus, the globus pallidus, and parts of the internal capsule, amongst other structures (Mawdesley, 1975). The exact location of these lesions, when a number of the treated brains became available for post-mortem examination, proved to be rather less accurate than had been expected, but there were nevertheless therapeutic gains.

In about nine out of ten patients, the primary tremor and rigidity which so disable Parkinsonian patients were abolished, with a concomitant increase in motor proficiency. The surgery has been less successful, however, at improving the impoverishment of motor behaviour and the difficulties in the initiation of motor acts which many of these patients also have. Disequilibrium and akinesia were also often not significantly improved. Nevertheless, mortality from the procedure is low, and despite some troublesome side-effects in speech production for a number of patients, daily function could be considerably improved. A large number of these operations were performed in the 1960s and into the 1970s, but the advent of new drugs for the treatment of this disorder, notably L-Dopa, amongst a variety of others (see Pincus and Tucker, 1978), resulted in a decline in popularity of the operation. Because its results in everyday function were not more impressive (Hoehn and Yahr, 1967), and certain cognitive functions were affected, albeit not seriously (Darley, Brown and Swenson, 1975; Riklan and Levita, 1969) drug treatment was usually preferred to surgery. Nevertheless, stereotactic surgery for Parkinsonism remains a good example of a discrete, controlled and successful treatment for a condition with neuropsychological aspects.

Focal Epilepsy

Certain forms of epilepsy, where there is an identified 'focus' in the cortex which is considered to trigger off the epileptic seizures, can be treated by surgical removal of the epileptogenic tissue (Rasmussen, 1979; Sweet, 1977). The results in terms of relief from seizures caused by lesions other than tumours are in general good, with typically about two-thirds of the patients showing a marked reduction in seizures, including about a third who become immediately or eventually seizure-free, and the remaining third generally showing a moderate or small reduction in seizure frequency. There is a very low operative mortality and few reports of significant unwanted effects. The figures are naturally less good when the lesion is a tumour, largely because of the tendency of tumours to recur. These results are impressive (particularly as they come from a large number of patients: 1277 in the Canadian series), and doubts about the efficacy of the treatment must be set against the side-effects of anticonvulsive medication. Drugs administered for epilepsy can be seriously disabling, particularly in retarding cognitive function, which adds to the attraction of the neurosurgical alternative in appropriate cases.

Another particular form of surgery for epilepsy is anterior temporal lobectomy. (In *lobectomy* the lobe, or part of it, is removed; in *lobotomy* the connections to the lobe are severed; in *leucotomy* more discrete interruptions in fibre tracts are made.) The operation is indicated

when pathological tissue has been demonstrated in the anterior
temporal lobe. The use of the Wada technique to establish speech
lateralization in connection with this procedure has already been
mentioned (p. 80). The results on seizure frequency are generally
good. Of particular interest, however, are the deficits in cognitive
performance which follow temporal removals, and which have already
been discussed in Chapter 4 (Milner, 1975). The operation has been
used successfully with children and adolescents, and has been considered by some to be particularly valuable where abnormalities of
the electrical activity of the temporal lobe are associated with violent
and aggressive outbursts (Blumer, 1975; Falconer, 1974).

PSYCHOSURGERY

Prefrontal Leucotomy

The current debate over psychosurgery is strongly influenced by the
history of the leucotomy operation. Although there were earlier
experiments, it was Moniz who introduced the operation in 1936 for
serious psychiatric illnesses, including schizophrenia. It was soon
adapted into its most common form, the 'standard leucotomy', by
Freeman and Watts. In this form, burr holes were drilled at each side
of the head, a cutting instrument inserted, and swivelled up and down
in a broad arc, so severing a major part of the connections coming up
into the frontal lobe (see Fig. 8.1). There were several refinements of

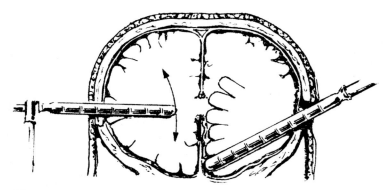

Figure 8.1. The leucotomy procedure developed by Freeman and Watts.
(After Freeman and Watts, 1950)

this operation, including 'orbital undercutting', developed by Scoville in 1948 (Fig. 8.2), but all used relatively crude techniques with the object of disconnecting centres in the frontal lobe from subcortical circuits in the limbic system. An enormous number of these operations were performed, with estimates of up to 100,000 world-wide, and an extensive account of the history of the operation will be found in Valenstein (1980).

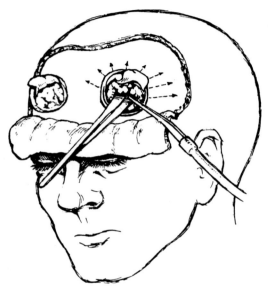

Figure 8.2. The orbital undercutting operation developed by Scoville.
(After Asenjo, 1963)

As with many treatments in psychiatry, it was taken up with fervent enthusiasm, and a proper evaluation of its effectiveness was too long delayed (see Clare 1980; and for a discussion of other shortcomings in the history of psychiatry). While there were earlier reviews, the first major study was that of Tooth and Newton (1961), who examined 10,365 cases in the United Kingdom in the years 1942–52. Forty-six per cent were discharged from hospital (although this does not mean fully recovered), but 4 per cent died, 3 per cent had major undesired effects, including chronic epilepsy, and 2 per cent became significantly worse. It should be noted that the assessments of outcome were often not independent or objective, and the criteria of improvement were fairly minimal. On the other hand, we should recognize that many of the patients would now be regarded as most unsuitable material for this kind of operation, and that many had an extremely long history of psychiatric illness (41 per cent had been ill for more than six years).

More recent assessments have not been more encouraging about the success of the operation. Post, Linford-Rees and Schurr (1968), examining patients who had undergone a modified leucotomy operation, found undesirable permanent side-effects in 59 per cent of the patients, and troublesome symptoms in a further 21 per cent. Such symptoms included various degrees of epilepsy, incontinence of urine and faeces, and motor impairments. Nevertheless, it was concluded that in 40 per cent of patients the operation initiated lasting changes for the better, particularly if the illness was chronic depression or anxiety rather than schizophrenia.

Robin and Macdonald (1975) also reported on a series of studies, both retrospective and prospective, of the effects of different leucotomy operations. They attempted to match control subjects within their studies and found no better prospect of discharge from hospital after leucotomy for either schizophrenia or depression, and inconclusive results for severe phobic and obsessional disorders. Although there were some differences in improvement within the institutional setting, drugs were as effective as the surgical operations. Surgery might in some cases affect certain symptoms but did not result in general clinical improvement. Post-operative deaths were still found to be rather high (2 per cent), and the rate of epilepsy was as high as 5 per cent over a long follow-up period. They also reported intellectual deficits in the surgical patients.

There have been many other studies, but there is now general agreement, even among the proponents of psychosurgery, that leucotomy operations at best fell short of success, and at worst are a scandal in the history of psychiatry. If they were to be successful (as some related operations now are), they should preferably have been undertaken on chronically depressed and anxious patients, and certainly not on schizophrenics. It should, however, be remembered that the operation was introduced in the 1950s, in the period before the revolution brought about by psychotropic drugs, when psychiatrists were desperate to prevent the decline of psychotic patients into a chronic retarded state, a progress they were largely powerless to halt. Nevertheless, despite the apparent scientific rationale which was used to justify the operation, it was not well founded theoretically, the operative procedure was primitive and crude, and it was applied to large numbers of unsuitable patients. The history of leucotomy should rightly teach us a lesson about the care which must attend the introduction of novel treatments, but we should also not allow the failure of these earlier techniques to cloud our judgement of modern psychosurgical techniques.

Modern Psychosurgery

There are a variety of operative procedures used in modern psychosurgery, with certain operations being favoured in certain centres, but they fall roughly into four groups.

The first of the contemporary procedures was *stereotactic subcaudate tractotomy*, which is essentially a much refined version of the earlier frontal lobe operations. In devising it, Knight developed a method of stereotactically placing tiny ceramic rods containing radioactive yttrium at the site for the lesion, which is in the white matter beneath and in front of the caudate nucleus (below the septal region), extending into the frontal central white matter (see Fig. 8.3 and Fig. 2.5). The yttrium decays quite rapidly, as its half-life is only 62 hours, and leaves a lesion of about 25 × 15 × 5 mm in the standard operation with six rods. Introducing the rods can be undertaken with relative accuracy and causes very little trauma, and the operation may be performed entirely under general anaesthetic. Assessments of the effectiveness of this operation (Bridges, 1978; Bridges and Bartlett, 1977) show that there is a 'good response' in about 60 per cent of severely depressed patients, and in about 50 per cent of those with chronic anxiety or obsessional neurosis. Unintended effects on the personality were reported in about 5 per cent, but these were by and

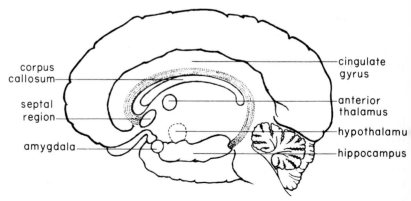

Figure 8.3. Some of the subcortical sites which are targets in psychosurgical procedures.

large not considered 'socially disabling'. The number of patients developing fits was low, and there was only one fatality among the 418 cases reported. The clinical assessments of outcome are supported by some objective psychological test data, and there was a dramatic decline in the number of suicide attempts in comparable periods before and after operation.

A second contemporary operation is *limbic leucotomy* and is very similar to subcaudate tractotomy. The lesions are usually created by freezing or electrocoagulation, but are placed by stereotactic means at two sites. One site is in the subcaudate area, as in the tractotomy although the lesion is smaller, the other is in the cingulum bundle. This operation has been performed less commonly than the tractotomy, but the results suggest that the effectiveness of the two operations is roughly comparable. It has been suggested that limbic leucotomy is more effective for obsessional neurosis and less good in anxiety states, although there is some controversy over this point. Unlike the tractotomy, however, it has been performed in highly selected cases of schizophrenia, with a surprisingly good outcome.

The third group of operations is aimed at the *cingulate region* alone. In a prospective study of 85 patients (Corkin, 1980), which included extensive follow-up data and careful objective assessment, no lasting neurological or behavioural deficits were found. There was therapeutic improvement in many although not all of the patients, the best outcome being in chronic pain or depression. Some of the earlier studies had suggested that this operation was less safe than the others just mentioned, but the latest developments of the technique seem to have avoided the major side-effects seen earlier.

Most controversial is the fourth group of operations, aimed at the *amygdala* or the *posterior hypothalamus*. This operation is considered for cases of severe, pathological and uncontrollable aggressiveness, particularly if there are clear signs of a neurological abnormality, usually seen in abnormal electrical activity of the brain. Much of the opposition to this operation springs from its earlier use in the United States with violent offenders, and the resulting argument that a behavioural rather than a neurological disorder was being treated by the operation. This has resulted in very strict legal controls on the operation in the United States, although it is performed in at least one centre in the United Kingdom. It appears effective in reducing emotional excitability, and in improving the patient's social adaptation, without significant effects on cognitive abilities.

There are other operative procedures, including methods by which arrays of electrodes are implanted in frontal lobe sites, so that small serial lesions can be produced over a period of time while the therapeutic progress is being monitored. The variety of operations practised in the United States is also wider than this account perhaps suggests, but the above four groups contain the essential elements to be found in any of these procedures.

Some general points should be made about the modern operations. The first is that they are performed only as a 'treatment of last resort', that is, after all other treatments have been tried and failed. Some critics of psychosurgery have raised the quite reasonable point that if it is believed to be effective, why should it be reserved in this way? While a good point, it is a little unfair, for the caution exercised by most psychosurgeons is urged upon them by the operations' opponents. However, it does mean that the patients who undergo the operations are severe and intractible cases, and have generally been seriously ill for a protracted period. That the outcome statistics are as good as they are is perhaps more remarkable in the light of this consideration, given the severe nature of the illnesses being treated. Nevertheless, the cases are still highly selected as to their suitability for surgery, which tempers the force of this point.

The number of psychosurgical operations performed each year is, in any case, extremely small. In the early 1970s the number of operations in the UK was about 200–250 each year, as against about 400 in the USA, the operations therefore being relatively more common in the UK. Since this time there has been a decline in numbers, with about 150 each year in the UK by 1976, and a comparable decline in the USA. Most of these operations are performed in a small number of units which specialize in particular operations. A statement which clearly lays out the indications for the treatments practised at certain of these centres was recently published by Bartlett, Bridges and Kelly (1981).

Taking an overview of these modern operations, it seems that objective (although not always independent) assessments show them to be effective for chronic depression, anxiety, neurosis, obsessionality, somatic complaints, tension and phobias. Undesirable cognitive effects are only rarely manifested, and tend to be in learning and memory or language. These deficits were most commonly associated with thalamic operations, which are now much less frequently practised. The psychiatric and neurological ratings of improvement are generally favourable, if schizophrenia and drug addiction are excepted, and the rate of post-operative complications has declined steadily over the years, so that it is now acceptably low. The suggestion that psychosurgery merely produces overall indiscriminate emotional blunting and cognitive slowing, with the result that the patient becomes an incomplete and damaged person, is not really supported by any of the studies of the modern operations. One concern, however, is the extent of (scientifically) unreported psychosurgery, particularly in the United States, where as many as three out of four surgeons have not published their results in the literature (Valenstein, 1980). This is to be regretted.

Undoubtedly there are ethical problems which attach to psychosurgery, particularly the problem as to whether a patient can really consent to any procedure the outcome of which he has no way of knowing in advance. As all of the patients have relatively severe psychiatric disorders, this problem is doubly difficult. However, it is also important to balance the distress experienced by these patients, and the very real risks from suicide in many cases (perhaps 15 per cent), if they are untreated, against the limits of the effectiveness of the operations. There is also something in the criticism that these operations are still relatively crude and are not based on any clear scientific rationale. However, if treated as experimental medicine and employed with great caution, the information which we have suggests that the operations should continue to be used in highly selected cases, with careful independent assessment of outcome and full reporting of the results. What of course is needed is a sound controlled trial of psychosurgery, but for ethical and methodological reasons it is probably impossible to achieve. Patients cannot ethically be randomly assigned to treatment and no-treatment control groups; the treatment cannot be applied to a control group not possessing the normal indications for the therapy; it is very difficult to have an independent yet thorough assessment of post-operative state by an examiner who is 'blind' as to whether the operation has been performed or not; and it is certainly impossible for the patient to remain ignorant about whether the treatment has been applied (as is the case with placebo controls for drug therapy). In the meantime, psychosurgery probably has a place in neuropsychiatry, while more is discovered about both the disorders and the full effects of the operations.

CONCLUSION

Almost all lesions of the brain have subcortical as well as cortical effects, although these have historically been much neglected by human neuropsychologists. This is, however, one area where comparative neuropsychology can contribute invaluable evidence from studies of animals which help us to understand the subcortical systems of man. The effects of major subcortical lesions are often so radical that the cognitive deficits are either extremely gross or unimportant in comparison with the major functional impairments of consciousness or basic drives.

In considering the subcortex, neurosurgery and psychosurgery are of some interest. There is much routine and uncontroversial neurosurgery practised with effects upon behaviour, often demanded by one of a number of life threatening processes. Some examples have been given, however, where neurosurgery is not an emergency procedure, where it is aimed at behavioural deficits among others, and where the rationale and success of the methods have clearly justified their use.

Psychosurgical methods have also been described. While the historical operations fell far short of real success, the modern operations are by contrast well controlled and relatively successful. They raise serious ethical and scientific issues, but unbiased appraisal of the evidence suggests that they should have a place in contemporary medicine, even if that place is under continual critical review.

FURTHER READING

There are many excellent texts on physiological psychology which review the functions of subcortical structures, but two which can be recommended are:

Brown, T. S. and Wallace, P. M., *Physiological Psychology* (New York, Academic Press, 1980). A relatively elementary introduction.

Carlson, N. R., *Physiology of Behavior*, 2nd edition (Boston, Mass., Allyn and Bacon, 1981). This takes the reader to a more advanced level.

On the topic of neurosurgery, there are two very clear introductions to the procedural aspects:

Hayward, R., *Essentials of Psychosurgery* (Oxford, Blackwell Scientific Publications, 1980).

Jennett, B., *An Introduction to Neurosurgery*, 3rd edition (London, Heinemann Medical Books, 1977).

The following cover the broader aspects of surgery and psychiatry:

Pincus, J. H. and Tucker, G. J., *Behavioural Neurology*, 2nd edition (New York, Oxford University Press, 1978). This includes some well presented introductory material.

Rasmussen, T. and Marino, R., eds., *Functional Neurosurgery* (New York, Raven Press, 1979). This includes more detailed papers on a number of aspects.

More specifically addressed to psychosurgery are the following:

Clare, A., *Psychiatry in Dissent*, 2nd edition (London, Tavistock Publications, 1980). In addition this covers a range of controversial topics in psychiatry.

Smith, J. S. and Kiloh, L. G., eds., *Psychosurgery and Society* (Oxford, Pergamon Press, 1977). This book discusses not only the scientific aspects, but also social attitudes and implications, especially in the American and Australian context.

Smith, W. L. and Kling, A., eds., *Issues in Brain/Behavior Control* (New York, Spectrum Books, 1976). This volume contains a variety of contributions on philosophical, social and scientific aspects.

Valenstein, E. S., ed., *The Psychosurgery Debate: Scientific, Legal and Ethical Perspectives* (San Francisco, W. H. Freeman, 1980). This is undoubtedly the best single book on psychosurgery. It contains excellent coverage of the historical and present scientific status of the various operations, and represents critical opinion fairly. It also includes discussion of the ethical and legal position (although primarily with respect to the United States), and an account of the reports submitted to the US National Commission for the Protection of Human Subjects of Biomedical and Behavioral Research.

REFERENCES

Asenjo, A., *Neurosurgical Techniques* (Springfield, Illinois, Charles C. Thomas, 1950).

Bartlett, J., Bridges, P. and Kelly, D., 'Contemporary Indications for Psychosurgery', *British Journal of Psychiatry*, 138 (1981), 507–511.

Bridges, P. K., 'A Contemporary View of Psychosurgery', in R. N. Gaind and B. L. Hudson, eds., *Current Themes in Psychiatry 1* (London, Macmillan, 1978).

Bridges, P. K. and Bartlett, J. R., 'Psychosurgery: Yesterday and Today', *British Journal of Psychiatry*, 131 (1977), 249–260.

Blumer, D., 'Temporal Lobe Epilepsy and Its Psychiatric Significance', in D. F. Benson and D. Blumer, eds., *Psychiatric Aspects of Neurological Disease* (New York, Grune and Stratton, 1975).

Clare, A., *Psychiatry in Dissent*, 2nd edition (London, Tavistock Publications, 1980).

Corkin, S., 'A Prospective Study of Cingulotomy', in E. S. Valenstein, ed., *The Psychosurgery Debate: Scientific, Legal and Ethical Perspectives* (San Francisco, W. H. Freeman, 1980).

Darley, F. L., Brown, J. R. and Swenson, W. M., 'Language Changes after Neurosurgery for Parkinsonism', *Brain and Language*, 2 (1975), 65–69.

Falconer, M. A., 'Mesial Temporal (Ammon's Horn) Sclerosis as a Common Cause of Epilepsy. Aetiology, treatment and prevention', *Lancet*, 2 (7883), (1974) 767–770.

Fedio, P. and Van Buren, J. M., 'Memory and Perceptual Deficits during Electrical Stimulation in the Left and Right Thalamus and Parietal Subcortex', *Brain and Language*, 2 (1975), 78–100.

Freeman, W. and Watts, J. W., *Psychosurgery in the Treatment of Mental Disorders and Intractable Pain*, 2nd edition (Springfield, Illinois, Charles C. Thomas, 1963).

Hoehn, M. M. and Yahr, M. D., 'Parkinsonism: Onset, Prognosis and Mortality', *Neurology*, 17 (1967), 427–442.

Lansdell, H. and Clayton-Davies, J., 'Massa Intermedia: Possible Relation to Intelligence', *Neuropsychologia*, 10 (1972), 207–210.

Mawdesley, C., 'Parkinson's Disease', in W. B. Matthews, ed., *Recent Advances in Clinical Neurology, No. 1* (Edinburgh, Churchill-Livingstone, 1975).

Milner, B., 'Psychological Aspects of Focal Epilepsy and its Neurosurgical Management', in D. P. Purpura, J. K. Penry and R. D. Walter, eds., *Advances in Neurology*, vol. 8 (New York, Raven Press, 1975).

Pincus, J. H. and Tucker, G. J., *Behavioral Neurology*, 2nd edition (New York, Oxford University Press, 1978).

Post, F., Linford-Rees, W. and Schurr, P., 'An Evaluation of Bimedial Leucotomy', *British Journal of Psychiatry*, 114 (1968), 1223–1246.

Rasmussen, T., 'Cortical Resection for Medically Refractory Focal Epilepsy: Results, Lessons and Questions', in T. Rasmussen and R. Marino, eds., *Functional Neurosurgery* (New York, Raven Press, 1979).

Riklan, M. and Levita, E., *Subcortical Aspects of Human Behaviour* (Baltimore, Maryland, Williams and Wilkins, 1969).

Robin, A. and Macdonald, D., *Lessons of Leucotomy* (London, Henry Kimpton, 1975).

Sweet, W. H., ed., *Neurosurgical Treatment in Psychiatry, Pain and Epilepsy* (Baltimore, Maryland, University Park Press, 1977).

Tooth, G. C. and Newton, M. P., 'Leucotomy in England and Wales 1942–1954', *Reports on Public Health and Medical Subjects No. 104* (London, HMSO, 1961).

Valenstein, E. S., ed., *The Psychosurgery Debate: Scientific, Legal and Ethical Perspectives* (San Francisco, W. H. Freeman, 1980).

Vilkki, J., 'Effects of Thalamic Lesions on Complex Perception and Memory', *Neuropsychologia*, 16 (1978), 427–437.

Watson, P. J., 'Nonmotor Functions of the Cerebellum', *Psychological Bulletin* 85 (1978), 944–967.

III

Experimental Studies

CHAPTER 9

Split Brains and Dual Minds

Split brain patients, or in more formal terms those who have undergone *cerebral commissurotomy*, provide a natural link between the clinical and experimental studies of the organization of the human brain. These patients are clinical subjects who have undergone neurosurgery, and yet the data which they provide is treated as if it were derived from an experimental procedure. The focus of the research is on understanding the brain, not on helping the patient. Historically, split brain studies also provided a particular stimulus for the development of laboratory techniques for use with intact human subjects.

The commissurotomy operation was introduced by Van Wagenen in 1940 as a treatment for certain severe and intractible forms of epilepsy, characterized by a focus in one hemisphere triggering off a major fit which spreads across the corpus callosum to involve both hemispheres. The idea was, simply, that cutting the corpus callosum and the other forebrain commissures would restrict the seizure to one hemisphere. In the event, it was found that even better relief from the epilepsy could be obtained, and that the frequency as well as the extent of seizure activity could be dramatically improved by the operation. A series of patients was operated upon, but interest was lost in the operation until the early 1960s when Sperry, in collaboration with the neurologist Joseph Bogen and the surgeon Philip Vogel, instituted a new series of operations. (For a full treatment of the theoretical background to this work, see Bogen, 1979.)

Sperry had been working in the 1950s on experimental split brain preparations in animals, and it was he who saw the significance of the operation for theories about the organization of the brain. A curious fact about the earlier series was that almost no handicaps in everyday life had been reported, despite the radical nature of the surgery. Relatively sophisticated experimental investigations, for the time, were also carried out without significant deficits being revealed.

However, Sperry, working with Michael Gazzaniga, was able to show by elegant techniques that the patients in the Bogen and Vogel series did suffer from certain subtle deficits which were not apparent in their everyday activity. These deficits will be described shortly.

Following the Bogen and Vogel series, a further series of patients has been operated upon by Wilson, and a number of patients have also received commissurotomy for the treatment of intraventricular and midline tumours, and for abnormalities of the cerebrovascular system.

THE COMMISSUROTOMY OPERATION AND THE PATIENTS

The operation in its full form involves complete section of the corpus callosum, the anterior and hippocampal commissures, and the massa intermedia (see Fig. 9.1). It therefore divides all direct cortical links between the two cerebral hemispheres, isolating the cortex of each hemisphere from its partner. From this division comes the term 'split brain', and also the importance of these patients in helping to construct models of the function of the right and left halves of the human brain. A number of patients have also undergone partial commissurotomy (incomplete section of the corpus callosum), and while data from these patients is of considerable importance, in the interests of clarity only the complete 'splits' will be discussed in this chapter. The related operation of hemispherectomy, in which an entire hemisphere is removed, and the naturally occurring cases of absence of the corpus callosum ('callosal agenesis') are also relevant, but will not be

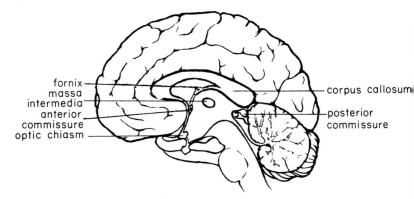

Figure 9.1. The major interhemispheric cerebral commissures.

treated here. Reviews may be found in Kinsbourne and Smith (1974) and Milner and Jeeves (1979).

Before we go on to examine the effects of commissurotomy, several points should be made clear. The first is that although split brain patients are treated as a single group, the operations performed in the three series do differ in significant ways (and this may partly account for the failure to find in the first series some of the deficits which were observed in the later series). In particular, not all the operations involved cutting the anterior commissure, which is now known to be capable of transferring quite considerable amounts of information between the two hemispheres (Risse, LeDoux, Springer, Wilson and Gazzaniga, 1978). Within the Wilson series, there are two subseries, the anterior commissure being sectioned in the first, but not the later, set of patients (Wilson, Reeves and Gazzaniga, 1978). The operation performed by Van Wagenen was undertaken in stages, while later series used a single operation. We do not have space here to go into the significance of these differences, but a careful study of the effects of commissurotomy should take account of these factors.

Perhaps more important is a word of caution about the patients. The number of patients operated upon is small, and the number reported in the (very extensive) literature is a minority of these. The total number of patients available is probably no more than about 30, and the vast bulk of the literature concerns no more than about half a dozen of these. Particularly as these patients differ greatly in their performance on the experimental tasks set for them, it is dangerous to regard them as an homogeneous group. Beware of any conclusion based upon the mean performance of a group of these patients, as it is likely to be misleading. In fact, the practice has grown of reporting the data from the patients as a set of single case studies, which seems more reasonable but is not universally adopted.

It is also tempting to treat the data as if split brain patients presented us with neat controlled experimental results. This is not so. These are surgical lesions in *abnormal* brains. The patients each have a long and complex neurological history, reflected in their pre- and post-operative neurological status. Many have lesions in other parts of the brain; some have had lesions from birth (with the suspicion that the organization of the brain has developed atypically); and some have had the operation at a relatively early age, when a degree of plasticity still remains in the brain. A detailed illustration of how these factors make interpretation of the data from split brain patients extremely difficult has been provided by Whitaker and Ojemann (1977).

All these factors – the small number of patients, their different pre- and post-operative histories and response to the operation, the precise nature of the surgery they have received, and their current anticon- vulsive medication – point to caution in treating the patients as a single group, and in treating the findings as if they came from experi- mental lesions in a previously normal brain.

THE EFFECTS OF COMMISSUROTOMY

The most striking result of commissurotomy remains the lack of handicap experienced by most patients. There is an interesting film of one of the patients, a housewife, doing domestic tasks like beating eggs, and also swimming, activities which involve integration be- tween the two sides of the body, and doing them quite successfully. Nevertheless, by ensuring that information coming from the external world is restricted to one side of sensory space, and external means of communication between the two sides of the body are prevented (more of this later), the independence of the two cerebral hemispheres, and consequent deficits in integration between the two sides of the body, can be demonstrated.

The clearest example of this is when visual information is presented in the *left or right visual field*. Stimuli which appear to the left of the point on which a subject is fixating are projected initially only to the right occipital cortex, while those to the right of fixation (in the 'right visual field') are projected to the left occipital cortex. Therefore, if the subject's fixation is controlled, this 'divided visual field' technique can be used to present visual information to either the left or the right hemisphere alone. While in normal subjects the information is then distributed through the entire brain (see Chapter 10), in split brain patients it is confined to the hemisphere of original reception.

If a visual stimulus is shown in the right visual field, and projects to the left hemisphere (which possesses speech), then the stimulus can be verbally identified, and can be picked out from a set of possible responses by the right hand (also controlled by the left hemisphere). It cannot, however, be selected by the left hand (controlled by the right hemisphere). Conversely, a stimulus presented in the left visual field will go to the right hemisphere and can be indicated by the left hand, but not by the right hand, or by speech. The information is restricted to the hemisphere of reception, and can only be linked to response processes which are controlled by that hemisphere. This basic pattern of response to visual stimuli occurs whether the task is to match a visual picture to a real object, to another picture, to a word, or to try to name it; or whether it is to match a word to another word, to a picture, an object, or to speak it.

Some curious phenomena can be observed as a result of this dissociation between the hemispheres. If a word with two component parts, for example 'heart' (he-art), is presented very briefly so that the subject is fixating between the 'e' and the 'a', then the patient will say that he saw 'art' while the left hand hand will, at the same time, pick out (from among an array of possible responses) 'he' as the stimulus. This behaviour can be seen at its clearest in the 'chimeric figure' experiments (Levy, Trevarthen and Sperry, 1972). Chimeric figures are constructed of two half-figures arranged so that the patient fixates upon the vertical division between the two half stimuli (see Fig. 9.2). These stimuli may be constructed from outline drawings or more complex figural stimuli like faces. As we might expect, shown a chimeric figure composed of the left half-face of an old man with a beard wearing a hat and the right half-face of a young blonde, the patient says that he has seen an attractive young woman, as the left speaking hemisphere only knows about the right half of the stimulus. Incidentally, the patient does not know of the chimeric nature of the stimuli and reports nothing unusual about what he has seen. At the same time, the left hand will select the old man from among a

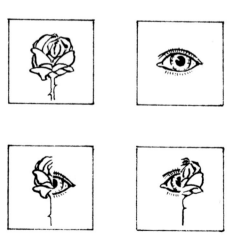

Figure 9.2. Chimeric figures. The chimeric figures (below) are constructed from the whole stimuli (above) which are used to test recognition.
(After Levy, Trevarthen and Sperry, 1972)

selection of whole faces which include the complete faces of the old man and the blonde. If the anomaly of his response is pointed out to the patient, he may well appear confused, and may make some comment such as that the hairstyle looked rather like a hat, in an attempt to resolve the confusion.

Stimuli may also be lateralized by *somaesthetic presentation*, following the same logic as divided visual field presentation. The patient may be touched at some point on his body and asked to report where he has been stimulated or in what fashion (by light touch, pinprick, and so on), or asked to point to the spot with either the right or the left hand. Objects may be placed in one hand (out of sight) and haptically explored for naming, or for matching to another object among an array using either the same or the opposite hand. Hand postures may be set up on one hand (again out of sight) to be reproduced by the opposite hand, or a representation of a gesture presented in one of the visual fields to be reproduced by the ipsilateral or contralateral hand. There are a rich variety of possibilities for the ingenious investigator, and many of the changes have been rung on this kind of experiment. What the results boil down to is, however, that split brain patients have difficulty in integrating information across the body midline: pointing with one hand to places on the opposite side of the body, passing information from one hand to the other, or relating visual information on one side of the body to movement and sensation on the other. Further, there is difficulty in expressing the results of right hemisphere processing or left sided stimulation in speech.

This conclusion concerning somaesthesis has to be qualified a little. The lateralization of somaesthesis is most complete in relation to the more distal parts of the body, and especially if finely controlled or skilled movements are required. The effects are seen most clearly, therefore, in the hands and especially the fingertips. Taking more gross body movements, and sensation from the more proximal body areas such as the trunk, the lateral differentiation is less clear. This is almost certainly because of the existence of ipsilateral connections to these areas for both sensation and motor control (see Gazzaniga and LeDoux, 1978).

Audition turns out to be rather less straightforward than vision. This is because the projections from the ears to the brain are not exclusively contralateral, but are to some extent bilateral (see p. 69). Nevertheless, the dominance of the crossed contralateral pathway can be observed in the suppression which follows *dichotic* (bilateral simultaneous) presentation. Split brain patients can report stimuli presented to either ear if the stimuli are presented singly, but if two stimuli are presented at the same time to the two ears, there will be a massive bias to report the right ear stimulus (which passes to the left hemisphere by the dominant crossed pathway). It is assumed that the ipsilateral projection from left ear to left hemisphere is suppressed in dichotic presentation, although, while the spoken response may favour the right ear, there may be evidence of reception of the left ear stimulus in response by the left hand (Gordon, 1980; Springer, Sidtis, Wilson and Gazzaniga, 1978).

While the question of speech function in the two hemispheres is clearly answered by the commissurotomy evidence, the question of the extent of *right hemisphere language* is not. The left hemisphere clearly has the capacity to generate speech, but there is no evidence to suggest that in the normally developed and lateralized brain this capacity is also present in the right (outside automatic speech and swearing). In early studies there was a tendency to confuse 'speech' and 'language', and to assume that language functions were as completely lateralized. There has since been a gradual and continuing revision of this assumption, with the right hemisphere being credited with increasingly sophisticated linguistic abilities, short of speech output.

Early reports tended to suggest that the comprehension of language stimuli presented to the right hemisphere was very limited, and that beyond the recognition of simple and common concrete nouns there was little linguistic ability present. It is now clear that while an asymmetry undoubtedly exists, in that the right hemisphere is simply not as good at performing language functions as the left, the right hemisphere nevertheless possesses a significant degree of linguistic skill. Various studies have now shown that the right hemisphere can understand abstract words and a variety of syntactic structures including verbs, sentence transformations and long non-redundant and semantically abstract references; is competent at semantic matching; can perform rhyme matches; and can understand mental associations based upon semantically coordinate, contingent and superordinate relationships. In addition, they have shown that the inability to name objects held in the left hand is only an inability to generate the name; it does not imply a failure to comprehend the nature of the object, or to construct semantic associations with it which may be manipulated and expressed in language, although not in speech. A degree of writing is possible for the left hand, although some of the patients show difficulty with this (in contrast with left hand performance in drawing and spatial manipulation which is superior to the right). The precise extent of right hemisphere language is still a matter of debate, despite extensive and elegant studies (notably by Eran Zaidel). Reviews of the work on right hemisphere speech are to be found in Searleman (1977) and in Eran Zaidel (1978a, b). Perhaps the most interesting and telling finding is that of Eran Zaidel (1979) who also compared the performance of the separated hemispheres with the performance in 'free vision' (allowing the hemispheres to cooperate), and found that the two hemispheres together produced better performance than either alone.

Relevant to this issue of the abilities of the right hemisphere are the most elegant '*metacontrol*' experiments of Levy and Trevarthen (1976). These studies employed chimeric figures which were outline drawings but which were cleverly selected so that the half-stimuli could be matched to complete stimuli on the basis of identity, or on physical similarity, or by semantic functional association (see Fig. 9.3). It was found, as had been expected, that the right hemisphere was relatively proficient at, and generally assumed control of, appearance matches, while the left hemisphere controlled function matches. From these findings come the theoretical arguments for a difference between the two hemispheres which is based upon modes of processing rather than upon the nature of the material or of the response which is demanded. It is suggested that it is the nature of the cognitive operations required which determine the relative proficiency of the two hemispheres. However, we must be careful to note that this result is only one of *relative* specialization. The data show that while there is an asymmetry between the performance of the two hemispheres, there was a significant number of trials when the 'wrong' hemisphere assumed control of the match. In other words, while the right hemisphere may prefer, or be more competent at, appearance matches (for whatever reason), it is not without the ability to undertake function matches. Dissociations between controlling hemisphere and the strategy employed occurred on a significant number of trials, and therefore the asymmetry is certainly far from absolute.

As reviews of the effects of commissurotomy have tended to emphasize the division and independence of the two hemisphere systems, and to maximize the asymmetries in performance which may be observed, some evidence which points to the limitations of this view should also be noted. I have argued elsewhere (Beaumont, 1981) that the published literature has significantly misrepresented the nature of the effects of commissurotomy by presenting an oversimplified and over generalized picture, and I am wary of repeating the error myself here. The problem, historically, was undoubtedly the influence exercised on Sperry's thinking by the initial one or two

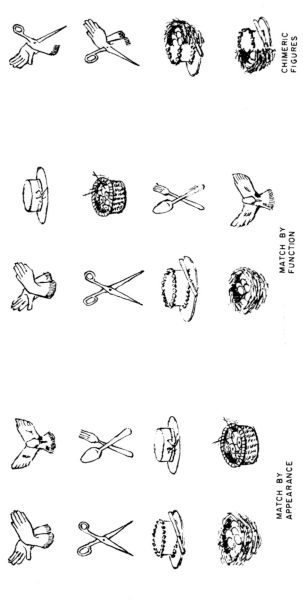

Figure 9.3. Chimeric stimuli in metacontrol experiments. The whole stimuli which the chimeric figures (right) imply can be matched by appearance (left) or by function (centre). (After Levy and Trevarthen, 1976)

patients in the Bogen and Vogel series. These turned out to be not entirely typical for a variety of reasons, and the rather bold and dramatic conclusions which he drew have had to be tempered in a number of ways.

Firstly, there are clear exceptions to the general statements made above about the effects of the operation. For instance, some of the patients are able to indicate with a given hand points stimulated on the opposite side of the body. (The variation in the degree of left hand agraphia has already been noted.) There are also opportunities for the interhemispheric transfer (obviously by routes other than the commissures which have been sectioned) of certain types of information, transfer of the size-weight illusion (Gandevia, 1978) being just one illustration. Other evidence has emphasized the continuity of the integrated and articulated operation of the total cerebral system. LeDoux, Risse, Springer, Wilson and Gazzaniga (1977) examined the performance of one of the patients on a complex, high level concept attainment and hypothesis testing task, in which there seems no doubt that the cooperation of both hemispheres was required for satisfactory performance. The patient was assessed both pre- and post-operatively, and no post-operative deficit was found, but rather an improvement in performance. They conclude that complex cognitive processes are not dependent upon the function of the corpus callosum.

A problem in assessing the significance of some of the exceptions to the 'expected' findings (although the last-named study seems free of this suspicion) is that many of the patients develop subtle *cross-cuing* strategies, that is, they develop ways to circumvent their handicap by using external routes for the lateral transfer of information. For example, sound cues may be passed from objects in the left hand to the left hemisphere via the right ear. Also, emotional signals may transfer easily by subcortical routes, so that by feeling a generalized arousal response a correct response may be deduced. The left hemisphere may conduct a speech commentary upon the responses of the left hand which it can see in free vision in the right visual field, and so transmit guidance to the right hemisphere. But perhaps the most subtle strategy concerns eye movements, which can transfer subcortically, so that even the extent of eye movement required to inspect a stimulus may give the essential clue to stimulus identity if the range of possibilities is sufficiently small (Gazzaniga, 1970; Gazzaniga and Hillyard, 1971).

These examples alone show how carefully controlled must be the experiments, and how vigilant the experimenter, if the possibility of this kind of external transfer is to be ruled out. Also, it becomes less surprising that the patients suffer little handicap in everyday life, particularly as they can manipulate what appears in which field of vision and employ both hands in order to implement strategies to share information between the hemispheres.

There are numerous reviews of this field in the literature, among which the most useful are perhaps Bogen (1979), Dimond (1972), Gazzaniga and LeDoux (1978), Levy (1980) and Sperry (1973, 1974). Excellent discussions of the theoretical models employed may also be found in Trevarthen (1975) and E. Zaidel (1978c). As has already been made clear, care should be exercised in evaluating the accuracy of some of these reviews. It may nevertheless be concluded that split brain patients have a deficit in the cross-integration of information, at least under experimental conditions. In a limited sense it is possible to accept the conclusion of Sperry that the patients exhibit 'two independent streams of conscious awareness' which are out of contact with each other, each with its own 'separate and private sensations; its own perceptions; and its own impulses to act' (Sperry, 1968, p. 724). Whether this really implies that the consciousness of these patients is divided or in some way doubled, and whether this holds implications for the processes which normally underlie consciousness, are questions to which we now turn.

CONSCIOUSNESS DIVIDED?

In a recent publication, Charles Furst claimed that 'split brain research has opened a new frontier of scientific investigations into the physical basis of consciousness. The vistas which lie beyond this frontier will perhaps revolutionize our traditional ways of understanding the human mind'. (1979, p. 161). Is this neuro-science or neuro-fantasy?

The separation between the cognitive activities of the two hemispheres has led various writers to suggest that dividing the cerebral commissures produces two independent minds. This notion was taken up most energetically by Roger Sperry, who proposed that the split brain patient has two separate minds within the one body, each with its own will as well as its own perceptions and memories (Sperry, 1976). This model, with minor variations, has been the most popular, and it is possible to find several examples of it in the literature (see Beaumont, 1981).

The only major opponent of this theoretical position has been Eccles (1977). He has suggested that, while commissurotomy divides higher level functions between the two hemispheres, only the left hemisphere contains the seat of consciousness. The right hemisphere is considered as an automatically acting subordinate partner with rather less than normal human attributes. He bases this position largely on the inability of the right hemisphere to produce speech, which he regards as the necessary test of the possession of conscious awareness.

It may have occurred to you to wonder what is meant by 'consciousness'. Indeed, much of the debate might be resolved if those who construct theories about this topic were themselves more clear. Some writers, particularly those who espouse double mind theories, include any evidence of intelligent responsiveness, attention and awareness as indicating consciousness. Eccles, however, uses the very much more restricted requirement that the organism must declare itself conscious by speech. I do not intend to try to resolve this matter here, but it seems to many people that Eccles' definition is too restrictive. It demands, for instance, that we remain agnostic about whether the congenitally dumb are conscious. It also implies that it is not possible to know if a person possesses consciousness when he has lost his voice from a sore throat. This is patently absurd. On the other hand, 'any intelligent cognitive act' seems too loose a definition, for it forces us to attribute consciousness even to lowly animals if they show that they can learn some simple experimental task, although we are generally not sure that this demands 'consciousness'. Possibly a solution can be found by demanding some evidence of self-awareness and purposeful cognitive activity, although this is inadequate as a formal definition. A fuller discussion of this problem may be found in Savage (1976).

By now it may also be clear to you that the debate is embroiled in philosophical mind-body issues (see p. 7). There are many fascinating discussions by both neuroscientists and philosophers of these problems, including the prospect of transplanting separated hemispheres into different bodies and then recombining them at a later date (Bell, 1975; Globus, 1976; Nagel, 1971; Puccetti, 1973). Such issues raise fundamental questions about our conception of personal identity, but they have to be sidestepped here for want of space. However, if my argument is accepted that it is not sensible to regard the minds of commissurotomy patients as divided, many of the questions become academic.

To return to the scientific evidence, there are five central questions which we should ask before deciding on the structure of consciousness in split brain patients.

1. *Does the right hemisphere possess language?* This question has already been broached, with the conclusion that the right hemisphere may be effectively mute, and is certainly less proficient at most linguistic tasks, but that it does possess a remarkable variety of linguistic skills. As a result, the right half-brain of a split brain patient cannot be considered to lack language. It is, of course, possible that this evidence is in part a consequence of the patient's early neurological history, and that it does not imply that language is similarly represented in the right hemisphere of a normal brain. The speech developed in association with the right hemisphere by a patient known as PS, who was operated upon at the age of fifteen and whose neuropsychological development was almost certainly not normal, provides an illustration of how atypical organization may occur in these patients (Gazzaniga, Volpe, Smylie, Wilson and LeDoux, 1979). However, the point still stands that split brain patients have some right hemisphere language capability.

2. *Are there other abilities which the right hemisphere may lack?* While there is much evidence for the *relative* specialization of the two hemispheres, with some functions better performed by the right and some better performed by the left, no abilities other than speech and language have been proposed as absent from the left hemisphere. In fact, the trend has increasingly been to credit the right hemisphere with sophisticated abilities. The most striking example is the demonstration by Sperry, Zaidel and Zaidel (1979) of self-recognition and social awareness in the right hemisphere of two of the patients. Arrays of pictures and photographs which included some with personal and emotional reference among similar neutral stimuli were presented. The detailed accounts of the patients' responses leave little doubt that while the patients have great difficulty in describing their thoughts about the stimuli through speech, a characteristic social, political, personal and self-awareness, such as we should expect for the left, was present in the right hemisphere. For example, a woman was shown (to her right hemisphere) four photographs of men which included one of her son. She readily picked out her son as the one she recognized, but could not say who it was. She reported good feelings about the image and suggested the names of her daughter and husband, but remained confused. Following further questions to which she indicated further positive feelings ('Yea, it's fine, it's beautiful.'), she pointed to the picture of her son and said, 'The best looking one there.' Examiner: 'Is it you? . . . Your husband?' (Patient does not

respond) '. . . your son?' Patient (in a very definite decisive tone); 'Yeah.' Thus helped to overcome the handicap of limited speech output, the right hemisphere showed every sign of being characteristically human.

It has also been suggested that there is a lack of awareness of right hemisphere processes, based on some rather slender evidence, such as the denial of left hand control, the failure to recognize the anomaly in chimeric figures (although normal subjects may also miss the anomaly under certain circumstances), and the maintenance of independent response probabilities by the two hemispheres in a learning task. This evidence is not sufficiently strong to deny awareness of right hemisphere processes, particularly in view of the kind of demonstration above.

3. *Is there any cross-integration between the disconnected hemispheres?* It has already been hinted that the separation of the hemispheres is not as complete as is sometimes suggested. There is intermanual transfer of maze learning, accurate target-directed reaching across the midline and completion across the midline for incomplete geometric figures, pictures and words. The ambient space around the body, in vision outside the central field, is not divided for the perception of space relations or motion in space (Trevarthen, 1974). Bimanual skills are relatively preserved (Preilowski, 1975).

It is clear that the assumption that cross-integration is impossible for these patients is incorrect. It is possible to demonstrate deficits in this function in a rigorous experimental situation and on a particular task, but for most cognitive activities (certainly in the unrestricted patient) there are mechanisms which allow substantial cross-integration.

4. *Are the separated hemispheres ever in conflict?* It is more difficult to decide the answer to this question because the relevant evidence is anecdotal. There are various accounts of conflicting activity by the two hands: one hand pulling trousers up, while the other pulled them down; one hand seeking help from the patient's wife while the other pushed her away. At one time it seemed that most of these accounts came from one patient, and in the early period following surgery, but they have been amplified and extended by a range of personal accounts collected by Stuart Dimond (1979). One patient said: 'You wouldn't want to hear some of the things this left hand has done – you wouldn't believe it. It acts independently a lot of times. I don't even tell it to – I don't know it's going to do anything. . . . It seems to have a mind of its own.' (p. 213).

It is still difficult to know what to make of such accounts, particularly as many of the patients are not ignorant of the literature written about them. I feel that these are rare incidents which are not fundamentally different from a variety of the silly errors we all occasionally make (unwrapping a sweet, holding the wrapper and sweet in opposite hands and then throwing the sweet in the bin and placing the wrapper in your mouth). Experimental attempts to document the conflict have failed, and great significance should not be attached to such anecdotal reports.

5. *Are there qualitative changes in thinking?* This is another question which is difficult to answer. There are again intriguing reports, but little firm evidence. Different strategies in performance have been assigned to the two hemispheres on the basis of performance on cognitive tasks, but other reports are essentially anecdotal. It may well be that split brain patients do suffer changes in the nature of their thinking, but as yet such changes have not been satisfactorily demonstrated.

In view of the answers to our five questions, can we regard the consciousness of commissurotomy patients as abnormal? I do not think so. It is first of all clear that the right hemisphere does not seem in any way basically different from the left, except in speech production. The patients appear to possess high level abilities, conceptualization and self-awareness within the right hemisphere, and to be aware, although perhaps to a limited extent, of right hemisphere processes. It seems wrong, in the face of this evidence, to deny consciousness to the right hemisphere, and we can therefore reject Eccles' model.

If consciousness resides in both hemispheres, is it divided? The answers to our questions again suggest that outside very special, highly controlled and artificial circumstances, it is not. It may be possible, particularly with cognitive tasks in the laboratory, to demonstrate some dissociation between the two hemisphere systems. This is no more remarkable than the fact that I can talk while holding a cup of coffee in one hand and scratching my ear with the other. There is extremely slight evidence for conflicting wills in the two hemisphere systems, and a fair amount of evidence for cross-integration between the two lateral systems. There is none for significant qualitative changes in the thinking, everyday responsiveness, or awareness of these patients. On consideration, this is hardly surprising. Both cortical systems are fundamentally bound on to a subcortical substrate with massive integrated bilateral structures, and they cannot sensibly be considered independently from this substrate. The two hemispheres in split brain patients are no more disconnected than are my two hands. Under certain circumstances they may be observed to be undertaking different but simultaneous activities, and they may retain certain properties of their own, but they are part of a more general system which maintains the integrity of the mind, just as the hands are joined to the arms and trunk, so maintaining the integrity of the body.

Split brain patients have prompted a valuable debate about the nature of consciousness and its relation to mental processes. However, it seems a mistake to think that the state of consciousness of these patients has been altered in any radical fashion, or to consider that the studies should lead us to revise our traditional model of a single and unitary mind associated with the entire organ of the brain, forming an integral part of a single physical body.

CONCLUSION

Considerable significance has been attached to the studies of patients who have undergone commissurotomy. It has been considered that they provide essential evidence about the independence of the two cerebral hemispheres and their lateral specialization. The evidence suggests that, while there is a degree of disconnection between the two hemispheres in these patients so that under laboratory conditions it can be shown that information cannot be transferred between the two sides of the brain, we should be cautious about overstating the importance of these findings. Split brain patients do, however, possess cortical hemispheres which can independently perceive, remember, think and respond, to some degree outside the awareness of the other.

It has also been suggested that these patients show evidence of divided consciousness. From a brief review, it is concluded that this view cannot be supported. Certain unusual phenomena may be demonstrated in these patients, but there is no good reason to believe that they possess two independent minds as a result of the operation, or that they tell us very much about the normal operation of consciousness.

The true significance of split brain studies is the dramatic stimulus which they have given to the development of neuropsychological techniques and theoretical models, which will be discussed in the following chapters.

FURTHER READING

The most accessible recent reviews of the effects of commissurotomy are to be found in:

Bogen, J. E., 'The Callosal Syndrome', in K. M. Heilman and E. Valenstein, eds., *Clinical Neuropsychology* (New York, Oxford University Press, 1979).

Gazzaniga, M. S. and LeDoux, J. E., *The Integrated Mind* (New York, Plenum Press, 1978).

Discussions of consciousness and split brains are to be found in:

Beaumont, J. G., 'Split Brain Studies and the Duality of Consciousness', in G. Underwood and R. Stevens, eds., *Aspects of Consciousness*, vol. 2 (London, Academic Press, 1981).

Dimond, S. J., 'Symmetry and Asymmetry in the Vertebrate Brain', in D. A. Oakley and H. C. Plotkin, eds., *Brain, Behaviour and Evolution* (London, Methuen, 1979).

Sperry, R. W., 'Consciousness, Freewill and Personal Identity', in Oakley and Plotkin, op. cit.

REFERENCES

Beaumont, J. G., 'Split Brain Studies and the Duality of Consciousness', in G. Underwood and R. Stevens, eds., *Aspects of Consciousness*, vol. 2 (London, Academic Press, 1981).

Bell, G. A., 'The Double Brain and Mind Brain Relationship', *Journal of Behavioral Science*, 2 (1975), 161–167.

Bogen, J. E., 'The Callosal Syndrome', in K. M. Heilman and E. Valenstein, eds., *Clinical Neuropsychology* (New York, Oxford University Press, 1979).

Dimond, S. J., *The Double Brain* (Edinburgh, Churchill-Livingstone, 1972).

Dimond, S. J., 'Symmetry and Asymmetry in the Vertebrate Brain', in D. A. Oakley and H. C. Plotkin, eds., *Brain, Behaviour and Evolution* (London, Methuen, 1979).

Eccles, J. C., *The Understanding of the Brain*, 2nd edition (New York, McGraw Hill, 1977).

Furst, C., *Origins of the Mind* (Englewood Cliffs, N. J. Prentice-Hall, 1979).

Gandevia, S. C., 'The Sensation of Heaviness after Surgical Disconnection of the Cerebral Hemispheres in Man', *Brain*, 101 (1978), 295–306.

Gazzaniga, M. S., *The Bisected Brain* (New York, Appleton-Century-Crofts, 1970).

Gazzaniga, M. S. and Hillyard, S. A., 'Language and Speech Capacity of the Right Hemisphere', *Neuropsychologia*, 9 (1971), 273–280.

Gazzaniga, M. S. and LeDoux, J. E., *The Integrated Mind* (New York, Plenum Press, 1978).

Gazzaniga, M. S., Volpe, B. T., Smylie, C. S., Wilson, D. H. and LeDoux,

J. E., 'Plasticity in Speech Organisation following Commissurotomy', *Brain*, 102 (1979), 805–815.

Globus, G. G., 'Mind, Structure and Contradiction', in G. G. Globus, G. Maxwell and I. Savodnik, eds., *Consciousness and the Brain: a Scientific and Philosophic Enquiry* (New York, Plenum Press, 1976).

Gordon, H. W., 'Right Hemisphere Comprehension of Verbs in Patients with Complete Forebrain Commissurotomy: Use of the Dichotic Method and Manual Performance', *Brain and Language*, 11 (1980), 76–86.

Kinsbourne, M. and Smith, W. L., eds., *Hemispheric Disconnection and Cerebral Function* (Springfield, Illinois, Charles C. Thomas, 1974).

LeDoux, J. E., Risse, G. L., Springer, S. P., Wilson, D. H. and Gazzaniga, M. S.,'Cognition and Commissurotomy', *Brain*, 100 (1977), 87–104.

Levy, J., 'Cerebral Asymmetry and the Psychology of Man', in M. C. Wittrock, ed., *The Brain and Psychology* (New York, Academic Press, 1980).

Levy, J. and Trevarthen, C., 'Metacontrol of Hemispheric Function in Human Split-Brain Patients', *Journal of Experimental Psychology: Human Perception and Performance*, 2 (1976), 299–312.

Levy, J., Trevarthen, C. and Sperry, R. W., 'Perception of Bilateral Chimeric Figures following Hemispheric Disconnexion', *Brain*, 95 (1972), 61–78.

Milner, A. D. and Jeeves, M. A., 'A Review of Behavioural Studies of Agenesis of the Corpus Callosum', in I. Steele Russell, M. W. Van Hof and G. Berlucchi, eds., *Structure and Function of Cerebral Commissures* (London, Macmillan, 1979).

Nagel, T., 'Brain Bisection and the Unity of Consciousness', *Synthese*, 22 (1971), 396–413.

Preilowski, B., 'Bilateral Motor Interaction: Perceptual-motor Performance of Partial and Complete 'Split-brain' Patients', in K. J. Zülch, O. Creutzfeldt and G. C. Galbraith, eds., *Cerebral Localization* (Berlin, Springer-Verlag, 1975).

Puccetti, R., 'Multiple Identity', *The Personalist*, 54 (1973), 203–215.

Risse, G. L., LeDoux, J., Springer, S. P., Wilson, D. H. and Gazzaniga, M. S., 'The Anterior Commissure in Man: Functional Variation in a Multi-sensory System', *Neuropsychologia*, 16 (1978), 23–31.

Savage, C. W., 'An Old Ghost in a New Body', in G. G. Globus, G. Maxwell and I. Savodnik, eds., *Consciousness and the Brain: a Scientific and Philosophic Enquiry* (New York, Plenum Press, 1976).

Searleman, A., 'A Review of Right Hemisphere Linguistic Capabilities', *Psychological Bulletin*, 84 (1977), 503–528.

Sperry, R. W., Hemisphere Deconnection and Unity in Conscious Awareness', *American Psychologist*, 23 (1968), 723–733.

Sperry, R. W., 'Lateral Specialisation of Cerebral Function in the Surgically Separated Hemispheres', in F. J. McGuigan and R. A. Schoonover, eds., *The Psychophysiology of Thinking* (New York, Academic Press, 1973).

Sperry, R. W., 'Lateral Specialisation in the Surgically Separated Hemispheres', in F. O. Schmitt and F. G. Worden, eds., *The Neurosciences: Third Study Program* (Cambridge, Mass., MIT Press, 1974).

Sperry, R. W., 'Mental Phenomena as Causal Determinants in Brain Function', in G. G. Globus, G. Maxwell and I. Savodnik, eds., *Consciousness and the Brain: a Scientific and Philosophic Enquiry* (New York, Plenum Press, 1976).

Sperry, R. W., Zaidel, E. and Zaidel, D., 'Self-recognition and Social Awareness in the Deconnected Minor Hemisphere', *Neuropsychologia*, 17 (1979), 153–166.

Springer, S. P., Sidtis, J., Wilson, D. and Gazzaniga, M. S., 'Left Ear Performance in Dichotic Listening following Commissurotomy', *Neuropsychologia*, 16 (1978), 305–312.

Trevarthen, C., 'Analysis of Cerebral Activities that Generate and Regulate Consciousness in Commissurotomy Patients', in S. J. Dimond and J. G. Beaumont, eds., *Hemisphere Function in the Human Brain* (London, Elek Science, 1974).

Trevarthen, C., 'Psychological Activities after Forebrain Commissurotomy in Man: Concepts and Methodological Hurdles in Testing', in F. Michel and B. Schott, eds., *Les Syndromes de Disconnexion Calleuse chez L'Homme* (Lyon, Hôpital Neurologique, 1975).

Whitaker, H. A. and Ojemann, G. A., 'Lateralization of Higher Cortical Functions: a Critique', *Annals of the New York Academy of Sciences*, 299 (1977), 459–473.

Wilson, D. H., Reeves, A. and Gazzaniga, M. S., 'Division of the Corpus Callosum for Uncontrollable Epilepsy', *Neurology*, 28 (1978), 649–653.

Zaidel, C., 'Auditory Language Comprehension in the Right Hemisphere following Cerebral Commissurotomy and Hemispherectomy: a Comparison with Child Language and Aphasia', in A. Caramazza and E. B. Zurif, eds., *Language Acquisition and Language Breakdown* (Baltimore, Maryland, The Johns Hopkins University Press, 1978a).

Zaidel, E., 'Lexical Organisation in the Right Hemisphere', in P. A. Buser and A. Rougeul-Buser, eds., *Cerebral Correlates of Conscious Experience* (Amsterdam, North-Holland, 1978b).

Zaidel, E., 'Concepts of Cerebral Dominance in the Split Brain', in P. A. Buser and A. Rougeul-Buser, eds., *Cerebral Correlates of Conscious Experience* (Amsterdam, North-Holland, 1978c).

Zaidel, E., 'Performance on the ITPA following Cerebral Commissurotomy and Hemispherectomy', *Neuropsychologia*, 17 (1979), 259–280.

CHAPTER 10

Divided Visual Field Studies

The perception of briefly presented lateralized stimuli has been studied by experimental psychologists throughout this century. Much work was done in the 1950s to investigate the superior recognition of words presented in the right visual field, but while reference was made to 'cerebral dominance', other factors such as reading habits and post-exposural scanning were considered important in explaining the findings. It was the study of split brain patients in the early 1960s by Sperry and Gazzaniga which led to the technique of divided visual field presentation being used to investigate the cerebral organization of normal intact subjects in the laboratory, and laid the foundation for contemporary experimental human neuropsychology.

Since the mid 1960s, and especially in the last decade, an enormous number of studies have used the technique, which now forms the most important method of investigation in experimental neuropsychology. A recent and far from comprehensive review contains a bibliography of over 1,000 references, mostly published within the last ten years, and this is some indication of the importance of the technique. If the experimental studies were unanimous in their findings, it would be possible to report dramatic progress in this field, but in fact it is difficult to draw firm conclusions from them. This is partly because of the indifferent scientific quality of many of the studies, and partly because of the complexity of the system under study. Nevertheless, some fairly clear conclusions may be drawn.

THE TECHNIQUE

The logic of the technique of divided visual field presentation is simple and elegant, and has been referred to in the previous chapter: if a visual stimulus is presented in the left visual field, then it is projected initially only to the right occipital cortex, if presented in the right visual field, it is projected only to the left occipital cortex, and therefore if the subject's fixation is controlled, stimuli can be injected into one or the other hemisphere. Because the technique usually involves binocular vision, and the stimulus in a given visual field travels through both eyes and via one crossed and one uncrossed pathway to the contralateral hemisphere, differences between the eyes and the visual pathways are balanced out (see Fig. 10.1). The subject's performance in terms of accuracy of report or speed of response can then be studied as a function of the hemisphere of initial presentation, even though processes following initial reception may result in the stimulus information being distributed to both hemispheres of the brain.

The technique relies on accurate *control of fixation*, and this is usually

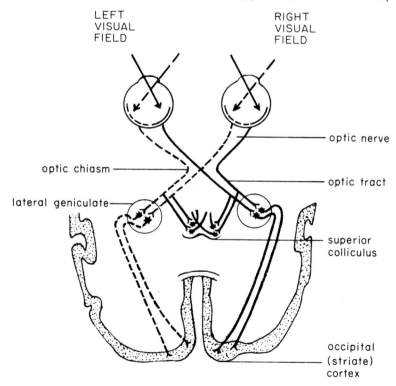

Figure. 10.1. Anatomy of the visual pathways. Note how the left visual field projects to the right visual cortex (solid lines) and the right visual field to the left visual cortex (broken lines).

achieved by directing the subject's fixation to a desired point. The stimulus is then presented for a brief duration, too short to allow the subject voluntarily to orient his eyes to the stimulus location. It is difficult to determine just how long an exposure may be before such eye movements can be brought into play, but a conservative estimate suggests 150 msec., and exposures up to 200 msec. may be acceptable. A tachistoscope (or its microcomputer simulation) is the most common method for presentation of stimuli, but other methods have been used (see Dimond and Beaumont, 1974). The use of half-occluding contact lenses to limit vision to one visual field for longer periods, allowing the presentation of a wider variety of forms of stimulation including films and very complex detailed displays, is an exciting development, although the technique may not be entirely reliable (Dimond, Bureš, Farrington, and Brouwers, 1975; Zaidel, 1975).

It is obviously wise to maintain a check on the direction of fixation at the time of stimulus presentation, although this has been done less commonly than one might wish. However, both direct video and electro-oculographic monitoring of eye movements are possible and have been used with success (Dimond and Beaumont, 1972; Young, Bion and Ellis, 1980). It has also generally been considered advisable to present stimuli unilaterally, that is, in one field at a time, and in a random sequence so that the subject cannot anticipate where the next stimulus will occur. This guards against the loss of accurate central fixation, and might be especially important where concurrent monitoring of fixation is not undertaken. However, quite a number of studies have used bilateral presentation, or 'blocked' unilateral presentation in which a series of stimuli all appear at the same side. There is remarkably good agreement between the bilateral and random unilateral studies, particularly where these involve some additional control over fixation, and where the bilateral studies report the order in which stimuli have been presented (either from the right, or left, visual field first). This is surprising in view of the general level of disagreement among published results and the heated debate which has surrounded the topic.

One extension of the technique, particularly with bilateral studies, has been the presentation of a 'neutral' stimulus at central fixation, which is reported before the lateral stimuli as an aid to ensure accurate central fixation. It has been feared that this addition might affect the subsequent perception of the lateral stimuli because of the need to process and report the stimulus in the centre, and although such an effect has never been clearly demonstrated, the method has become less popular as a result of this concern.

A final methodological question concerns the degree of overlap down the central meridian of the visual fields, and the eccentricity of the stimuli necessary to ensure lateralized presentation. We noted in Chapter 6 how there was an area of bilateral projection around central fixation which was often spared following unilateral lesions. There is also an area served with direct interhemispheric links through the splenium of the corpus callosum, around central vision. The precise extent of these two areas is not clearly established for man, and it seems wise to avoid the central three degrees of vision around fixation when placing lateralized stimuli, although studies have reported visual field asymmetries with less eccentric stimuli.

Despite the fact that the method is in principle simple and elegant, some of the methodological problems connected with it are more than trivial (see Beaumont, 1982a; Young, 1982). There has even been doubt cast over the whole field at various times, with suggestions that the findings might be due to something quite other than cerebral organization. However, none of these suggestions has ever satisfactorily explained away the very impressive body of evidence which has been accumulated. While the widespread adoption of the technique has been accompanied by some methodological laxity, the relatively coherent results which have been obtained in scores of different laboratories suggest that the technique is robust and generally reliable. It is now accepted as a valid method of investigating cerebral organization for performance in normal humans.

THE EVIDENCE

With such a large body of evidence to review, it is difficult to know how to divide it up sensibly for clear presentation. However, one of the earliest variables thought to underlie the appearance of a left or right visual field advantage was the verbal or non-verbal nature of the stimulus material, and this remains a useful way in which to classify the studies and the one that will be used here. Nevertheless, it should not be taken to indicate that this is the basis on which the observed hemisphere asymmetries rest. It is now clear, as we shall see, that a whole host of variables may influence any lateral advantage that emerges.

A comment is necessary about the terms *visual field asymmetry* and *advantage*. An asymmetry may be shown by either a right or a left visual field advantage (some people prefer to speak more accurately about the *hemi*fields, and a hemifield advantage). A right visual field advantage, for example, is when performance shows either more accurate or more rapid response following stimulus presentation to the right of fixation than to the left. It is inferred that reception of the stimulus by the left cerebral hemisphere confers some advantage for the speed or accuracy of subsequent processing. Just how and why this occurs is the subject of the theoretical models which we shall discuss shortly. It should be noted as well that the reported lateral advantage or *lateral asymmetry* is usually based upon the mean results of a number of subjects whose data has been grouped together for statistical analysis. While an asymmetry may be clear from such data, it does not mean that these average results will be typical of each subject. There are wide individual differences (see Chapter 13), and this variability has been of concern to some writers (Colbourn, 1978).

Non-verbal Stimuli

Poffenberger in 1912 is generally credited as the first to show that there are asymmetries in the detection of simple undifferentiated stimuli such as patches of light. His results have been confirmed by modern experiments, and consist of two main findings. The first is that for a stimulus on a given side of the body, there will be a faster response with the hand on the same side than with the opposite hand. This is interpreted as reflecting the difference between the direct pathway in which detection and response initiation can be performed by the same hemisphere (see Fig. 10.2), and the indirect pathway in

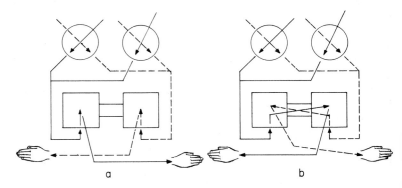

Figure 10.2. Direct (a) and indirect (b) pathways. With the direct pathway, the right hand responds to the right visual field (solid line), and only one hemisphere, the left, is involved. With the indirect pathway, the left hand responds to the right visual field (solid line), and both hemispheres and the corpus callosum are involved.

which information must be passed across the corpus callosum after stimulus detection for response initiation by the opposite hemisphere. Some workers have suggested that this model enables an estimate to be made of the time taken to transfer information across the callosum (IHTT: interhemispheric transfer time), with a typical result of about 4 msec. for a simple experiment of this kind. However, it is clear that the model involving a single callosal transfer is too simple, particularly with more complex stimuli and tasks, and that is why firm values for IHTT have not been obtained. Incidentally, the values for IHTT of up to 50 msec., which are often found, are very much greater than would be expected from what is known about physiological rates of neural transmission across the commissures.

It might well be pointed out that *compatibility* between stimulus and response is an established phenomenon in human performance, and that to respond with the hand on the same side as the stimulus is a more compatible response. Whether this might explain the finding has been elegantly tested by Berlucchi and co-workers, by the simple expedient of requiring subjects to undertake trials in which the hands were crossed over, thus associating the compatible alternative with the indirect, not the direct, route (Berlucchi, Crea, DiStefano and Tassinari, 1977). Their results show that while response compatibility is a factor in determining the differences between hands, the anatomical differences between direct and indirect routes are more important.

The second main finding to come out of these experiments is that superimposed upon the advantage of direct over indirect routes is a *lateral asymmetry*, with the advantage for stimuli in the left visual field. This finding applies not only to flashes of light, but also to other simple stimuli to be detected, such as a solid filled dot amongst an array of unfilled dots. The finding is not universal (almost none is, using this technique), but there seems general agreement on a right hemisphere advantage for simple stimulus detection.

A similar advantage has been found for sustained attention in a *vigilance* paradigm by Dimond (1979), who has suggested that the right hemisphere might contain the primary mechanisms for watch-keeping, although not all workers have agreed with this interpretation. Similar fundamental differences have been suggested by others to account for asymmetries in elementary perceptual processes. The masking and visual persistence investigations which experimental psychologists use to study the initial stages of perception have been undertaken in this context. During such stages, stimuli have to be selected from a barrage of sensory stimulation, and processed ready for categorization and subsequent processing for recognition and storage. There is some evidence that these pre-categorical mechanisms may differ between the hemispheres, favouring the right, but there is also criticism of the experiments which have been performed (Cohen, 1976; Hellige and Webster, 1979).

Hemisphere asymmetries have also been sought for a variety of *simple perceptual variables.* Judgement of brightness has been shown to result in reports of greater brightness associated with the right hemisphere. Similarly, colour perception seems to be better performed by the right hemisphere, although only if a relatively difficult discrimination is demanded. This last aspect is a general feature of these studies. It seems that the task must be perceptually demanding, either because the stimuli are hard to discriminate or because they are relatively complex, if the right hemisphere advantage is to be observed. Another aspect of this is the extent to which stimuli might be named, which brings us directly to the fundamental problem with our scheme: it is very difficult to decide when a stimulus is 'verbal' or 'non-verbal'. Stimuli which are figural and meaningful are often relatively easy to name or to 'verbalize', which brings verbal characteristics into our 'non-verbal' stimulus. Conversely, even words have outlines, length, and so on, and although primarily verbal they have non-verbal attributes. It is sometimes suggested that for a right hemisphere advantage to be clearly observed, stimuli should be perceptually complex and difficult to verbalize, and that this is what is implied by 'non-verbal'.

Not only brightness and colour, but also depth perception, especially in binocular vision, motion perception, and stimulus enumeration, seems generally to be associated with a right hemisphere advantage. Detection of the length of lines is very difficult to test if a verbal response is to be avoided (so as not to encourage verbalization) and other lateral asymmetries in perception are not to interfere with the result. The findings for stimulus duration are similarly rather unclear because of some difficult procedural and methodological problems. It seems at least possible, however, that some aspects of the perception of duration are linked with a left hemisphere advantage. Two final stimulus variables, localization and orientation, have been associated with mixed results, although once again some sense can be made of the data by considering verbal codability. In general a right hemisphere advantage has been observed, and when a left hemisphere advantage has been found it can be explained by the inclusion of a frame or some other background which might aid coding. Even with stimuli which are (arguably) quite codable, such as a clock-face, or with horizontal or vertical stimuli, a left visual field superiority has been found.

Form perception has produced unclear results. White in his review (1972) found no evidence of an asymmetry, and the picture is no less uncertain now. To some extent the outcome depends on the complexity of the stimuli, as studies which have used the classic Vanderplas and Garvin figures in identification or matching tasks (see Fig. 10.3) have shown. Even so, the results are not simply that more complex figures (with more corners) produce a right hemisphere advantage, or that the 'association value' of the stimuli (which is an index of how verbalizable they are) predicts the asymmetry observed. What is clear is that when complex representations of nameable objects are presented, which are presumably readily associated with a name, then a left hemisphere advantage normally ensues.

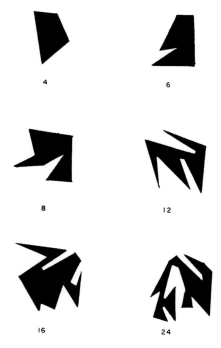

Figure 10.3. Examples of the Vanderplas and Garvin random shapes, with the number of corners as shown.

(After J. M. Vanderplas and E. A. Garvin, 1959, *Journal of Experimental Psychology*, 57, 147–154)

Some interesting results have been found with the *signs* used by the deaf. Adults who cannot 'read' them, and for whom they are a meaningless configuration, generally show a left visual field advantage when they are shown, but hearing adults who understand them show, like the deaf, a right visual field advantage. This fits with the idea that it is semantic or linguistic properties which are linked with a left hemisphere advantage.

Faces have been much investigated as stimuli. In general they yield a right hemisphere advantage, although the results are rather complex. Interestingly, schematic faces produce a much less clear asymmetry than do photographs of real faces. However, the right hemisphere seems better at recognizing and matching faces than the left, and also at recognizing emotions. It was suggested at one time that the hemispheres, right and left, might be linked with negative and positive emotions respectively, but it now seems more likely that the right hemisphere is superior at emotional perception from faces, whatever the emotion.

If the face is to be named, what should we expect: a right hemisphere advantage because it is a face, or a left hemisphere advantage because it has to be named? In fact, researchers have disagreed, although the balance of evidence seems slightly in favour of a right hemisphere advantage. The duration of presentation may be important here. In some experiments the faces were presented for less time than it normally takes to recognize them in central vision, with the result that basic perceptual aspects of the stimuli may have been emphasized at the expense of the properties which would normally be attended to. Upright and inverted faces have been contrasted in an attempt to control for the perceptual aspects of the stimuli, but just what cognitive processes are invoked by an inverted face seems unclear (Leehey and Cahn, 1979; Young and Bion, 1981).

It is difficult to summarize the above information on visual field advantages without doing grave misjustice to it. Those interested in this topic are advised to consult the excellent and extensive recent review by Davidoff (1982). However, repeating the warning that there are many contrary findings, it seems that if basic low level perceptual functions are examined, then some, but not all, may yield visual field asymmetries. When an asymmetry is found, it tends to be a right hemisphere advantage. Stimulus complexity and duration (with shorter durations producing perceptually more difficult discriminations) are implicated in determining a right hemisphere superiority. With more complex stimuli, familiar drawings with names produce a left hemisphere advantage, while faces and certain shapes may be associated with a right hemisphere advantage. The verbalizability of the stimuli may be an important variable, as may its symbolic content.

Verbal Stimuli

The results of studies using 'verbal' stimuli have been less contradictory than the 'non-verbal' studies. Certainly if stimuli such as words, strings of letters, single letters or digits are presented for identification or matching, a strong left hemisphere (right visual field) advantage is normally found (Beaumont, 1982b). In the cases where the effect has not been found, there is often reason to suspect that the stimuli have been processed on their perceptual rather than their verbal attributes. When words or letter strings are presented, the right hemisphere superiority is found whether the presentation is horizontal or vertical, although the horizontal orientation tends to produce the stronger effect. This demonstrates that while left-to-right scanning patterns, perhaps based upon reading habits, may have some influences on the left field superiority, they cannot be a complete explanation (Day, 1979).

What is surprising about these studies in view of the conclusions we drew previously is that *linguistic parameters* do not seem to relate directly to the left hemisphere advantage. The use of concrete nouns contrasted with abstract nouns, the manipulation of imageability, nouns opposed to verbs, or the effects of word frequency do not seem to relate in any coherent way to the left hemisphere superiority (Day, 1977; Bradshaw and Gates, 1978). Having previously found a lateral asymmetry for the recognition of linguistic stimuli, it was confidently expected that the more 'verbal' and less 'non-verbal' a stimulus (for example, abstract versus concrete nouns), then the stronger would be the lateral advantage. This has not been clearly demonstrated. Even with strings of letters, or 'nonsense' words, it does not seem to be the case that there is a left visual advantage if the string is more pronounceable ('BOV' rather than 'ZVH'), or more similar to meaningful English words (Leiber, 1976). This very much undermines the assumption that left hemisphere superiority is determined by the operation of purely linguistic processes.

Although identification of stimuli for simple report or matching has been the task most commonly employed, certain more demanding tasks have also been used. A particularly important one has been the presentation of letter stimuli for physical and nominal matching (Cohen, 1972; Hellige, Cox and Litvac, 1979; Ledlow, Swanson and Kinsbourne, 1978). This is a task much studied in cognitive psychology, and requires the subject to determine if two letters are identical (physical match: 'AA' but not 'Aa'), or similar in name (nominal match: 'AA' or 'Aa', but not 'AB'). Specific instructions are given to the subject as to which type of match to perform, and thus determine the *cognitive* demands of the task. In general, the requirement to make a physical match is associated with a right hemisphere advantage, at least for the 'same' responses, although this has not always been found. Where a nominal match is required, then a left hemisphere superiority is almost universally found, although it is again clearer for 'same' responses.

It is interesting that the distinction between nominal and physical matching may reflect on tasks where the type of match required is not clearly specified. Although the type of matching may be inherently clear in the form of stimuli presented, subjects may nevertheless adopt different *cognitive strategies* (Bryden, 1978), that is, they will adopt some preferred or habitual approach to solving the problem of determining a match. If different subjects select different strategies, then this may account for some of the variability found in the research reports. Also, the fact that a left hemisphere advantage is generally found for simple word or letter matching implies that although a physical matching strategy might be sufficient, subjects nevertheless generally adopt a nominal matching strategy. The extent to which very subtle aspects of the experimental instructions and procedure may influence the adoption of cognitive strategies is also of concern to some investigators.

A delay may be introduced between the elements to be matched in the physical/nominal matching paradigm, in order to investigate the role of memory components in determining lateral asymmetry. Some workers have found that introducing a delay in physical matching produces a shift from right to left hemisphere advantage, implying the necessity of verbally encoding the stimulus, but this has been contested in recent reports (McCarthy, 1980). Nevertheless, what these experiments clearly demonstrate is that purely cognitive factors may influence lateral asymmetry, so that even though the stimuli and presentation conditions may be identical, the task demanded may determine whether a left or right hemisphere advantage is found.

An obvious question which arises is the part played by the *response* in producing a lateral asymmetry. If a left hemisphere advantage were only to be found when a vocal or right hand response was demanded (both initiated presumably by the left hemisphere), this might well explain the phenomenon. The problem is that it is very difficult to change the response without to some degree changing the task. However, when a manual response is required, most workers have demanded responses with each of the hands in a balanced order, and some have subsequently analysed the effect of this variable (Besner, Grimsell and Davis, 1979; Segalowitz, Bebout and Lederman, 1979). The results are conflicting, and this may reflect the suspicion that quite subtle aspects of the response, such as how fine a movement is required (with more distinctly contralateral control), may be crucial variables.

It is more difficult to compare manual with vocal responses than responses with the two hands, although in general the evidence is that vocalization *per se* is not critical in determining the left hemisphere advantage. This has been shown by contrasting a meaningful response with a vocal, but meaningless, response (such as 'bonk') in a go/no-go paradigm where the subject either responds or refrains from responding. Bradshaw and Gates (1978), studying lexical decision ('Is the stimulus a word?'), found a stronger left hemisphere advantage with overt naming than with manual response. Most workers have been content to assume that response systems are relatively independent of other cognitive operations and, beyond balancing hand of response, have not taken much account of response variables.

Another factor which, it has been suggested, is important in determining lateral asymmetries is the *size of the stimulus set* (Hardyck, Tzeng and Wang, 1978). This conclusion was based upon a series of experiments in which matching was performed between various combinations of English words and Chinese characters by English and bilingual Chinese subjects. Part of the aim of the experiment was to compare the lateral advantage for perceptually complex characters when they were meaningless (English subjects) or possessed semantic properties (Chinese subjects). It was found, however, that asymmetries only appeared when a very restricted set of possible stimulus items was employed. The suggestion is that the subject must know the range of possible stimuli, or rapidly deduce it, and then adopt a strategy which involves 'referencing a table of known values', if a left hemisphere advantage is to be found with verbal stimuli. However, there has been no formal analysis of the literature to support this hypothesis, and many examples can be found where new information is presented on each trial and a right visual field superiority is nevertheless found.

Memory of course plays some role in almost any experiment, but does it play some fundamental role in lateral asymmetry? Studies which have explicitly required a target item or a target set to be held in memory, and to which later stimuli must be matched, have generally yielded a left hemisphere advantage. This might be expected on the basis of the verbal material alone. However, that requiring memory for verbal items does not necessarily produce a left hemisphere advantage is shown by the experiment of Klatzky and Atkinson (1971) who asked subjects to hold verbal items in memory and then presented either single letters or pictures of objects. The initial letter of the depicted object, or the letter presented, were to be matched to items in memory. A left hemisphere advantage emerged for the pictures, but not the letters. All this brings us back to the problem of strategies. We cannot know that subjects will necessarily adopt semantic coding for verbal items, for they might alternatively attend to the spatioperceptual elements of the stimulus, and attempts to manipulate such strategies directly have not generated clear results (Metzger and Antes, 1976). Memory components are clearly implicated in lateralized cognitive processing, but there is no reason to believe that they are entirely responsible for lateral visual asymmetries.

Practice is another variable which complicates the investigation of hemisphere specialization (Jonides, 1979; Ward and Ross, 1977). Practice clearly does have some effect, but just how is not yet clear. The nature of the stimuli and the task, the difficulty of the task, the familiarity of the material and the experimental paradigm, the compatibility of the response, the pattern of test trials and rest pauses, all interact with the effects of practice. Two factors may be at work, however. One is that with increasing familiarity with the stimuli and task, there is a shift from attention to the spatial and configurational properties of the stimulus material to a processing mode with important verbal and semantic components. This would be reflected in a shift from right hemisphere advantage to left hemisphere advantage. At the same time, increasing familiarity with the task might reduce the task's difficulty and consequently the strength of lateral asymmetry. These two factors will work to some extent in opposition, and interacting with the host of other variables may result in the very complex results which have been reported.

Finally, we might note that *additional tasks* have sometimes been added to the primary visual field task in an attempt to elucidate the nature of the lateralized processes (Kinsbourne and Hicks, 1978). In general the addition of a concurrent verbal task to a divided visual field task has been found to reduce or reverse the left hemisphere advantage normally observed. There are difficulties, however, in interpreting such studies (Cohen, 1979; Hellige, Cox and Litvac,

1979). One simple problem is the ambiguity of *activation* and *interference*. Interpretations have suggested that the secondary task may activate one hemisphere and so make its contribution to processing the divided visual field task more prominent. On the other hand, it may interfere with processing, and so cause greater participation of the opposite hemisphere. Such activation and interference will result in opposite effects on lateral asymmetry, but there is no way of knowing which will apply, so that although with increasing secondary task difficulty there may be a shift from activation to interference, there is no independent way of knowing when this will occur. These concepts have tended to result in most unsatisfactory *post hoc* explanations of experimental results, which have done little to further our understanding of lateralized cognitive processes.

In conclusion, a clear left hemisphere advantage is generally found in studies which require identification of 'verbal' stimuli, such as words, letters, letter strings or digits. The role played by semantic and linguistic parameters remains unclear, but does not at present satisfactorily explain the left hemisphere advantage. If physical matching is required, a right hemisphere advantage may be found, depending upon cognitive variables inherent in the task. These results are relatively independent of response mode, although both this and mnemonic processes may play some part in determining lateral asymmetry. Practice is a complex variable which deserves more study, and the whole picture is further complicated by other subject and task variables. Nevertheless, over a very considerable number of experiments, the stability and importance of the left hemisphere advantage in association with verbal stimuli remain clear. (A more detailed and fully referenced review is to be found in Beaumont, 1982b.)

THE THEORIES

There has been a tendency for divided visual field studies to be reported independently of any explicit theoretical foundation. Visual field differences have thus been reported as if they were little nuggets of fact which had simply been dug up and deposited on a mound of knowledge. Such an approach is limited. At best, data accumulate and can constitute a resource for those who want to understand the processes which underlie performance asymmetries. At worst, the hypotheses and assumptions made in collecting the data are never made explicit and yet play a part in determining the findings which are reported. An associated problem, deriving from the ease with which divided visual field experiments may be carried out, is the large number of small-scale isolated studies which report on a particular task under a single set of conditions. What the theory builder needs are extended studies in which conditions are systematically varied in order to clarify the mechanisms which produce the phenomenon under study.

While several theories accounting for lateral asymmetries have been proposed, there has been little critical conceptual analysis of the various theoretical positions. However, in addition to Bryden's 1978 review, we now have an invaluable analysis by Cohen (1982). Indeed, the classification of theoretical models of hemisphere specialization suggested below (and see Table 10.1) owes a great deal to her insightful and creative review.

TABLE 10.1 THEORETICAL MODELS OF HEMISPHERE
SPECIALIZATION (MODIFIED FROM COHEN, 1982)

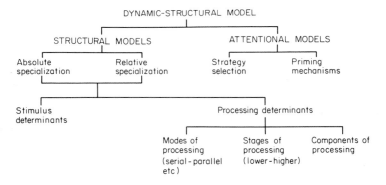

Structural Models

This has been the most common variety of model adopted in divided visual field researches. If a model is implicit, then it is usually a structural model which is assumed. The general idea behind these models is that psychological functions may show lateral asymmetries, as we know from the behavioural data, and these functions may be localized in cerebral structures which are lateralized to one of the cerebral hemispheres. In this the models reflect current concepts in clinical neuropsychology.

Structural models do not necessarily exclude a variety of other factors which may contribute to lateral asymmetries, such as post-exposural scanning or the influence of reading habits. They do, however, assume that when such factors are not themselves a function of cerebral lateralization, they are of minor importance by comparison with the structural cerebral factors.

This raises a whole host of conceptual issues about the allocation of *cognitive* functions to *physiological* structures, and accounts for the rather unsatisfactory status of some of the concepts used in building structural models. There is insufficient space to deal with the topic here (see Beaumont, 1982c), but greater attention should be devoted to this philosophical problem.

Structural models may be based upon either absolute or relative specialization. Where the specialization is thought to be *absolute*, some mechanism must be proposed to effect the transfer of stimulus information if it arrives at the 'wrong' hemisphere. This transfer might be automatic, so that all information is transferred and is available to both hemispheres, but only the appropriate hemisphere takes up the processing. Transfer might be conditional, either following assignment by some initial sorting mechanism, or following the failure of the receiving hemisphere to complete the required processing. Alternatively, transfer may occur and be followed by both hemispheres processing the material, with the specialized hemisphere reaching a conclusion faster, or some mechanism arbitrating on the results. Davis and Schmit (1973) provide an example of such a model. There are problems with all these alternatives. They all seem to rely on mechanisms (for allocation of processing, for deciding when processing has failed, or for arbitrating between solutions) which have an unspecified location and for which there is little evidence. Moreover, in certain cases the systems are wasteful and implausible, such as dual simultaneous processing.

There is also difficulty in squaring absolute specialization models with the split brain evidence we noted in the last chapter, which suggests (albeit in abnormal patients) that both hemispheres possess some capacity for most functions. Differential error rates may be attributed to 'degradation' in callosal transfer, which seems implausible in the large degree often claimed, when other transmission pathways, from primary up to tertiary cortex, are used with much higher fidelity. The failure to establish good stable estimates of IHTT and to account for within-individual shifts in laterality also argues against the adoption of an absolute specialization model.

On the other hand *relative specialization* models, in which both hemispheres are believed to be capable of performing most functions but with different levels of efficiency, have the problem that they are too imprecise. They fit very well with most of the data from a variety of sources, but it is very difficult to derive firm predictions from them. Even the inference that increasing difficulty should be associated with greater asymmetry cannot generate firm hypotheses because of the inadequate definition of difficulty, and this imprecision is in turn reflected in confusion among the findings. Thus, although the relative specialization model in many ways seems more acceptable than the absolute model, it only gains its acceptability by a serious loss in explanatory power.

Structural models may be based on either stimulus or processing determinants. We have already seen how inadequate was the division of stimulus type into 'verbal' and 'non-verbal' as a predictor of lateral asymmetry. It nevertheless figured prominently in early theories, and still underlies the assumptions in many procedures designed to exercise left or right hemisphere functioning.

It is now more fashionable to consider *processing determinants*. These were initially considered in terms of a number of dichotomies which assigned serial, sequential, temporal or analytic processing to the left hemisphere and parallel, holistic or gestalt processing to the right. Many have treated these terms as roughly equivalent, which they are not. The description of the processes has frequently been *post hoc*, and firm criteria for the identification of such processes have almost always been omitted. Although experimental techniques exist for the identification of such processes, they have rarely been employed, and when they have been used, the results have not always been clear (Cohen, 1973; Patterson and Bradshaw, 1975). Of the mode of processing schemes, none accounts well for the experimental data.

The most recent formulations feature *stages of processing*. These may be in terms of Component Operations (Cohen, 1977) or Information Processing Models (Moscovitch, 1979). The Component Operations Model features the contribution of a number of elementary components in cognitive processing, each of which may be characterized by hemisphere specialization. Lateralization will then be determined by the specialization inherent in visual analysis, phonological analysis or semantic analysis as each is called into operation. This approach is useful in that it allows for some flexibility in the operation of the contributory processes, and it can account for task variability if this is mediated by strategy selection. It suggests a way forward in the attempt to identify and specify the exact nature of the contribution of each element. However, like relative specialization, it is weak at generating firm and testable hypotheses, and perhaps only succeeds in shifting the phenomenon of lateralization to another part of the model without explaining it.

By contrast the Information Processing Model is more precise. It assumes a model with a clear sequence of processes from perception through categorization to memory and response (from low-level through to high-level). Lateralization is presumed to be characteristic of certain of these stages (mid- and high-level) and is carried through to later stages. The attraction of the model is that it has clear reference to general models in cognitive psychology, although cybernetic models now seem a little old-fashioned in this context. The problem is that while the model is precise and relatively well formulated (although Cohen is highly critical of certain aspects), it does not always fit well with the data, and is for this reason not entirely acceptable.

Attentional Models

Attentional models are a more recent development and have not gained such wide popularity. The idea underlying them is that the cerebral system has a certain capacity which can be allocated in a flexible way. Arousal, activation and expectancy will result in attention and associated processing capacity being dedicated (and divided between the hemispheres) in a particular way. The most notable exponent of this form of model has been Kinsbourne (1975).

Such models do not deny the existence of structural differences but claim that these are small in relation to the effects of attentional variables. These effects can be best seen, and are accessible for study, in the mechanism of *priming*. Priming may be determined by stimulus location, by stimulus type, or by a concurrent task. When the stimulus location is predictable (or when the subject adopts a strategy of expecting stimuli at a given location, even if presentation is random), then the subject may direct his attention (although *not* necessarily his gaze) to that area of space, resulting in better perception of stimuli at that location.

The stimulus type may prime the hemispheres either by putting the 'appropriate' hemisphere in readiness for a certain type of stimulus, or by directing attention to the side of sensory space opposite the appropriately primed hemisphere. Both these mechanisms would result in better performance in the lateral visual field opposite the more specialized hemisphere. The degree to which such a mechanism is supported by the evidence is uncertain. Some experiments using mixed trials find effects which could be explained in terms of stimulus priming (Berlucchi, Brizzolara, Marzi, Rizzolatti and Umiltà, 1974), but others have failed to find any specific effect of stimulus type expectancy, even when the expectancy can be shown to have an effect on overall performance. Beaumont and Colley (1980), for example, presented subjects with a mixed sequence of shapes or words which appeared randomly in the left or right visual field. In a given set either shapes or words were more common, and the subject was clearly informed about this. While subjects responded more rapidly to the more common type of stimulus in any set, whether a stimulus type was more or less common did not affect the asymmetry for that stimulus type, as attentional models would predict. The effects of perception in the unprimed hemisphere are not, however, always as would be expected from attentional models: presenting pairs of stimuli which could be any pairing from among words, faces and shapes, presented in balanced order to the two hemispheres, Hines (1975) found only limited support for an attentional explanation of the results.

Reference has already been made to the use of concurrent tasks and the difficulties of interpreting the results of such studies. Nevertheless, some support for attentional models comes from such work. Kinsbourne (1973) required subjects to report the location of a small gap in the outline of a square while performing a concurrent task. When this task was to hold a string of words in memory, a left hemisphere advantage was found, but when remembering a melody, a right hemisphere advantage. Such studies are difficult to explain without recourse to attentional mechanisms, but models which rely on secondary task performance are nevertheless generally inadequate in their explanatory power.

The Dynamic-Structural Model

Despite its rather grand title, this model really does no more than accept that at present there is good evidence for both structural and attentional models. Both have weaknesses and strengths. While the dynamic-structural model has not yet been clearly formulated, the approach is implicit in much current research, and seems the only sensible way to proceed for the moment. Most workers would regard the structural aspects as more important than the attentional processes, but few wish to deny the real contribution of attentional mechanisms. We are left, therefore, with a model which combines structural features with attentional processes. The structural components confer relative specialization determined by the contribution of particular cognitive processes. The attentional mechanisms include priming in association with cognitive strategy selection. We cannot pretend that this is a satisfactory model of cerebral specialization, but it seems to be the best sense that we can make of the experimental findings which have been accumulated to date.

CONCLUSION

The divided visual field technique has been the principal method of investigation in experimental human neuropsychology, and has been employed in a large body of research. Somewhat confused findings have resulted but nevertheless, out of this mass of data, a number of conclusions have emerged. These conclusions are now accepted as showing that there are lateral differences in the specialization of the cerebral hemispheres for psychological function. These differences seem, in general, to reflect the form of cerebral organization which has been inferred from the study of clinical patients.

The mechanisms which produce these lateral asymmetries are still unclear. It is not possible to say why, for example, the recognition of words is associated with superior right visual field performance. However, it is reasonable to believe that certain aspects of cognitive processing, as yet poorly specified but in terms, perhaps, of linguistic or phonological or semantic analysis, are more effectively performed in the left cerebral hemisphere. The lateral advantage observed in such processes may be modified by the operation of attentional variables.

This may seem a rather weak conclusion, in view of the research effort devoted to the topic. Nevertheless it comprises a significant advance in understanding a very complex dynamic system which, until the introduction of methods such as the divided visual field technique, remained a dark mystery, largely hidden to scientific investigation.

FURTHER READING

There is happily a recent single and comprehensive review which provides the obvious source for further study of divided visual field presentation:

Beaumont, J. G., ed., *Divided Visual Field Studies of Cerebral Organisation* (London, Academic Press, 1982).

Some useful and relevant contributions will also be found in:

Dimond, S. J. and Beaumont, J. G., eds., *Hemisphere Function in the Human Brain* (London, Elek Science, 1974).

Kinsbourne, M., ed., *Asymmetrical Function of the Brain* (Cambridge, Cambridge University Press, 1978).

Kinsbourne, M. and Smith, W. L., eds., *Hemispheric Disconnection and Cerebral Function* (Springfield, Illinois, Charles C. Thomas, 1974).

REFERENCES

Beaumont, J. G., 'Methods for Studying Cerebral Hemisphere Function', in A. W. Young, ed., *Functions of the Right Cerebral Hemisphere* (London, Academic Press, 1982a).

Beaumont, J. G., 'Studies with Verbal Stimuli', in J. G. Beaumont, ed., *Divided Visual Field Studies of Cerebral Organisation* (London, Academic Press, 1982b).

Beaumont, J. G., 'Neuropsychology and the Organisation of Behaviour', in A. Gale and J. Edwards, eds., *Physiological Correlates of Human Behaviour* (London, Academic Press, 1982c).

Beaumont, J. G. and Colley, M., 'Attentional Bias and Visual Field Asymmetry', *Cortex*, 16 (1980), 391–396.

Berlucchi, G., Brizzolara, D., Marzi, C. A., Rizzolatti, G. and Umiltà, C., 'Can Lateral Asymmetries in Attention Explain Interfield Differences in Visual Perception?', *Cortex*, 10 (1974), 177–185.

Berlucchi, G., Crea, F., DiStefano, M. and Tassinari, G., 'Influence of Spatial Stimulus-Response Compatability on Reaction Time of Ipsilateral and Contralateral Hand to Lateralized Light Stimuli', *Journal of Experimental Psychology: Human Perception and Performance*, 3 (1977), 505–517.

Besner, D., Grimsell, D. and Davis, R., 'The Mind's Eye and the Comparative Judgement of Number', *Neuropsychologia*, 17 (1979), 373–380.

Bradshaw, J. L. and Gates, E. A., 'Visual Field Differences in Verbal Tasks: Effects of Task Familiarity and Sex of Subject', *Brain and Language*, 5 (1978), 166–187.

Bryden, M. P., 'Strategy Effects in the Assessment of Hemispheric Asymmetry', in G. Underwood, ed., *Strategies of Information Processing* (London, Academic Press, 1978).

Cohen, G., 'Hemisphere Differences in a Letter Classification Task', *Perception and Psychophysics*, 11 (1972), 139–142.

Cohen, G., 'Hemispheric Differences in Serial Versus Parallel Processing', *Journal of Experimental Psychology*, 97 (1973), 349–356.

Cohen, G., 'Components of the Laterality Effect in Letter Recognition: Asymmetries in Iconic Storage', *Quarterly Journal of Experimental Psychology*, 28 (1976), 105–114.

Cohen, G., *The Psychology of Cognition* (London, Academic Press, 1977).

Cohen, G., 'Comment on "Information Processing in the Cerebral Hemispheres: Selective Attention and Capacity Limitations" by Hellige, Cox and Litvac', *Journal of Experimental Psychology: General*, 108 (1979), 309–315

Cohen, G., 'Theoretical Interpretations of Lateral Asymmetries', in J. G. Beaumont, ed., *Divided Visual Field Studies of Cerebral Organisation* (London, Academic Press, 1982).

Colbourn, C. J., 'Can Laterality be Measured?', *Neuropsychologia*, 16 (1978), 283–289.

Davidoff, J., 'Studies with Nonverbal Stimuli', in J. G. Beaumont, ed., *Divided Visual Field Studies of Cerebral Organisation* (London, Academic Press, 1982).

Davis, R. and Schmit, V., 'Visual and Verbal Coding in the Interhemispheric Transfer of Information', *Acta Psychologica*, 37 (1973), 229–240.

Day, J., 'Right Hemisphere Language Processing in Normal Right Handers', *Journal of Experimental Psychology: Human Perception and Performance*, 3 (1977), 518–528.

Day, J., 'Visual Half Field Word Recognition as a Function of Syntactic Class and Imageability', *Neuropsychologia*, 17 (1979), 515–519.

Dimond, S. J., 'Symmetry and Asymmetry in the Vertebrate Brain', in D. A. Oakley and H. C. Plotkin, eds., *Brain, Behaviour and Evolution* (London, Methuen, 1979).

Dimond, S. J. and Beaumont, J. G., 'On the Nature of the Interhemispheric Effects of Fatigue', *Acta Psychologica*, 36 (1972), 443–449.

Dimond, S. J. and Beaumont, J. G., 'Experimental Studies of Hemisphere Function in the Human Brain', in S. J. Dimond and J. G. Beaumont, eds., *Hemisphere Function in the Human Brain* (London, Elek Science, 1974).

Dimond, S. J., Bureš, J., Farrington, L. J. and Brouwers, E. Y. M., 'The Use of Contact Lenses for the Lateralisation of Visual Input in Man', *Acta Psychologica*, 39 (1975), 341–349.

Hardyck, C., Tzeng, O. J. L. and Wang, W. S.-Y., 'Cerebral Lateralization of Function and Bilingual Decision Processes: Is Thinking Lateralized?', *Brain and Language*, 5 (1978), 56–71.

Hellige, J. B. and Webster, R., 'Right Hemisphere Superiority for Initial Stages of Letter Processing', *Neuropsychologia*, 17 (1979), 653–660.

Hellige, J. B., Cox, P. J. and Litvac, L., 'Information Processing in the Cerebral Hemispheres: Selective Hemispheric Activation and Capacity Limitations', *Journal of Experimental Psychology: General* 108 (1979), 251–279.

Hines, D., 'Independent Functioning of the Two Cerebral Hemispheres for Recognising Bilaterally Presented Visual Half Field Stimuli', *Cortex*, 11 (1975), 132–143.

Jonides, J., 'Left and Right Visual Field Superiority for Letter Classification', *Quarterly Journal of Experimental Psychology*, 31 (1979), 423–439.

Kinsbourne, M., 'The Control of Attention by Interaction between the Cerebral Hemispheres', in S. Kornblum, ed., *Attention and Performance IV* (New York, Academic Press, 1973).

Kinsbourne, M., 'The Mechanism of Hemispheric Control of the Lateral Gradient of Attention', in P. M. A. Rabbitt and S. Dornic, eds., *Attention and Performance V* (London, Academic Press, 1975).

Kinsbourne, M. and Hicks, R. E., 'Functional Cerebral Space: a Model for Overflow, Transfer and Inteference Effects in Human Performance: a Tutorial Review', in J. Requin, ed., *Attention and Performance VII* (Hillsdale, N. J., Lawrence Erlbaum Associates, 1978).

Klatzky, R. L. and Atkinson, R. C., 'Specialisation of the Cerebral Hemispheres in Scanning for Information in Short-term Memory', *Perception and Psychophysics*, 10 (1971), 335–338.

Ledlow, A., Swanson, J. M. and Kinsbourne, M., 'Reaction Times and Evoked Potentials as Indicators of Hemispheric Differences for Laterally Presented Name and Physical Matches', *Journal of Experimental Psychology: Human Perception and Performance*, 4 (1978), 440–454.

Leehey, S. C. and Cahn, A., 'Lateral Asymmetries in the Recognition of Words, Familiar Faces and Unfamiliar Faces', *Neuropsychologia*, 17 (1979), 619–635.

Leiber, L., 'Lexical Decisions in the Right and Left Cerebral Hemispheres', *Brain and Language*, 3 (1976), 443–450.

McCarthy, R. A., 'Visual Field Differences in Sequential Letter Classification', unpublished Ph.D. thesis, University of Leicester (1980).

Metzger, R. L. and Antes, J. R., 'Sex and Coding Strategy Effects on Reaction Time to Hemisphere Probes', *Memory and Cognition*, 4 (1976), 157–171.

Moscovitch, M., 'Information Processing and the Cerebral Hemispheres', in M. S. Gazzaniga, ed., *Handbook of Behavioural Neurobiology, vol. 2: Neuropsychology* (New York, Plenum Press, 1979).

Patterson, K. and Bradshaw, J. L., 'Differential Hemispheric Mediation of Nonverbal Stimuli', *Journal of Experimental Psychology: Human Perception and Performance*, 1 (1975), 246–252.

Segalowitz, S. J., Bebout, L. J. and Lederman, S. J., 'Lateralisation for Reading Musical Chords: Disentangling Symbolic, Analytic and Phonological Aspects of Reading', *Brain and Language*, 8 (1979), 315–323.

Ward, T. B. and Ross, L. E., 'Laterality Differences and Practice Effects under Central Backward Masking Conditions', *Memory and Cognition*, 5 (1977), 221–226.

White, M. J., 'Hemispheric Asymmetries in Tachistoscopic Information-processing', *British Journal of Psychology*, 63 (1972), 497–508.

Young, A. W., 'Methodological and Theoretical Bases of Visual Hemifield Studies', in J. G. Beaumont, ed., *Divided Visual Field Studies of Cerebral Organisation* (London, Academic Press, 1982).

Young, A. W. and Bion, P. J., 'Accuracy of Naming Laterally Presented Known Faces by Children and Adults', *Cortex*, 17 (1981), 97–106.

Young, A. W., Bion, P. J. and Ellis, A. W., 'Studies toward a Model of Laterality Effects for Picture and Word Naming', *Brain and Language*, 11 (1980), 54–65.

Zaidel, E., 'A Technique for Presenting Lateralized Input with Prolonged Exposure', *Vision Research*, 15 (1975), 283–289.

CHAPTER 11

Dichotic Listening

The technique of dichotic listening is the auditory parallel to divided visual field presentation. Like the latter, it was first developed within experimental psychology, and its relevance to neuropsychology was recognized only later. It was Kimura (1961) who first pointed out that the asymmetry which had already been observed could be attributed to cerebral lateralization, thus introducing the technique into human experimental neuropsychology at about the same time as the divided visual field technique was being explored with split brain patients.

Although dichotic listening has not attracted as much attention as divided visual field presentation, perhaps because of the added technical difficulty of creating the stimuli, three to four hundred studies using the technique have been published.

THE TECHNIQUE

The logic which underlies dichotic listening is exactly as in the visual technique. Stimuli presented to the right ear are considered to be directed to the left hemisphere, and via the left ear to the right hemisphere. Subsequent performance measured by accuracy or response latency can be taken to reflect the operation of systems lateralized to the two hemispheres. The only significant difference is that in dichotic listening stimuli are presented to the two ears *simultaneously*, although associated procedures of lateralized auditory presentation are also used, in which stimuli are not bilateral and simultaneous. These are not, however, properly termed 'dichotic'.

As has already been pointed out in Chapter 4, while the primary projection of the visual system is completely lateralized, that of the auditory system is not (see Fig. 4.2). For this reason, the technique is not quite as simple as divided visual field presentation. Dichotic listening relies on the dominance of the crossed contralateral pathways over the ipsilateral uncrossed pathways. The clinical evidence supports this contralateral dominance, at least under conditions of bilateral competition, as does the evidence from split brain patients (which was discussed in Chapter 9). There are also physiological differences in the size of the auditory pathways, the crossed tracts being larger.

Recently, the extent of the crossed dominance in audition has been questioned. Some workers have shown that the suppression effect seen in split brain patients (see p. 170) only operates for dichotic speech stimuli and not for pure tones (Efron, Bogen and Yund, 1977). It has also been suggested that the apparent suppression of left ear material may result from spectral-temporal overlap between stimuli, and so be a more peripheral perceptual phenomenon than has generally been thought (Springer, Sidtis, Wilson and Gazzaniga, 1978). These studies indicate that the dominance of the crossed pathway is not so clearly established as was once thought, but for the present we will accept that crossed dominance applies because it enables us to make sense of the experimental findings. Nevertheless, we should remember that if crossed dominance did not apply to a certain auditory stimulus, the logic of the technique used with normal human subjects would be completely undermined.

Careful attention must be paid to the construction of stimulus tapes for dichotic listening. The characteristics of the stimuli which arrive at the two ears must be carefully balanced, and the onset of the two stimuli carefully aligned. It has become increasingly common to use computers to generate and control the presentation of dichotic stimuli, and this allows very precise control of not only the onset but also the duration of the stimuli.

The way in which subjects are asked to respond is also very important, although it has been little studied. Given that the subject will hear pairs of simultaneous stimuli, whether he is asked to report one or both the items, and which is to be given first if both are to be reported, will greatly affect the results. Many workers have simply allowed free report in which subjects must report as many items as they can. Others have directed attention to one or the other ear, or controlled the order of reporting from the two ears. The findings from what little study there has been of the effect of response mode are equivocal. However, while certain forms of reponse are more appropriate to specific experimental designs, controlled report must in general be superior to free report.

Much study has been made of how to score the results, which is a much less simple problem than it might appear. The asymmetry observed is usually described in terms of a left or right *ear advantage*, and this description must account for the effects of overal accuracy and the effects of guessing in forced choice response modes. The simplest solution of taking the difference between the scores at the two ears and dividing by the total score ((Right − Left) ÷ (Right + Left)) is not really satisfactory. The difficulty partly hinges on whether we consider that a performance of 20 per cent in the right ear and 10 per cent in the left ear represents the same asymmetry as 80 per cent in the right and 70 per cent in the left. And what if the scores are 100 per cent in the right and 95 per cent in the left: is that the effect of a 'ceiling' on performance? Decisions about how to treat such scores will have a fundamental effect on the interpretation of the results of the experiment (see Berlin and Cullen, 1977). Various solutions have been proposed and the most generally accepted is a slightly complicated index (the 'e' and 'e$_g$' coefficients) developed by Repp (1977). Few studies have, however, employed the more sophisticated scoring methods.

A more detailed discussion of the problems in the dichotic listening technique will be found in Beaumont (1982). For the present, we must recognize that there are some methodological difficulties inherent in it. The production of stimuli may be critical, as may the method of scoring, and there is some niggling uncertainty about the physiological substrate of the technique. Nevertheless, as we shall see, findings using dichotic listening have been remarkably consonant with those from other neuropsychological methods, and this must increase our confidence in its use.

LATERAL EAR ASYMMETRIES

In the classic dichotic listening experiment, three or four pairs of stimuli, one of each pair to each ear, are presented at a rate of one pair every one or two seconds. At the end of the series the subject must report the stimuli. The ear associated with more correct responses (or occasionally the earlier responses) is described as showing an ear advantage. Kimura's 1961 study had used digits as stimuli and found a right ear advantage. Such stimuli have been the most consistent in producing a clear right sided advantage, but the effect is not limited to numbers. A right ear advantage is also generally observed for words, and not only for meaningful but also nonsense words. Even artificially generated consonant-vowel (CV) syllables yield a stable right ear advantage, indicating that left hemisphere processes are not associated only with linguistically meaningful material. Studies have proceeded to investigate most linguistic aspects of verbal stimuli. These studies are important in revealing, by the degree of lateral asymmetry which may be observed, the processes involved in producing the lateral advantage. They also provide important information for those investigating speech perception and language comprehension. The common factor, however, is that most speech-like and language-related stimuli are reported more accurately from the right ear if presented in dichotic pairs.

By contrast, certain stimuli are associated with a left ear advantage. These include melodies, sonar signals, environmental sounds and 'nonverbal vocal tract sounds'. Environmental sounds might be a running tap, traffic, or teeth being brushed, and vocal tract sounds might be coughs, hums, or grunts. These stimuli seem to have in common that they are patterned and nonverbal. In particular they are not at all speech-like, and this may be an important feature in determining the involvement of the right hemisphere.

The simplest model which can be set up for dichotic listening performance looks very much like that for divided visual field performance. Speech and language stimuli are associated with a left hemisphere advantage, while nonverbal stimuli are associated with a right hemisphere advantage.

Before looking at how this model has been developed, it is worth asking if there is an asymmetry in response to very simple stimuli, reflecting findings in the visual modality. Obviously we cannot perform a parallel dichotic experiment, but we can test the reaction time, shown by the hands, to simple auditory tones presented to the right and left ears. From this test it seems there is some evidence that faster reaction times are associated with the 'direct' route from ear to ipsilateral hand, in contrast with the crossed indirect pathway from ear to contralateral hand (Provins and Jeeves, 1975). However, asking subjects to attend only to one ear modifies this effect: if subjects attend to the right ear, the difference in reaction times between hands disappears, if to the left ear, the left hemisphere advantage is retained and there is a faster reaction shown by the left hand (Spellacy and Wilson, 1978). This emphasizes the importance of central, cortically mediated, mechanisms in modifying performance through selective attention.

Left Hemisphere Processes

What precisely underlies the left hemisphere advantage? An early idea was that the left hemisphere might be particularly equipped to deal with speech perception. Speech perception is more difficult to study than might at first appear, as is reflected in the slow progress being made with automatic systems for speech recognition. The difficulty is that the sounds which go to make up a word are not strung together simply. Many of the component sounds arrive in parallel, so that in the word 'big', for example, the 'b' sound continues through the first two-thirds of the word and the vowel through the entire word. Note the sudden transition you must make when sounding out this word for a young child: at some point you stop being able to blend 'b--i--g . . . b-i-g' and must directly pronounce 'big'. The difficulty in speech perception is therefore to unravel parallel components, a process referred to as *drastic restructuring* (see Liberman, 1974; Springer, 1979). This difficulty is increased because a perceived phonetic segment may result from different acoustic cues in different contexts, that is, the same sound may come from differing physical stimuli.

Drastic restructuring has been linked with right ear advantage when hard-to-decode stimuli have been contrasted with easy-to-decode stimuli. Stop consonants (/b/,/d/,/g/,/p/,/t/,/k/) need more restructuring than isolated vowels, and stop consonants with an added /a/ vowel produce a right ear advantage, while synthetic vowels do not. In nonsense words, if the consonants are contrasted ('BIP' versus 'GIP') then a larger right ear superiority will result than if the vowels are contrasted ('BIP' versus 'BAP'). Sounds which require intermediate levels of restructuring, such as liquid consonants (/r/,/l/), semivowels (/y/,/w/), and fricatives (/s/,/v/,/f/,/z/), have been reported to produce an intermediate right ear advantage.

Darwin (1971) showed the importance of the presence of formant transitions (certain features of speech stimuli) for speech perception, thus supporting the restructuring hypothesis. Other linguistic factors have also been shown to be related to right ear superiority: if grammatical structure is present, even in a sentence of nonsense words ('The wak jud shendily' has grammatical structure, 'Bul hudky gu nee' has not; Zurif and Sait, 1970), then it may produce the right ear superiority. Linguistic tone (intonation) may also be involved: if a language like Thai is used (with Thai speakers as subjects) in which the same sound with different intonation can have quite disparate meanings ('naa' can mean 'aunt' or 'field'), then a right ear advantage can be seen for stimuli which differ only in tone.

However, that the right ear advantage reflects the involvement of speech perception can only be a partial explanation. For one thing, this advantage may be seen for language stimuli which do not involve the effect of formant transitions. Some very elementary aspects of stimuli, such as intensity, time and frequency, may also moderate the right ear advantage (Berlin, 1977). And using vowels, but masking them by adding white noise, has also been shown to produce a right ear superiority (Weiss and House, 1973). Both these results indicate that purely acoustic factors may also be linked to left hemisphere processes. Some of these processes may still be linked to language perception, but it cannot be language perception alone which is lateralized to the left hemisphere.

Cutting (1974) compared performance using CV stimuli with that using appropriate or inappropriate formant transitions. Both types of stimuli yielded right ear advantages. However, only the stimuli with appropriate formants produced a discrimination curve which would be expected for language-related perception. This seems to point to a purely auditory component in the processing of CV syllables with inappropriate formants, yet they produced a right sided advantage. Godfrey (1974) has systematically manipulated such features as the signal-noise ratio, acoustic-phonetic distinctness and vowel duration, and his results also suggest that the effects are being created at the auditory rather than the phonetic level of processing.

This literature can be rather technical for those not expert in linguistics and speech processing. However, most workers now accept that there may be two types of processor associated with left hemisphere specialization (Bub and Whitaker, 1980; Springer, 1979). One of these is related to the restructuring and encoding of speech stimuli, and operates at a phonetic level. The other operates at a purely acoustic level, and will function in any difficult acoustic discrimination, even if nonlinguistic in character. It has been suggested that this second processor may be set to detect rapidly changing frequency information, or that it performs temporal order judgements. None of these hypotheses can be regarded as a very satisfactory explanation of the data, and it may be that some better model may yet be found. Nevertheless, it is clear that, while the left hemisphere is implicated in speech and language processing, this is not a sufficient explanation of many of the right ear advantages which have been reported.

Right Hemisphere Processes

That certain nonspeech-like sounds can produce a left ear advantage is undisputed; but what processes actually determine right hemisphere lateralization? From what has been said of the left hemisphere, it seems unlikely to be a matter of nonverbal auditory discrimination.

This question has been most commonly tackled through the study of musical stimuli. Certain kinds of musical stimuli produce a clear left ear advantage, and it is possible to manipulate different aspects of such stimuli to discover just what determines the advantage. At least, that has been the strategy behind research in this area. Unfortunately, the results have not yet enabled any clear conclusions to be drawn about the processors resident in the right hemisphere (for reviews, see Craig, 1979; Damásio and Damásio, 1977; Gates and Bradshaw, 1977a; Wyke, 1977).

Kimura, in 1964, described a left ear advantage for dichotic melodies, but this result has not always been supported by similar experiments. For instance, Gordon (1970) found no lateral asymmetry for melodies, although he did find an effect for dichotic chords. Taking even simpler stimuli, the ear advantage for pitch (or frequency) has not been clearly established. There is some suspicion that this may be because pitch is also critically involved in speech perception, and the context of the stimuli may therefore be important in determining whether they are treated as being more or less speech-like. Other factors which have been shown to be relevant are the delay between the stimulus and a subsequent comparison stimulus; the complexity of the stimulus; and the subject's expectation as to which ear will receive the stimulus. The results with timbre are equally inconsistent, and time and rhythm have received little attention.

It is possible to make some sense of this data, however, by considering just how subjects are likely to treat the stimuli. One difficulty of decomposing complex stimuli into their components is that subjects may not process them in the same manner. As 'musical' stimuli become more and more simplified, they are less and less distinct from simplified speech sounds, and it becomes more likely that subjects will process them as if they were speech sounds. This is supported by two pieces of evidence: that, by and large, the right hemisphere advantage is found more readily with structured musical passages, and that characteristics of the subjects themselves can have a profound effect on the lateral advantage observed.

Some of the conflict, between the findings of Kimura and Gordon with respect to melodies, for example, can be resolved by reference to the subjects employed. A number of studies have specifically examined the effects of the musical training and experience of the subjects. For example, in a study by Johnson, Bowers, Gamble,

Lyons, Presbrey and Vetter (1977) musicians were asked to recognize conventional melodies or random note sequences. All subjects showed a left ear advantage for the random note sequences. With the melodies, however, the results were especially interesting, for trained musicians who could transcribe music showed a right ear advantage, but the trained musicians who could not transcribe music showed a left ear advantage. The interpretation of these findings is that complex musical stimuli are processed by right hemisphere mechanisms unless the stimuli are both meaningful and can be encoded in a formal symbolic way. If they can be so encoded, as they may be by those who can transcribe music, then left hemisphere mechanisms may be called into play.

This finding has an interesting parallel in an experiment with morse code (Papçun, Krashen, Terbeck, Remington and Harshman, 1974). Morse code was presented dichotically to morse code operators and to these unfamiliar with morse code. The operators showed a consistent right ear advantage, but subjects unfamiliar with morse code only showed a right ear advantage if there were seven or less pairs of elements. With longer lists, which they were presumably unable to process semantically, or which could not be handled by the sequential analysis of components of the stimulus train, there was a left ear advantage, reflecting a switch to right hemisphere based functions.

However, not all studies with trained musicians have found a right ear advantage for complex stimuli: both Gordon (1980) and Zatorre (1979) found a left ear advantage and no effect of the degree of musical training. Also, in an elegant study of the parallel effects of verbal and musical components of the stimulus, which used either numbers superimposed upon piano notes or digits sung in a tonal pattern, a separate right ear superiority for the verbal elements and left ear superiority for the musical elements was maintained.

No doubt the solution to this conflicting evidence lies in the precise nature of the experimental task and the expectations of the subjects. Gates and Bradshaw (1977b), following a complex and thorough series of experiments on the detection of pitch, rhythm and harmony changes, emphasized the importance of the different strategies adopted by subjects, as well as the familiarity of the type of material employed. Musical perception may well rely on contributions by both the cerebral hemispheres, in different forms in different subjects, and this makes it difficult to determine just what is the unique contribution of the right hemisphere.

ATTENTION

Both the structural and attentional models can be applied to dichotic listening data, in the same way that they were applied to divided visual field research (see p. 198). We have already seen how the structural model can be used to interpret a lateral ear advantage, but is it sufficient to explain all the results? Various forms of evidence are relevant in answering this question.

The first is whether competition is necessary to establish a lateral asymmetry, that is, can an ear difference be established using *monaural* instead of dichotic presentation? While the asymmetry is smaller and less stable with monaural stimuli, it seems that it can be observed (Henry, 1979). The study by Kallman (1977) serves as a good example of an experiment which was parallel to the usual dichotic procedure, and yet used monaural presentation. Both speech and nonverbal stimuli were used and the expected interactions between the type of stimulus and performance at the two ears was found. Belmore (1980) even managed to demonstrate an asymmetry using monaurally presented sentences, although only when the task demanded attention to the meaning of the stimulus material. Results of this kind support the importance of a structural explanation.

There are, however, findings that do not fit so neatly into a structural model. One is that monaural competing stimuli presented to the *same* ear can yield a right ear advantage (Bradshaw, Farrelly and Taylor, 1981). This could be interpreted as a simple lateral advantage, but does suggest that the effects of competition do not necessarily arise from interference between different lateral input channels.

That the laterality effect does not depend on physical separation of the stimuli is demonstrated most clearly by the fact that a right ear advantage can still be found even when the stimuli are not presented through headphones but through loudspeakers at the left and right of the subject (Morais and Bertelson, 1973). The effect must in this case be due to the physical location of the stimuli in space, to the left or right, and not to the arrival of the stimuli by different anatomical channels, because the stimuli at each side enter by both ears. Even more remarkable is that the laterality effect can be produced by *apparent* rather than real physical location to one side of space. We determine the location of sounds by various cues, the most important of which are intensity and time differences. A stimulus to our left, for example, will be louder and will arrive earlier at the left than at the right ear, and this difference in intensity and time of arrival tells us the location of the stimulus. It is therefore possible, by simply manipulating the time and intensity differences between two stimuli, to produce an apparent origin for the sounds which they do not have in reality. That a sound is apparently located to the right side of the body is sufficient for it to be associated with superior performance (Morais and Bertelson, 1975).

Findings of this kind are difficult to explain by a structural model, and support the importance of attentional factors. The contribution of such factors has been assessed in a related phenomenon, the 'ventriloquism' effect (Morais, 1975). Subjects were seated with four loudspeakers visible to them, at 45 degrees and 90 degrees to the left and right of the direction in which they were facing. Behind each of these visible speakers, which were dummies, was a curtain and beyond that an active speaker. The subjects were told to which speakers they should attend for subsequent recall of the stimuli. Simultaneous messages, which might or might not come from the locations expected by the subject, were then presented. Among some rather complex results, the right side advantage was only found when subjects expected the message to be 90 degrees to the right and it was actually located there. This finding clearly shows that neither the structural nor the attentional model is sufficient in itself, both must be involved. If the structural model is a sufficient explanation, the subject's attention would be irrelevant; there would be a right side advantage whenever the stimulus was at that side. Similarly, if the attentional model is a sufficient explanation, the actual location would be unimportant, and the subject's expectation would alone determine the advantage.

A similar experiment, but actually using dichotic presentation, examined the effects of ear of entry and subjective location by directing different formants of the stimulus to different ears (Darwin, Howell and Brady, 1978). Again, the ear of entry was in itself a significant factor, but an additional right ear advantage was attributed to the effects of subjective location.

A useful discussion of the competing claims of the structural and attentional models was presented by Studdert-Kennedy in introducing a special issue of *Brain and Language* in 1975 devoted to dichotic listening. He sensibly suggested that an experiment with mixed materials in a random sequence might help to resolve the issue. A structural model would predict that the usual asymmetries for each type of material would be preserved, while an attentional model would predict reduced lateral advantages. An experiment of this type has been reported by Kallman (1978). The speech stimuli produced the expected right ear advantage, while the musical stimuli which were mixed with them tended to give a left ear advantage. The results again indicate that attentional factors, if involved, are not themselves sufficient to explain the lateral asymmetries.

Finally, the fact that the subject's *response strategy* can affect the results is pertinent to any model of the processes involved. Both Bryden (1978) and Freides (1977) have shown this to be the case. Both workers contrasted a free recall condition with conditions in which attention and report order were more strictly controlled. Both found that the report instructions influenced which ear advantage was found. However, they differed in the significance which they placed upon the result. Freides strongly made the point that if response strategy is such an important determinant of the lateral advantage, then competitional methods such as dichotic listening might be merely measuring the subject's response strategy rather than something more fundamental about brain organization. Bryden, on the other hand, emphasized how the subject's strategy reflected the operation of attentional and cognitive factors within the processing system. Whichever view is taken, the effects of cognitive strategy, in the context of our general models of cerebral lateralization, illustrate the contribution of variables other than those related directly to structural mechanisms. Just as with the visual studies, the evidence clearly points to a dynamic-structural model.

AN INDEX OF LATERALIZATION

Many writers have been keen to point out that the right ear advantage for digits, while associated with cerebral laterality, cannot be used as an index of lateralization (Berlin, 1977; Colbourn, 1978; Teng, 1981). The problem arises from the variability both of different subjects and of any one subject over time. It is easy to be misled by the clear average ear advantage shown by group data, and assume that dichotic performance could be an index of speech lateralization in individual subjects. Studies regularly appear in which dichotic listening data are used in this way.

The evidence is clearly against the use of such an index, with one notable exception: the Dichotic Monitoring Test of Geffen, Traub and Stierman (1978). This test involves the dichotic presentation of monosyllabic word pairs which include the target word 'DOG' among eight 'noise words' in each channel that share two phonemes in common with the target (e.g. 'DIG' or 'LOG'), as well as fifty-two dissimilar words. The subject must detect the target word, and both his reaction time and accuracy are recorded in response to occurrences of the target word. The test was given to four patients who had undergone the Wada Test to establish speech lateralization and to thirty-one patients whose speech laterality had been assessed by the presence of (temporary) dysphasia following the unilateral administration of electroconvulsive therapy (ECT), and extremely good agreement about language lateralization was shown between the physical tests and the dichotic procedure. An extension of this study by Geffen and Caudrey (1981), reported an agreement of ninety-five per cent, and a test-retest study for reliability found a shift in assessed laterality in only three of eighty-six subjects. This procedure appears more reliable and more valid than previous attempts to develop an index of speech lateralization that could be used in normal subjects but we must wait to see if it fulfils its promise.

If either dichotic listening or divided visual field methods could yield an index of cerebral lateralization, we should expect a correlation between the asymmetries found using the two techniques in any individual subject. Fennell, Bowers and Satz (1977) examined just this issue, using a sequence of four tests of dichotic listening to concrete words and divided visual field presentation of letters. They found both the expected right visual field and right ear advantages. The dichotic asymmetry was relatively stable across the four occasions of testing, although the visual asymmetry was significant only after the first occasion. The correlation between the two modalities was also found to be reliable and stable, particularly on the final two occasions of testing.

This study has now been subjected to extremely searching criticism in terms of the general methodological problems inherent in the measures, the composition of the samples, and the statistical treatments used (Berenbaum and Harshman, 1980). The authors of this criticism urge scepticism about the findings of the study by Fennell *et al.*, and it seems at least prudent to await further investigation of the issue. Other data, collected with a primary interest in the effects of the subject variables of sex and handedness, also suggests that there can be a significant dissociation between the asymmetries observed in different modalities (Searleman, 1980).

CONCLUSION

While dichotic listening studies have made a major contribution to experimental neuropsychology, they have been less numerous than studies in the visual modality. This is due both to the technical demands of the technique and to the added problems which the bilateral nature of auditory projection brings to interpretation of the results. In consequence, studies in recent years have concentrated more on linguistic variables than on the general principles underlying cerebral lateralization.

The studies have nevertheless provided evidence of lateral specialization in the brain. The left hemisphere seems to be associated with two kinds of processing: one phonetic, the other acoustic. The phonetic processor deals with speech and speech-like stimuli in terms of their linguistic composition. The acoustic processor deals more generally with complex auditory stimuli, and may be involved in temporal order perception. It does not deal merely with speech stimuli.

The right hemisphere has been associated with 'nonverbal' sounds and with complex musical stimuli. Not all aspects of music are processed preferentially in the right hemisphere, and music perception (like most real-life tasks) involves the contribution of both the hemispheres.

It will by now be apparent that the research undertaken in a purely experimental context is generally of a much higher standard than that performed with clinical patients (discussed in Section II). This mainly reflects the difficulty of doing scientifically sound research in a clinical context, but the general level of both methodological sophistication and theoretical discussion has been superior in experimental neuropsychology.

Direct comparison between experimental and clinical findings is difficult, partly because clinical work has concentrated on localization, which has been ignored in experimental research in favour of lateralization. Also, many of the tests and tasks employed in clinical research cannot be presented, for procedural reasons, in experimental paradigms. Integration of the two approaches has not been attempted in any systematic fashion, although there seem to be few fundamental disagreements between the two areas of research. The evidence from dichotic listening agrees remarkably well with both clinical findings and data from divided visual field studies.

The only model which at present accounts well for the whole body of dichotic research is the dynamic-structural model, which is also the model supported by visual studies. Attentional and cognitive factors play a significant role in auditory as in visual lateralization.

Dichotic listening has proved neither sufficiently reliable nor sufficiently stable to allow the determination of speech lateralization in individual subjects. Recent research may, however, show that an index of this kind can be developed.

OTHER METHODS IN EXPERIMENTAL NEUROPSYCHOLOGY

While divided visual field and dichotic listening techniques far outweigh all other methods in importance, some of the alternative methods should be briefly mentioned. A review of all these methods is to be found in Beaumont (1982).

Lateralized stimulus presentation has also been used in *tactile perception*. Stimuli can be presented to the right and left hands and subsequent performance recorded. It has been possible to demonstrate lateral asymmetries in this way, but only when fairly fine manipulation or tactile exploration is required. The projection of tactile information to the cortex (see p. 89) involves both ipsilateral and contralateral pathways, and this means that it is difficult to be sure that stimulus presentation has been appropriately lateralized. However, a 'dichhaptic' technique originally developed by Witelson (1974) and involving bilateral simultaneous stimulation has been used in a number of studies and produced interesting results.

Lateral eye movements have also attracted some interest. Kinsbourne (1972) sparked off this work by the observation that solving 'verbal' problems was often accompanied by conjugate gaze deviation to the right, and solving 'spatial' problems by gaze deviation to the left. He explained this phenomenon in terms of his attentional model, hemisphere activation being considered to produce eye movement towards the opposite side of space. Following much debate about the reliability and validity of such observations, recent reviews have suggested that lateral eye movements can be reliably elicited and that they do reflect hemisphere lateralization (Ehrlichman and Weinberger, 1978). Whether the evidence justifies their use as an index of an individual's cerebral organization, as is sometimes done, seems doubtful.

Some lateral asymmetries are also to be observed in *free vision*, for example, there are lateral asymmetries in aesthetic composition which seem to relate to hemisphere specialization, although the mechanism behind such asymmetries is under dispute. It has also been reported that the left side of the face has been more commonly presented in formal portraiture, and this side of the face is also judged as more emotionally intense. Asymmetries in spatial orientation and judgement, as seen in map reading and direction finding, have also been demonstrated.

Finally, there are the *lateral performance asymmetries*, of which the most important is handedness. Differences between left and right handers are discussed at length in Chapter 13, but even in right handers the difference between the preferred and non-preferred hands can be studied as one aspect of cerebral organization. Various aspects of manual skill have been measured, and recently there has been a renewal of interest in tapping performance. As with tactile presentation, inferences about cerebral lateralization are complicated by the bilateral nature of certain aspects of neural organization. The Torque Test, which measures the direction of drawing tendencies as clockwise or anticlockwise, has been much discussed but has also been subjected to recent criticism.

All of these methods can contribute to our overall model of neuropsychological organization but because of methodological or theoretical complications none is as satisfactory or important as divided visual field and dichotic listening research. All experimental data have nevertheless some part to play, and the development of techniques in neuropsychology may well spring from refinements of these alternative methods.

FURTHER READING

There is an unfortunate dearth of good general accounts of dichotic listening research. Reviews of relatively specific aspects have been mentioned in the text, but study might best proceed with a look at the following:

Berlin, C. I., 'Hemispheric Asymmetry in Auditory Tasks', in S. Harnad, R. W. Doty, L. Goldstein, J. Jaynes and G. Krauthamer, eds., *Lateralization in the Nervous System* (New York, Academic Press, 1977).
Springer, S. P., 'Speech Perception and the Biology of Language', in M. S. Gazzaniga, ed., *Handbook of Behavioral Neurobiology*, vol. 2, *Neuropsychology* (New York, Plenum Press, 1979).

REFERENCES

Beaumont, J. G., 'Methods for Studying Cerebral Hemispheric Function', in A. W. Young, ed., *Functions of the Right Cerebral Hemisphere* (London, Academic Press, 1982).

Belmore, S. M., 'Depth of Processing and Ear Differences in Memory for Sentences', *Neuropsychologia*, 18 (1980), 657–663.

Berenbaum, S. A. and Harshman, R. A., 'On Testing Group Differences in Cognition Resulting from Differences in Lateral Specialisation: Reply to Fennell *et al.*', *Brain and Language*, 11 (1980), 209–220.

Berlin, C. I., 'Hemispheric Asymmetry in Auditory Tasks', in S. Harnad, R. W. Doty, L. Goldstein, J. Jaynes and G. Krauthamer, eds., *Lateralization in the Nervous System* (New York, Academic Press, 1977).

Berlin, C. I. and Cullen, J. K. Jr, 'Acoustic Problems in Dichotic Listening Tasks', in S. J. Segalowitz and F. A. Gruber, eds., *Language Development and Neurological Theory* (New York, Academic Press, 1977).

Bradshaw, J. L., Farrelly, J. and Taylor, M. J., 'Synonym and Antonym Pairs in the Detection of Dichotically and Monaurally Presented Targets: Competing Monaural Stimulation Can Generate a Substantial Right Ear Advantage', *Acta Psychologica*, 47 (1981), 189–205.

Bryden, M. P., 'Strategy Effects in the Assessment of Hemispheric Asymmetry', in G. Underwood, ed., *Strategies of Information Processing* (London, Academic Press, 1978).

Bub, D. and Whitaker, H. A., 'Language and Verbal Processes', in M. C. Wittrock, ed., *The Brain and Psychology* (New York, Academic Press, 1980).

Colbourn, C. J., 'Can Laterality be Measured?', *Neuropsychologia*, 16 (1978), 283–289.

Craig, J. D., 'Asymmetries in Processing Auditory Nonverbal Stimuli?', *Psychological Bulletin*, 86 (1979), 1339–1349.

Cutting, J. E., 'Different Speech-processing Mechanisms Can Be Reflected in the Results of Discrimination and Dichotic Listening Tasks', *Brain and Language*, 1 (1974), 363–375.

Damásio, A. R. and Damásio, H., 'Musical Faculty and Cerebral Dominance', in M. Critchley and R. A. Henson, eds., *Music and the Brain* (London, Heineman Medical Books, 1977).

Darwin, C. J., 'Ear Differences in the Recall of Fricatives and Vowels', *Quarterly Journal of Experimental Psychology*, 23 (1971), 46–62.

Darwin, C. J., Howell, P. and Brady, S. A., 'Laterality and Localisation: a "Right Ear Advantage" for Speech Heard on the Left', in J. Requin, ed., *Attention and Performance VII* (Hillsdale, N. J., Lawrence Erlbaum Associates, 1978).

Efron, R., Bogen, J. E. and Yund, E. W., 'Perception of Dichotic Chords by Normal and Commissurotomised Human Subjects', *Cortex*, 13 (1977), 137–149.

Ehrlichman, H. and Weinberger, A., 'Lateral Eye Movements and Hemispheric Asymmetry: a Critical Review', *Psychological Bulletin*, 85 (1978), 1080–1101.

Fennell, E. B., Bowers, D. and Satz, P., 'Within-modal and Cross-modal Reliabilities of Two Laterality Tests', *Brain and Language*, 4 (1977), 63–69.

Freides, D., 'Do Dichotic Listening Procedures Measure Lateralization of Information Processing or Retrieval Strategy?', *Perception and Psychophysics*, 21 (1977), 259–263.

Gates, A. and Bradshaw, J. L., 'The Role of the Cerebral Hemispheres in Music', *Brain and Language*, 4 (1977a), 403–431.

Gates, A. and Bradshaw, J. L., 'Music Perception and Cerebral Asymmetries', *Cortex*, 13 (1977b), 390–401.

Geffen, G. and Caudrey, D., 'Reliability and Validity of the Dichotic Monitoring Test for Language Laterality', *Neuropsychologia*, 19 (1981), 413–423.

Geffen, G., Traub, E. and Stierman, I., 'Language Laterality Assessed by Unilateral ECT and Dichotic Monitoring', *Journal of Neurology, Neurosurgery and Psychiatry*, 41 (1978), 354–360.

Godfrey, J. J., 'Perceptual Difficulty and the Right Ear Advantage for Vowels', *Brain and Language*, 1 (1974), 323–337.

Gordon, H. W., 'Hemispheric Asymmetries in the Perception of Musical Chords', *Cortex*, 6 (1970), 387–398.

Gordon, H. W., 'Degree of Ear Asymmetries for Perception of Dichotic Chords and for Illusory Chord Localisation in Musicians of Different Degrees of Competence', *Journal of Experimental Psychology: Human Perception and Performance*, 6 (1980), 516–527.

Henry, R. G., 'Monaural Studies Eliciting an Hemispheric Asymmetry: a Bibliography', *Perceptual and Motor Skills*, 48 (1979), 335–338.

Johnson, R. C., Bowers, J. K., Gamble, M., Lyons, F. M., Presbrey, T. W. and Vetter, R. R., 'Ability to Transcribe Music and Ear Superiority for Tone Sequences', *Cortex*, 13 (1977), 295–299.

Kallman, H. J., 'Ear Asymmetry and Monaurally-presented Sounds', *Neuropsychologia*, 15 (1977), 833–836.

Kallman, H. J., 'Can Expectancy Explain Reaction Time Ear Asymmetries?', *Neuropsychologia*, 16 (1978), 225–228.

Kimura, D., 'Cerebral Dominance and the Perception of Verbal Stimuli', *Canadian Journal of Psychology*, 15 (1961), 166–171.

Kimura, D., 'Left-right Differences in the Perception of Melodies', *Quarterly Journal of Experimental Psychology*, 16 (1964), 355–358.

Kinsbourne, M., 'Eye and Head Turning Indicates Cerebral Lateralization', *Science*, 176 (1972), 539–541.

Liberman, A. M., 'Ear Differences and Hemispheric Specialisation', in F. O. Schmitt and F. G. Worden, eds., *The Neurosciences: Third Study Program* (Cambridge, Mass., MIT Press, 1974).

Morais, J., 'The Effects of Ventriloquism on the Right Side Advantage for Verbal Material', *Cognition*, 3 (1975), 127–139.

Morais, J. and Bertelson, P., 'Laterality Effects in Diotic Listening', *Perception*, 2 (1973), 107–111.

Morais, J. and Bertelson, P., 'Spatial Position Versus Ear of Entry as Determinant of the Auditory Laterality Effects: a Stereophonic Test', *Journal of Experimental Psychology: Human Perception and Performance*, 1 (1975), 253–262.

Papçun, G., Krashen, S., Terbeck, D., Remington, R. and Harshman, R., 'Is the Left Hemisphere Specialised for Speech, Language and/or Something Else?', *Journal of the Acoustical Society of America*, 55 (1974), 319–327.

Provins, K. A. and Jeeves, M. A., 'Hemisphere Differences in Response Time to Simple Auditory Stimuli', *Neuropsychologia*, 13 (1975), 207–212.

Repp, B. H., 'Measuring Laterality Effects in Dichotic Listening', *Journal of the Acoustical Society of America*, 62 (1977), 720–737.

Searleman, A., 'Subject Variables and Cerebral Organisation for Language', *Cortex*, 16 (1980), 239–254.

Spellacy, F. and Wilson, A., 'Directed Attention and Perceptual Asymmetry to Monaurally Presented Tones', *Cortex*, 14 (1978), 71–77.

Springer, S. P., 'Speech Perception and the Biology of Language', in M. S. Gazzaniga, ed., *Handbook of Behavioral Neurobiology*, vol. 2, *Neuropsychology* (New York, Plenum Press, 1979).

Springer, S. P., Sidtis, J., Wilson, D. and Gazzaniga, M. S., 'Left Ear Performance in Dichotic Listening Following Commissurotomy', *Neuropsychologia*, 16 (1978), 305–312.

Studdert-Kennedy, M., 'Dichotic Studies II', *Brain and Language*, 2 (1975), 123–130.

Teng, E. L., 'Dichotic Ear Difference is a Poor Index for the Functional Asymmetry Between the Cerebral Hemispheres', *Neuropsychologia*, 19 (1981), 235–240.

Weiss, M. S. and House, A. S., 'Perception of Dichotically Presented Vowels', *Journal of the Acoustical Society of America*, 53 (1973), 51–58.

Witelson, S. F., 'Hemispheric Specialisation for Linguistic and Nonlinguistic Tactual Perception Using a Dichotomous Stimulation Technique', *Cortex*, 10 (1974), 3–17.

Wyke, M., 'Musical Ability: a Neuropsychological Interpretation', in M. Critchley and R. A. Henson, eds., *Music and the Brain* (London, Heineman Medical Books, 1977).

Zatorre, R. J., 'Recognition of Dichotic Melodies by Musicians and Non-musicians', *Neuropsychologia*, 17 (1979), 607–617.

Zurif, E. B. and Sait, P. E., 'The Role of Syntax in Dichotic Listening', *Neuropsychologia*, 8 (1970), 239–244.

CHAPTER 12

Electrophysiology

The introduction of electrophysiological techniques into neuropsychology has been one of the most exciting developments of recent years. For the first time it is possible to observe in 'real time', that is, as they happen, cognitive processes and the physiological events which are believed to be associated with them. Thus for the first time we have a technique which may make it possible to construct a bridge between mental and physiological events. If so, then we have a solution to the problem which has dogged so much of neuropsychology, that of directly investigating mind-body relationships.

However, before being carried away by such exciting possibilities, it has to be said that there are a number of difficult technical problems to be solved with these methods of investigation, and there is not yet any case in which a cognitive process has been shown to be associated unequivocally with a specific brain event. This area of research is probably the most technically demanding in human neuropsychology, and there are myriad experimental problems, as I hope to show. Nevertheless, despite the difficulties and some disappointments, we should not lose sight of what the techniques offer: to observe subjects engaged upon some intelligent task, and at the same time to observe the processes within the brain which are the physiological aspect of that mental activity.

Before introducing the techniques themselves, the distinction between clinical and research electroencephalography should be noted. Clinical electroencephalograms, or *EEG*s, are recordings of electrical activity in the brain used to investigate suspected pathological processes within the head. They are performed in a relatively standard way, using a variety of appropriate techniques, and play an important role in the physical investigation of neurological and psychiatric patients. Research electroencephalograms, however, are used to investigate brain activity in normal subjects, and involve a much less well defined set of techniques which have been derived from, and are associated with, the clinical techniques.

Electroencephalographical techniques fall into two principal groups: recording 'on-going' activity, and recording evoked potentials. The procedures involved in both groups will be described first, followed by some typical experiments and findings.

EEG RECORDING

The recording of the continuous electrical activity of the brain, or *'on-going' EEG*, has been practised for about fifty years. However, recent advances in amplifier design and the involvement of laboratory computers in analysing recordings have enabled the technique to be used more widely as a research tool.

If two electrodes, usually small silver cups coated with silver chloride and filled with a conducting gell, are glued at two positions on the scalp, with a third electrode attached elsewhere on the head to act as an earth, it is possible to detect a fluctuating potential difference between the two electrodes. This constantly changing potential difference can be amplified (about 20,000 times) and written out on a moving paper chart to form the EEG trace. It is unusual to record from more than a single pair of electrodes (a single *channel*) and a typical reording might have four, eight or more channels simultaneously recorded (up to twenty-four in clinical EEGs). The chart forms a convenient way of inspecting the recording, although the data written out on the chart will be fed directly into a laboratory computer for analysis. As the computer will sample the trace for each channel at least 128 times a second, yielding 61,440 numbers for each minute of activity across eight channels, a great deal of data is generated by even a relatively short period of recording. An example of a normal human EEG is shown in Fig. 12.1.

The first problems – of what exactly is being recorded and how to interpret the trace – arise when the sites for placing the electrodes are selected. Since the electrical activity of the brain is being recorded through the skull, scalp and other tissues, the electrode is picking up activity from a relatively large area of underlying cortex, and presenting a rather distorted aggregate image of what is going on in an area of about one square centimetre. However, it is known from comparing scalp recordings with recordings made directly on exposed brain tissue that there is some validity in the method and even if it is imperfect, it is all we have. Matters are sometimes further confused in

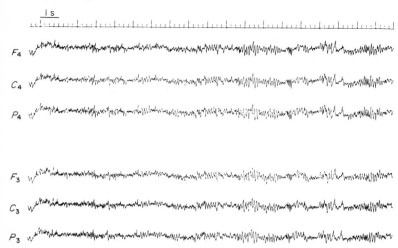

Figure 12.1. Normal human EEG: three channels recorded from the right (above) and left hemisphere (below); Common extracerebral reference. Bursts of alpha activity may be seen, especially to the right of centre.

that the electrode may pick up more activity from distant sites than from the directly underlying tissue, but these problems, caused by the directional nature of the propagation of the electrical activity, need not worry us for the present.

The electrodes are usually placed directly over the area of the brain which is of interest, and usually at points located with reference to a system of labelling known as the *Ten-Twenty system* (because it divides distances on the head in terms of 10 per cent and 20 per cent of the distance between fixed landmarks), which is shown in Fig. 12.2. A set of electrode positions is referred to as a *montage*.

Although, as mentioned previously, we cannot directly record the activity from one electrode, but only the difference between two electrodes, we can accept that we are recording the difference between two 'active' electrodes (both recording electrical activity from the brain) and so make a *bipolar* recording. Such recordings are quite common in clinical work, but they present difficulties in research. When the potential difference between electrodes changes, which electrode has changed? Almost certainly both will have changed, and it is impossible to unravel the contribution of each to the final observed change in the EEG.

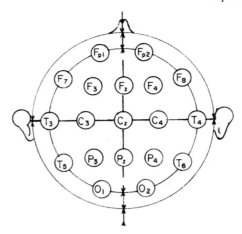

Figure 12.2. Principal points on the Ten-Twenty system of electrode placement.

In order to get round this problem we may choose to make a *monopolar* recording, where one of the two electrodes is relatively 'inactive'. However, it is almost impossible to find sites on the head at which brain electrical activity will not be recorded, including the tip of the nose or the tongue, and we must also avoid recording eye movements, muscle potentials and other artifacts. We might move our inactive electrode off the head (extracerebral reference), but then we find the activity of the heart and other bodily processes contaminating our recording, although there are techniques which allow these to be filtered out. The usual solution is therefore to choose a site which will pick up some EEG but which will be relatively inactive with respect to the activity in which we are interested. Such sites are often on the midline, and frequently the *vertex* (C_z) or midpoint on top of the head is chosen. The mastoid processes (behind the ears) and other sites are also used, sometimes in linked pairs to cut out any lateral bias (although linking is probably ineffective in doing this).

Further, it is common to employ a single reference for all the active electrodes being used, in a *common reference* recording. The reference may not be truly inactive, but at least when a comparison is made across channels, its contribution to each channel will be the same, and differences between the channels associated with active electrodes will reflect differences between the activity at those sites.

There are other more technical problems associated with a selection of electrode site and recording montage, especially if lateral asymmetries are to be investigated, which is the aim of much of the research in this field(see Beaumont, 1982a; Donchin, Kutas and McCarthy, 1977). Many of these problems can be solved by careful experimental design but one fundamental problem, as yet unsolved, is that of underlying asymmetries of the brain. We know that the brain is asymmetrical, particularly in certain regions, and there is a strong suspicion that these asymmetries have functional significance, but electrodes are applied to symmetrical points on the scalp. If we detect asymmetries in the EEG at homolateral points, do these represent lateral asymmetries in the activity of homolateral regions or merely indicate that we are not recording from anatomically homolateral points on the brain? This is an extremely worrying problem, which, until we can determine individual differences in anatomical asymmetries, is insoluble.

Once we have battled with all these problems, and have selected the task to set the subject (also fraught with difficulties which may produce artifactual results in the EEG) and have made our recording, the problems are not over. A form of data reduction and analysis must be selected. The difficulties here spring, quite simply, from ignorance: if we really understood what we see in the EEG trace, decisions about how to analyze it would be less arbitrary. While much is known about the origins of the EEG (see Thatcher and John, 1977, for a good introduction), we still do not know how a complex pattern of changes relates to mental events. It is usual however to analyse the frequencies present in the recording, and to divide these up into several frequency bands:

> Delta: 0 to 3.5 cycles/second
> Theta: 4 to 7.5 cycles/second
> Alpha: 8 to 12.5 cycles/second
> Beta 1: 13 to 19.5 cycles/second
> Beta 2: 20 to 29.5 cycles/second

These bands are not, however, precisely fixed, and there is some variation in the limits applied to them. Research has concentrated almost exclusively on alpha activity, although all the bands are potentially of interest and there is now a strong feeling that more interesting results may be found in other bands, especially theta and beta 1.

The *power* of a frequency band, or of a specific frequency, is usually calculated, and represents an overall measure of the strength of that component in the EEG during a specified period. Mental activity usually results in a decrease in the power of alpha activity, and an increase in the power of other frequency bands, especially beta 1. The former effect is referred to as alpha *attenuation* or alpha *abundance*, and the latter as *enhancement*. Power, however, confounds the amplitude with the duration of the component, that is, a very powerful component present for part of the time may result in the same overall power as a weaker component present for all of the period. These power analyses, however, are a useful if very crude way of quantifying the activity.

On-line computers have enabled a variety of more complex analyses to be performed, in particular certain forms of frequency analysis. One of the more promising of these is *coherence analysis*. This analysis takes a pair of channels and describes the amount of shared activity at the two channels at each frequency, but independently of the power of that frequency in the two channels (Shaw, 1981). The particular value of this form of analysis, apart from its independence from power, is the fact that it can be calculated from relatively short periods of EEG recording, down to about 0.5 sec., although a number of such short *epochs* have to be combined to provide a reliable estimate of the coherence. It is possible to identify some period when a particular cognitive process might be active, and then to examine the coherence between sites during that period. We can therefore begin to build up a dynamic map of the brain changes associated with relatively specific cognitive events, and to do this separately for each frequency across the range of the whole band of the EEG. Often associated with the *coherence spectrum*, as the plot of the coherence across the whole band of frequencies is called, is a *phase spectrum*, which can indicate which channel leads the other when the two share a significant amount of activity at some given frequency.

There are of course difficulties with coherence, technically and in interpretation. It is, for example, still uncertain whether we should expect coherence to increase or decrease with task-related activity in some region. It seems that there is a local increase, but a decrease with reference to more distant sites, and much more fundamental work is required before we can appreciate what this and other recently developed techniques can tell us.

In the EEG, we do have a fairly direct record of the activity of the brain, and while we may have difficult decisions to make about how to analyse the complexity of what is recorded, we are at least dealing with brain processes in a relatively immediate way. We can expect significant advances in understanding the EEG, and the brain processes which it reflects, in the near future.

RECORDING EVOKED POTENTIALS

Evoked potentials (EPs), also known as averaged evoked potentials (AEPs), averaged evoked responses (AERs) and event related potentials (ERPs), are an alternative way of studying psychological processes in the electrical activity of the brain. The common use of these abbreviations, further complicated by the addition of the modality of stimulation (hence visual, auditory and somatosensory evoked response: VER, AER, SER), can be somewhat confusing, but they all indicate measures based on the same basic technique.

This technique relies upon computer averaging, and has only been possible since the advent of relatively inexpensive laboratory computers. The idea behind it is that there is a relatively invariant response by the brain to a given sensory event. It is not possible to see this response in the EEG because it is masked by the large amount of background noise in which the response is embedded. However, if the noise is considered to be random, and if a number of examples of the response to a given event are collected and added together, then the noise at any time will tend to cancel out, allowing the event to emerge out of the background noise. Averaging, rather than simply summing, allows for the number of examples collected. An illustration of the principle behind the technique, using an artificial waveform, is shown in Fig. 12.3.

In practical terms, a simple sensory stimulus which can be accurately reproduced is selected, and this is presented a large number of times (commonly between 64 and 512) to the subject. Time-locked to the stimulus presentation, a short epoch of EEG is collected (between 500 and 1000 msec. around the stimulus), and stored in the computer. These epochs or samples are averaged as they are collected, and usually displayed during data collection. Subsequent analyses can then be performed. Examples of typical evoked potentials from different sensory modalities are shown in Fig. 12.4. (A note of warning here: physiologists prefer their graphs negative-up, while engineers and psychologists generally adopt positive-up, so take care about which way up an EP has been plotted.).

The recording electrodes and initial stages of the recording are just as for an on-going EEG and many of the problems about electrode placement apply equally to EP recording. A rather different set of problems arises, however, when we come to analyse the evoked potential records. Even though the absolute amount of data will be less than in an EEG record, there is still a formidable problem of data

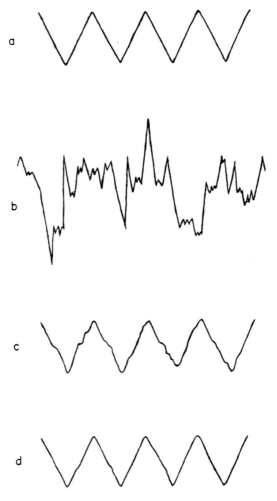

a

b

c

d

Figure 12.3. Illustration of the principal of waveform averaging: (a) the underlying waveform; (b) with added random noise; (c) after averaging 32 samples of the noisy signal; (d) after averaging 512 samples of the noisy signal, showing that the waveform has been accurately extracted.

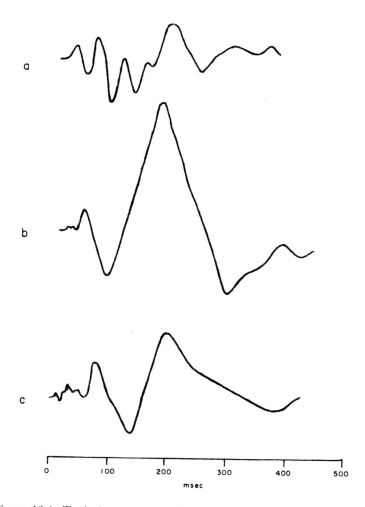

Figure 12.4. Typical average evoked potentials in (a) visual, (b) auditory, and (c) somatosensory modalities (positive up).

reduction. Again, our difficulties in deciding how to extract the most important features from the EP stem from our relative ignorance of what it is that we are looking for.

Most EPs contain a series of peaks and troughs, known as *components*, which presumably relate to significant brain events. It is usual to identify these components and to measure their location in time with respect to the stimulus event (*latency*), together with the *amplitude* of the response (commonly in the range ± 15 microvolts). We can then compare the amplitude and latency of given components across different recording sites and in different experimental conditions.

Things are rarely so simple, however. Although most subjects show a similar response pattern to a fairly clearly defined stimulus, a given component may simply not be present in the record from a certain subject. There may be two peaks of equal amplitude very close together: which is the component we are measuring, and should we average the latencies? One component may be superimposed upon another, and it may be difficult to extract the 'true' amplitude and latency information about both from the record which has been obtained. Also, the amplitude of one component may be influenced by the preceding component, and should this be taken into account? The use of peak-to-peak measurements of amplitude is one attempt to account for these sequential effects. What should be our baseline for measurement: is it zero volts, the average voltage of the whole response, or some prestimulus baseline?

None of these problems is readily soluble, although there are conventions which have been adopted to deal with most, and a number of computer algorithms which may help with the description of the components present in a set of evoked responses. There is however, a further problem: that of *latency jitter*. One of the assumptions of the averaging technique is that the underlying response is invariant. If, however, there is some basic variability in the latency of a component, this variability will only be seen in a reduction of the amplitude of the averaged component (see Fig. 12.5). Care must therefore be taken to ensure that amplitude differences between sites or conditions represent true amplitude differences and are not the effect of variable latency in the component. Inspection of the variability of the samples which make up the average, together with filtering techniques which correct for the latency of components, can help to deal with this problem. (Important discussions of EP methodology are to be found in Callaway, Tueting and Koslow, 1978, and Desmedt, 1977.)

There are some conventions about the labelling of commonly

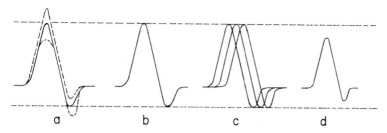

Figure 12.5. Latency jitter: averaging samples of differing amplitude but constant latency (a) yield the average (b); averaging samples of the same constant amplitude as (b) but with variable latency (c) yield the average (d), which is smaller in amplitude than (b).

occurring components seen in EPs but none of them is universally accepted. One approach is to number the components sequentially, so that P1 is the first main positive peak, N1 the first negative inflexion, followed by P2, N2, P3, and so on. This, however, tends to be rather confusing as the components tend to have different latencies with stimuli in different modalities. An alternative is to label the components as N100, P300, and so on, to indicate their polarity and approximate mean latency. An extension of this is that P300 comes to mean the theoretical component associated with P300, even if its latency is perhaps as long as 450 msec. from stimulus onset.

Unfortunately but inevitably this is confusing. However, it is worth noting that the two components which are perhaps most discussed are N1, which occurs in the visual modality at about 90–120 msec. from stimulus onset, and P300, which has a latency of 300–450 msec. Both these components have been clearly linked to cognitive processes. In general, the early components, up to about 100 msec. from stimulus onset, are thought of as being *exogenous* components, determined by the sensory reception and perception of the stimulus. The middle-range components which follow (100–300 msec.) and the subsequent late components (up to 1000 msec.) are thought of as *endogenous* and related to cognitive manipulation, stimulus evaluation and decision making. In one special case, the brain-stem evoked potential, it has been possible to identify components associated with each stage of the sensory transmission up to the cortex. With later endogenous components, things are much less well understood, although there are a number of theories about the cognitive significance of various components.

Mention should finally be made of the so-called *slow potentials*, generally seen as slow negative changes in the EEG preceding an expected event. These responses, or CNVs as they are sometimes called (contingent negative variation), can be recorded by similar averaging methods, and are thought to represent preparatory processes within the brain.

Evoked potential recording has been perhaps more successful than direct EEG studies in eliciting phenomena of psychological significance. particularly where the stimulus event and task are relatively simple and clearly defined, the technique is extremely valuable. With complex tasks and stimuli, it becomes more difficult to use the technique, and the need for a relatively large number of repetitious trials enforces a certain artificiality upon the experimental design. Despite this, and the numerous methodological problems and pitfalls, evoked potential recording has become an important specialism within neuropsychology.

LATERAL EEG ASYMMETRIES

As the bulk of research with on-going EEG measures has been directed to establishing lateral asymmetries in the EEG, a review of this topic will serve to illustrate the neuropsychological research using such measures.

All the recent reviews (Beaumont, 1982a; Donchin, Kutas and McCarthy, 1977; Marsh, 1978) have commented upon the methodological shortcomings of the studies which have been carried out. In fact it would not be unfair to say that *no* study (including those in which I have been involved) can be regarded as entirely methodologically sound. The view that one takes of the literature depends upon a judgement of the seriousness of the methodological shortcomings.

The approach in most research designs has been to set the subject some task or tasks to 'engage' the left or right hemispheres, and then to look for asymmetries in the accompanying EEG. These asymmetries might be seen by comparing the two hemispheres directly (between hemisphere effects) or by comparing intrahemispheric (within hemisphere) effects occuring on the left and on the right. The better studies have also recorded behavioural task performance alongside the EEG. This not only enables an examination of the relationship between EEG and performance parameters but, more mundanely, helps to ensure that the subject actually carries out the task which he has been set. It can also help to provide an independent measure of whether tasks selected to engage the left and right hemispheres have been satisfactorily matched in difficulty.

We might ask first whether there are relatively 'good' studies which do find an effect of cognitive task. Davidson, Taylor, Saron and Snyder (1980), for example, gave subjects tasks such as an embedded figures task, the Kohs' Blocks, and verbal analogies and reading comprehension tests, and found an asymmetry in right handed subjects, although only for those with sinistrals in the family. Ehrlichman and Wiener (1979, 1980) also used various verbal and spatial tasks and asymmetries in integrated alpha power, with a significant reduction in power (which is what would be expected) over the engaged hemisphere. They repeated their experiment using covert as well as overt responses, because of the suspicion that overt responding may introduce artifactual asymmetry into the EEG. It should be noted that their tasks are only *expected* to engage one of the hemispheres preferentially; there is no independent evidence to demonstrate that they will do so (apart from clinical investigations).

Tasks such as counting the words 'the' or 'a' in an auditory passage, or listening to music, were used by Moore (1979), and similar tasks but without counting were used by Moore and Haynes (1980), which resulted in different asymmetries for the two tasks, as was predicted. Parallel results have come from Ornstein, Johnstone, Herron and Swencionis (1980) and Rebert and Low (1978). The latter study also involved listening to verbal material, but had as the spatial component a block construction task performed entirely in imagination, which seems rather odd. Beaumont and Rugg (1979) used two memory tasks which were carefully matched for difficulty, for which there was clinical evidence of their association with left and right anterior lobes, and which involved judging which of a pair of either words or abstract paintings had been previously presented in a sequence of similar items. A task asymmetry in intrahemispheric coherence (see p. 230), at the expected cortical sites, was found. There are a number of other studies which would also support the existence of task-related asymmetries on various EEG variables.

We must also ask, however, whether there are 'good' studies which have failed to find the expected asymmetry. The study by Beaumont and Rugg just mentioned found the effects in coherence which were predicted, but found quite anomalous enhancement of alpha power with the cognitive task. In the study by Ornstein *et al.*, although task effects were found at centrally sited electrodes, they were not found at parietal placements. Rebert (1977) has also found alpha enhancement rather than attenuation, as expected, in the right hemisphere with a dot detection task, Rebert and Mahoney (1978) found no task effects at all in raw power measures taken during verbal and nonverbal target detection tasks. Visuospatial tasks designed to be analytic or synthetic in their cognitive demands failed to produce clear task-related effects (Tucker, 1976), and although Dolce with others (Dolce and Waldeier, 1974; Dolce and Decker, 1975) found complex and interesting effects in the beta, theta and delta ranges, no task effects upon alpha activity were seen. McCarthy and Donchin (1978) used a task derived from the 'chimeric metacontrol' studies with split brain patients, in a laudable attempt to produce well-matched 'left and right hemisphere tasks', but found no task-dependent asymmetries in alpha.

Finally, we must ask whether there are 'good' studies which find effects, but which suggest that the effect may be artifactual. The studies of Gevins and co-workers (Gevins *et al.*, 1979a, b; Gevins, 1981) are particularly relevant here. They conducted a series of experiments in which particular efforts were made to control for stimulus characteristics, the effects of eye and limb movements, and other performance-related factors, such as the subject's ability and task engagement. Their conclusion was quite clear: that when such factors were effectively controlled, task-related asymmetries which had been otherwise observed disappeared.

Other artifactual sources of asymmetry are suggested by the work of Amochaev and Salamy (1979) and Haynes (1980). In the first study, different sites for the reference electrode were compared, and they found the stability of the task effect, using a variety of tasks, to be related to the site chosen. The study by Haynes, in which subjects listened to sentences which were either to be imitated or followed by the construction of a new sentence, found left hemisphere activation only when imitation was demanded. This was interpreted in terms of the preparatory phases of motor programming for ensuing speech, and suggests that even when EEG is recorded during a period of inactivity, subvocal preparation, or preparation for other response processes, might contaminate the EEG.

What are we to conclude? If we adopt a fairly relaxed criterion of methodological rigour, then the bulk of studies point towards task-related asymmetries in the EEG. The asymmetries are those which would be predicted from the divided visual field and dichotic listening literature. That is the general trend of the results. However, the failure of a number of reputable studies to find effects, and the clear demonstration of a number of possible sources of artifact, must mean that we have to conclude that clear and reliable task-related effects have not as yet been demonstrated. It does not mean that the search for them should be abandoned, and improvements in methodology should lead to a clearer answer to whether asymmetries are to be observed in on-going EEG.

Evoked Potential Studies

When employing the evoked potential methodology to answer neuropsychological questions, there are two major strategies available. The stimuli which are used to elicit the EP may be task relevant (and may or may not be lateralized) or incidental to the task. If task relevant stimuli are used, there are problems about the control of such necessarily complex stimuli and also about obtaining strong potentials. On the other hand, it is not clear that if EPs are evoked incidentally during performance of some cognitive task by simple 'irrelevant' stimuli, the response to these 'probe' stimuli will reflect the concurrent task engagement. Studies have been reported using both approaches, and have tended to be in either the visual or auditory modalities.

Taking visual EPs first, a good example of a study using task relevant lateralized stimuli is that of Ledlow, Swanson and Kinsbourne (1978). They used the nominal/physical letter matching task (see p. 193) and collected performance data together with the EPs in order to establish independent evidence of lateral asymmetry in cognitive processing during the task. Their results are complex, but they found an overall difference in the amplitude of left and right hemisphere potentials, and for some components the direct pathway (when stimuli were presented to the hemisphere contralateral to response: see Fig. 10.2) was associated with responses of smaller amplitude but reduced latency. At P300 there were differences between direct and indirect stimulation which also varied with type of match (nominal or physical), and also an effect of same or different cases at P130 and N170.

A similar experimental design has been used by Rugg and Beaumont (1978). Letters were employed as stimuli throughout, but subjects were asked either to respond to letters containing an 'ee' sound (verbal task) or to letters containing a right-angle (spatial task). Variations in the amplitude of middle latency components with field of presentation were found which differed according to the cognitive task. A lateral asymmetry was found for late components, but only with the spatial task.

By contrast, Friedman, Simson, Ritter and Rapin (1975) collected responses to sequentially flashed words which made up one of three sentences: 'The wheel is on the axle', 'The heel is on the shoe', 'The peel is on the orange'. On some trials, the first part of the second word was not presented, so that from '-eel' the subject could not tell which sentence was being shown until the final word arrived. The second word therefore might deliver information or be indeterminate. The latency of P300 was longer for words delivering information, and 'syntactic closure' was also shown to affect P300 amplitude. However, they found no lateral asymmetries between the hemispheres.

McCarthy and Donchin (1978), as already indicated, have used the structural-functional matching task first used with split brain patients and have collected not only EEG data but also EP recordings. There was not only a visual EP to the stimulus figures, but also a warning tone which in some conditions served to indicate the type of match required and which evoked an auditory response. Although there was no effect of mode of matching on the EEG, during the preparatory period following the warning tone a component was seen which was sensitive to the mode required, and which had an asymmetrical distribution across the electrode sites employed.

The alternative of incidentally collecting EPs to flash stimuli during an on-going left or right hemisphere task was developed by Galin and Ellis (1975). They found changes in the asymmetry of the potentials recorded at left and right temporal and parietal areas which parallel task-dependent asymmetries in both EEG alpha power and in performance measures. These effects have, however, not always been confirmed by other workers (Beaumont and Mayes, 1977; Mayes and Beaumont, 1977).

Thatcher (1977) has extended this experimental approach by a probe technique which involves interspersing the relevant stimuli with random dot displays which evoke the potentials. On a delayed-letter matching task, he was able to show differences in the pattern of response to match and mismatch trials from a variety of posterior sites, primarily in the late component range.

In the auditory modality, the 'identical stimuli but variable task' design has also been used, for example by Wood (1977). Reaction times and EPs were collected during tasks which focussed upon various phonetic characteristics of the stimuli, with the result that differences were found in the left, but not the right, hemisphere between 60 and 140 msec. after stimulus onset. This was taken to support the independence of auditory and phonetic processes. Tanguay. Taub, Doubleday and Clarkson (1977) presented monaural voiced stop consonants (e.g. /ba/, /da/, /ga/) and found increased amplitude of response contralateral to the ear of presentation, but no hemisphere differences in latency or amplitude. Nevertheless, using musical chord stimuli, Taub, Tanguay, Doubleday, Clarkson, and Remington (1976) found lateral asymmetries as a function of hemisphere stimulated, in middle-range components and at sites close to Wernicke's area.

The auditory parallel to the visual ambiguity task, described above, has been extensively investigated by Brown and Marsh with others (see Brown, Marsh and Smith, 1979). They used sentences which contained an element with a given sound but with different meanings according to the context, for example, the word 'led' in 'The horse was led' or 'The metal was lead', and 'fire' in 'Ready, aim, fire' or 'Sit by the fire'. The results from these studies are complex, but effects have been found which are sensitive to parts of speech, as well as lateral asymmetries in certain components, some of which suggest the involvement of left anterior cerebral processes.

Task irrelevant probes with an on-going auditory task have been used by Shucard and Schucard (1979) and found to be associated with engagement in either musical or verbal tasks.

Both auditory and visual stimuli have been examined by Davis and Wada (1978), who performed spectral analysis on their EPs and found greater coherence in the left hemisphere with click stimuli, while flash stimuli produced this effect in the right. Not only were these hemisphere effects observed, but they were also found to vary with the speech lateralization of the subjects, which had been independently assessed.

Attentional variables have been assessed through evoked potential recording, and in both auditory and visual modalities. There is considerable debate about the effects of attention on EPs, especially upon the NI component (see Näätänen and Michie, 1979), with various groups of workers contributing elegant experiments. Most of these experiments rely upon the presentation of lateralized auditory material, with attention being directed to one of the ears. Lateralized recording sites have been included as well as central sites, and some but not all of these have revealed asymmetrical components. Notably, Buchsbaum and Drago (1977) have reported clear asymmetries in an N140 component with visual presentation, and which could be manipulated by attentional variables. The importance of these experiments lies not in the precise results, but in the fact that it can be shown that manipulation of the cognitive variable of attention may have effects which can be seen in electrophysiological recordings.

Research has not been limited entirely to the visual and auditory modalities, and somatosensory potentials (Barrett, Halliday and Halliday, 1978) as well as movement related effects (Kutas and Donchin, 1978; McCallum and Curry, 1979) have been shown to exhibit lateralized components.

The experiments mentioned above serve as examples of the kind of research which has been conducted using evoked potentials. The research literature is quite extensive, the pattern of results reported is extremely complex, and, as already indicated, methodological difficulties raise considerable problems in considering many of the studies. Happily there are several good reviews of the literature (Hillyard and Woods, 1979; Marsh, 1978; Rugg, 1982a, b), and there seems no reason not to accept what is the general opinion of these reviews: that EPs appear sensitive to both the locus of cognitive processes and to factors which reflect the mode of stimulus presentation, and the resulting effects upon EPs are the product of a complex interaction of such factors.

CONCLUSION

Having briefly outlined the techniques employed in electrophysiological investigations, and illustrated the kind of experiments which have been performed, what general result has emerged? On the one hand it would seem that there is remarkably good evidence, given the technical demands of the techniques, for the identification of cerebral processes which mirror those inferred from human performance studies. The results appear to fit remarkably well with what might be expected from divided visual field and dichotic listening research.

On the other hand, it is worth noting that there are considerable differences in the kinds of activity studied in clinical and experimental research. The experimental techniques, and especially the electrophysiological methods, demand a more passive involvement on the part of subjects, and it has to be recognized that rather different domains of behaviour are being studied by each of the different approaches and techniques.

It has also to be remembered that there are considerable methodological difficulties in both the EEG and EP literature. Close inspection of the reported results also reveals little unanimity about the precise effects to be observed, and there is little replication of experimental findings. Much of the interpretation of results is uncomfortably *post hoc*, and our ignorance about just what to look for in either the EEG or in EP components means that it is almost impossible to construct sound experimental tests of precise neuropsychological hypotheses.

Nevertheless, the techniques still hold considerable promise, and it may well be that the bridge will yet be established enabling us to link, precisely and accurately, the processes which we can observe in task performance with the associated cerebral events which we can observe in electrophysiological recordings.

MINOR PHYSIOLOGICAL TECHNIQUES

This seems an appropriate point at which to note that, while the major techniques employed in experimental neuropsychology have now been considered, there are a number of less widely used physiological techniques which have contributed to our present knowledge.

Regional cerebral blood flow (rCBF) has been used at a number of centres, and is in approach akin to electrophysiological indices. A radioactive material is introduced into the blood stream, usually by gas inhalation, which enables the amount of blood flowing to regions of the brain to be monitored by banks of detectors placed alongside the head. The results seem to show that increased local blood flow accompanies task engagement. However, the resolution of the technique is coarse and there are a variety of technical difficulties. A special issue of *Brain and Language* (1980, vol. 9, no. 1) is devoted to the technique and provides an excellent introduction.

Psychophysiological measures, such as skin conductance, muscle tension and finger pulse volume, have also been used, but the results, while interesting, are not entirely clear. The interpretation of results is complicated by the ipsilateral efferent projection of the autonomic nervous system, and it is difficult to predict the direction of change in autonomic variables.

Anatomical investigations are also of interest to neuropsychologists. It is now clearly established that there are certain marked anatomical asymmetries in the topography of the cerebral cortex, that these are present from birth, and that there is some reason to associate them with functional specialization (Galaburda, LeMay, Kemper and Geschwind, 1978). The advent of computerized axial tomography (CAT or 'EMI' scans) will probably lead to more studies which correlate anatomical variables with performance measures, and these should be of considerable interest. The contribution which might be made by such new techniques as positron emission tomography and by NMR scanners, with their improved spatial and temporal resolution for visualizing cerebral physiological processes, is an exciting prospect, but the relative cost of such investigations is likely to limit whatever contribution they might make. These techniques, together with even more esoteric methods, are reviewed in Beaumont (1982b).

FURTHER READING

A useful general introduction to the techniques introduced in this chapter, and associated methods, is to be found in:

Andreassi, J. L., _Psychophysiology: Human Behaviour and Physiological Response_ (New York, Oxford University Press, 1980).

The best souce for further information on EEG methodology is :

Cooper, R., Ossleton J. W. and Shaw, J. C., _EEG Technology_, 3rd edition (London, Butterworth, 1980).

And for EP techniques:

Callaway, E., Tueting, P. and Koslow, S. H., eds., _Event-related Brain Potentials in Man_ (New York, Academic Press, 1978).
Desmedt, J. E., ed., _Progress in Clinical Neurophysiology_, vols. 1 and 3 (Basel, S. Karger, 1977).

A useful introduction to recent findings can be found in these volumes, as well as in :

Begleiter, H., ed., _Evoked Brain Potentials and Behaviour_ (New York, Plenum Press, 1979).
Lehmann, D. and Callaway, E., eds., _Human Evoked Potentials: Applications and Problems_ (New York, Plenum Press, 1979).

More specific reviews of the literature include:

Beaumont, J. G., 'The EEG and Task Performance: a Tutorial Review', in A. W. K. Gaillard and W. Ritter, eds., _Tutorials in ERP Research– Endogenous Components_ (Amsterdam, North-Holland, 1982).
Donchin, E., McCarthy, G. and Kutas, M., 'Electroncephalographic Investigations of Hemispheric Specialization', in J. E. Desmedt, ed., _Progress in Clinical Neurophysiology_, vol. 3., _Language and Hemispheric Specialization in Man: Cerebral Event-related Potentials_ (Basel, S. Karger, 1977).
Hillyard, S. A. and Woods, D. L., 'Electrophysiological Analysis of Human Brain Function', in M. S. Gazzaniga, ed., _Handbook of Behavioral Neurobiology_, vol. 2, _Neuropsychology_ (New York, Plenum Press, 1979).
Marsh, G. R., 'Asymmetry of Electrophysiological Phenomena and its Relation to Behaviour in Humans', in M. Kinsbourne, ed., _Asymmetrical Function of the Brain_ (Cambridge, Cambridge University Press, 1978).

Rugg, M. D., 'The Relationship between Evoked Responses and Lateral Asymmetries of Processing', in A. W. K. Gaillard and W. Ritter, eds., *Tutorials in ERP Research – Endogenous Components* (Amsterdam, North-Holland, 1982).

REFERENCES

Amochaev, A. and Salamy, A., 'Stability of EEG Laterality Effects', *Psychophysiology*, 16 (1979), 242–246.

Barrett, G., Halliday, A. M. and Halliday, E., 'Asymmetries of the Late Evoked Potential Components and P300 Associated with Handedness and Side of Stimulus Delivery in a Somatosensory DetectionTask', *Electroencephalography and Clinical Neurophysiology*, 44 (1978), 791.

Beaumont, J. G., 'The EEG and Task Performance: a Tutorial Review', in A. W. K. Gaillard and W. Ritter, eds., *Tutorials in ERP Research – Endogenous Components* (Amsterdam, North-Holland, 1982a).

Beaumont, J. G., 'Methods for Studying Cerebral Hemispheric Function', in A. W. Young, ed., *Functions of the Right Cerebral Hemisphere* (London, Academic Press, 1982b).

Beaumont, J. G. and Mayes, A., 'Do Task and Sex Differences Influence the Visual Evoked Potential?', *Psychophysiology*, 14 (1977) 545–550.

Beaumont, J. G. and Rugg, M. D., 'The Specificity of Intrahemispheric EEG Alpha Coherence Asymmetry Related to Psychological Task', *Biological Psychology*, 9 (1979), 237–248.

Brown, W. S., Marsh, J. T. and Smith, J. C., 'Principal Component Analysis of ERP Differences Related to the Meaning of an Ambiguous Word', *Electroencephalography and Clinical Neurophysiology*, 46 (1979), 709–714.

Buchsbaum, M. and Drago, D., 'Hemispheric Asymmetry and the Effects of Attention on Visual Evoked Potentials', in J. E. Desmedt, ed., *Progress in Clinical Neurophysiology*, vol. 3, *Language and Hemispheric Specialization in Man: Cerebral Event-related Potentials* (Basel, S. Karger, 1977).

Callaway, E., Tueting, P. and Koslow, S. H., eds., *Event-related Brain Potentials in Man* (New York, Academic Press, 1978).

Davidson, R. J., Taylor, N., Saron, C. and Snyder, M., 'Individual Differences and Task Effects in EEG Measures of Hemispheric Activation. II: Effects of Familial Sinistrality', *Psychophysiology*, 17 (1980), 312.

Davis, A. E. and Wada, J. A., 'Speech Dominance and Handedness in the Normal Human', *Brain and Language*, 5 (1978), 42–55.

Desmedt, J. E., ed., *Progress in Clinical Neurophysiology*, vol. 1, *Attention, Voluntary Contraction and Event-related Cerebral Potentials* (Basel, S. Karger, 1977).

Dolce, G. and Decker, H., 'Application of Multivariate Statistical Methods in Analysis of Spectral Values of the EEG', in G. Dolce and H. Künkel, eds., *CEAN: Computerised EEG Analysis* (Stuttgart, Fischer Verlag, 1975).

Dolce, G. and Waldeier, H., 'Spectral and Multivariate Analysis of EEG Changes during Mental Activity in Man', *Electroencephalography and Clinical Neurophysiology*, 36 (1974), 577–584.

Donchin, E., Kutas, M. and McCarthy, G., 'Electrocortical Indices of Hemispheric Utilisation', in S. Harnad, R. W. Doty, L. Goldstein, J. Jaynes and G. Krauthamer, eds., *Lateralization in the Nervous System* (New York, Academic Press, 1977).

Ehrlichman, H. and Wiener, M. S. 'Consistency of Task-related EEG asymmetries', *Psychophysiology*, 16 (1979), 247–252.

Ehrlichman, E. and Wiener, M. S., 'EEG Asymmetry during Covert Mental Activity', *Psychophysiology*, 17 (1980), 228–235.

Friedman, D., Simson, R., Ritter, W. and Rapin, I., 'The Late Positive Component (P300) and Information Processing in Sentences', *Electroencephalography and Clinical Neurophysiology*, 38 (1975), 255–262.

Galaburda, A. M., LeMay, M., Kemper, T. L. and Geschwind, N., 'Right-left Asymmetries in the Brain', *Science*, 199 (1978), 852–856.

Galin, D. and Ellis, R. R., 'Asymmetry in Evoked Potentials as an Index of Lateralised Cognitive Processes: Relation to EEG Alpha Asymmetry', *Neuropsychologia*, 13 (1975), 45–50.

Gevins, A. S., 'The Use of Brain Electrical Potentials (BEP) to Study Localisation of Human Brain Function', *International Journal of Neuroscience*, 13 (1981), 27–41.

Gevins, A. S., Zeitlin, G. M., Yingling, C. D., Doyle, J. C., Dedon, M. F., Schaffer, R. E., Roumasset, J. T. and Yeager, C. L., 'EEG Patterns during "Cognitive" Tasks. I: Methodology and Analysis of Complex Behaviors', *Electroencephalography and Clinical Neurophysiology*, 47 (1979a), 693–703.

Gevins, A. S., Zeitlin, G. M., Doyle, J. C., Schaffer, R. E. and Callaway, E., 'EEG Patterns during "Cognitive" Tasks. II: Analysis of Controlled Tasks', *Electroencephalography and Clinical Neurophysiology*, 47 (1979b), 704–710.

Haynes, W. O., 'Task Effect and EEG Alpha Asymmetry: an Analysis of Linguistic Processing in Two Response Modes', *Cortex*, 16 (1980), 95–102.

Hillyard, S. A. and Woods, D. L., 'Electrophysiological Analysis of Human Brain Function', in M. S. Gazzaniga, ed., *Handbook of Behavioral Neurobiology*, vol. 2, *Neuropsychology* (New York, Plenum Press, 1979).

Kutas, M. and Donchin, E., 'The Effects of Subject Strategies on the Lateralisation of Movement Related Potentials', *Electroencephalography and Clinical Neurophysiology*, 45 (1978), 29P.

Ledlow, A., Swanson, J. M. and Kinsbourne, M., 'Reaction Times and Evoked Potentials as Indicators of Hemispheric Differences for Laterally Presented Name and Physical Matches', *Journal of Experimental Psychology: Human Perception and Performance*, 4 (1978), 440–454.

Marsh, G. R., 'Asymmetry of Electrophysiological Phenomena and its Relation to Behavior in Humans', in M. Kinsbourne, ed., *Asymmetrical Function of the Brain* (Cambridge, Cambridge University Press, 1978).

Mayes, A. and Beaumont, J. G., 'Does Visual Evoked Potential Asymmetry Index Cognitive Activity?', *Neuropsychologia*, 15 (1977), 249–256.

McCallum, W. S. and Curry, S. H., 'Hemisphere Differences in Event Related Potentials and CNV's Associated with Monaural Stimuli and Lateralised Motor Responses', in D. Lehmann and E. Callaway, eds., *Human Evoked Potentials: Applications and Problems* (New York, Plenum Press, 1979).

McCarthy, G. and Donchin, E., 'Brain Potentials Associated with Structural and Functional Visual Matching', *Neuropsychologia*, 16 (1978), 571–585.

Moore, W. H. Jr. 'Alpha Hemispheric Asymmetry of Males and Females on Verbal and Nonverbal Tasks: Some Preliminary Results', *Cortex*, 15 (1979), 321–326.

Moore, W. H. Jr and Haynes, W. O., 'A Study of Hemispheric Asymmetry for Verbal and Nonverbal Stimuli in Males and Females', *Brain and Language*, 9 (1980), 338–349.

Näätänen, R. and Michie, P. T., 'Early Selective-attention Effects on the Evoked Potential: a Critical Review and Reinterpretation', *Biological Psychology*, 8 (1979), 81–136.

Ornstein, R., Johnstone, J., Herron, J. and Swencionis, C., 'Differential Right Hemisphere Engagement in Visuospatial Tasks', *Neuropsychologia*, 18 (1980), 49–64.

Rebert, C. S., 'Functional Cerebral Asymmetry and Performance. I: Reaction Time to Words and Dot patterns as a Function of Electroencephalographic Alpha Asymmetry; II: Individual Differences in Reaction Time to Word and Pattern Stimuli Triggered by Asymmetric Alpha Bursts', *Behavioral Neuropsychiatry*, 8 (1977), 90–98, 99–103.

Rebert, C. S. and Low, D. W., 'Differential Hemispheric Activation during Complex Visuomotor Performance', *Electroencephalography and Clinical Neurophysiology*, 44 (1978), 724–734.

Rebert, C. S. and Mahoney, R. A., 'Functional Cerebral Asymmetry and performance. III: Reaction Time as a Function of Task, Hand, Sex, And EEG Asymmetry', *Psychophysiology*, 15 (1978), 9–16.

Rugg, M. D., 'The Relationship between Evoked Responses and Lateral Asymmetries of Processing', in A. W. K. Gaillard and W. Ritter, eds., *Tutorials in ERP Research – Endogenous Components* (Amsterdam, North-Holland, 1982a).

Rugg, M. D., 'Electrophysiological Studies of Divided Visual Field Stimulation', in J. G. Beaumont, ed., *Divided Visual Field Studies of Cerebral Organisation* (London, Academic Press, 1982b).

Rugg, M. D. and Beaumont, J. G., 'Interhemispheric Asymmetries in the Visual Evoked Response: Effects of Stimulus Lateralisation and Task', *Biological Psychology*, 6 (1978), 283–292.

Shaw, J. C., 'An Introduction to the Coherence Function and Its Use in Signal Analysis', *Journal of Medical Engineering and Technology*, 5 (1981), 279–288.

Shucard, D. W. and Shucard, J. L. 'Auditory Evoked Potentials as Probes of Lateralised Information Processing in Adults and Infants', in D. Lehmann and E. Callaway, eds., *Human Evoked Potentials: Applications and Problems* (New York, Plenum Press, 1979).

Tanguay, P. E., Taub, J. M., Doubleday, C. and Clarkson, D., 'An Interhemispheric Comparison of Auditory Evoked Responses to Consonant-vowel Stimuli', *Neuropsychologia*, 15 (1977), 123–131.

Taub. J. M., Tanguay, P. E., Doubleday, C. N., Clarkson, D. and Remington, R., 'Hemisphere and Ear Asymmetries in the Auditory Evoked Response to Musical Chord Stimuli', *Physiological Psychology*, 4 (1976), 11–17.

Thatcher, R. W., 'Evoked Potential Correlates of Delayed Letter-matching', *Behavioral Biology*, 19 (1977), 1–23.

Thatcher, R. W. and John, E. R., *Foundations of Cognitive Processes* (Hillsdale, N. J., Lawrence Erlbaum Associates, 1977).

Tucker, D. M., 'Sex Differences in Hemispheric Specialisation for Synthetic Visuospatial Functions', *Neuropsychologia*, 14 (1976), 447–454.

Wood, C. C., 'Average Evoked Potentials and Phonetic Processing in Speech Perception', in J. E. Desmedt, ed., *Progress in Clinical Neurophysiology*, vol. 3, *Language and Hemispheric Specialization in Man: Cerebral Event-related Potentials* (Basel, S. Karger, 1977).

CHAPTER 13

Individual Differences – Sex and Sinistrality

Happily we are not all alike, and one of the major historical themes of experimental psychology has been the investigation of just how and why we differ. This interest has inevitably been reflected in human neuropsychology.

There is a whole range of variables upon which individuals differ and which may be relevant to neuropsychological function. They include sensory function and perceptual abilities; metabolic and endocrine factors; motor skills and manipulative ability; intellectual performance and cognitive style. Even emotional traits, personality differences and anxiety may bear some relation to cerebral function. However, two particular characteristics of the individual subject have come under extensive scrutiny, and they are sex and handedness.

SEX DIFFERENCES IN CEREBRAL ORGANIZATION

The evidence in general psychology about sex differences in cognitive ability has pointed to a superiority among males for spatial and mechanical skills, and a superiority among females for verbal skills (Hutt, 1972; Maccoby and Jacklin, 1974). While this dichotomy has not been accepted uncritically (Fairweather, 1976), it is generally recognized that there are some differences between the sexes along these lines. Whether such differences can be attributed to biological factors, or result from social and cultural influences, is still hotly debated. It seems reasonable that both are involved, although the extent of the contribution of each is unclear.

It was almost inevitable that these ideas would be carried across into neuropsychology, particularly considering the battle to explain the very considerable degree of variability shown by subjects in performing experimental tasks. The kind of dichotomy proposed for sex differences also appeared to reflect, appealingly, contemporary ideas about the dichotomy between the specializations of the two hemispheres.

The work of Buffery and Gray (1972) gave a significant impetus to research by suggesting a model in which males were considered to possess less cerebral lateralization than females. The male brain was seen to have language represented more bilaterally, which in turn implied that spatial abilities must also be represented more bilaterally to occupy the remaining capacity. The result was, for males, a relative deficit in verbal ability, which suffers from bilateral representation, and a relative advantage in spatial ability, which might benefit from ambilaterality.

Subsequent research and theorization have almost unanimously failed to support the Buffery and Gray hypothesis. Nevertheless, it illustrates the kind of argument which has led to current theories. These, when they have accepted the presence of sex differences, have proposed that the brain of females is more bilaterally organized than that of males. The current debate is whether the evidence justifies such a conclusion. Fortunately, there are two good reviews which should help students to assess the current findings: Fairweather (1982) and McGlone (1980).

There is a particular difficulty about the manner in which much of the sex differences data has been collected. Particularly because of the general feeling that sex differences might be important, an experimenter will include equal numbers of males and females in his subject sample, and will probably include this factor in the statistical analysis of the results. If there is a significant effect of sex, it will be reported; if there is no significant effect, it may well not be reported at all. Even if such a bias were not present in the reporting of results, the incidental way in which information has accumulated, from studies not specifically designed to investigate sex differences, must be regarded as unsatisfactory.

The question as to whether there are differences between the sexes in the effects of clinical lesions raises another problem, which is the preponderance of males in clinical samples. Where comparable groups of male and female brain-injured patients are studied, there are almost inevitably differences between the two sex groups in terms of the cause of the lesion, the age of the patient, the severity of the lesion, and so on (see p. 46). McGlone, from the evidence of her 1978 study, and from her review of similar studies, reports that while males show effects of the laterality of the lesion on the Verbal-Performance

IQ discrepancy (left lesions affecting Verbal, and right lesions Performance, IQ on the Wechsler Adult Intelligence Scale), these effects are not to be found in females. It is also claimed that the aphasic effects of left hemisphere lesions are less severe in females, who also recover more rapidly. The commentaries which accompany McGlone's 1980 review together with the additional data presented there, and the data set out in Fairweather (1982) show that while some studies support the conclusion of female bilaterality on the basis of clinical evidence, there are also a number which do not.

Experimental neuropsychology has yielded a very confused set of results on sex differences. Using the divided visual field technique and verbal stimuli, some workers have found the predicted greater right visual field advantage among male subjects (Bradshaw and Gates, 1978; Kail and Siegel, 1978). However, there are also studies in which no evidence of a sex-related effect was apparent, for example, that of Hannay and Boyer (1978). Other workers have found differences, and then have failed to replicate them (McKeever and Van Deventer, 1977). A similar picture emerges from the studies employing non-verbal stimuli, with both positive (Davidoff, 1977; Rizzolatti and Buchtel, 1977; Saesanuma and Kobayashi, 1978) and negative (Bryden, 1976; Kail and Siegel, 1978) findings.

Merely totting up the number of studies which find a certain result, irrespective of their methodological adequacy, may be a dangerous procedure, but it is interesting that Fairweather (1982) calculated that among 49 studies with verbal stimuli, 42 found no sex effect, 5 found more lateralization among males, and 2 more lateralization among females; with nonverbal stimuli, of 62 studies, 13 showed greater lateralization for males and 4 for females. It is particularly striking that of the 111 studies reporting on sex differences, 87 found no effect of that variable. Fairweather concludes that there is no evidence for sex differences on verbal divided visual field tasks, and slender evidence for it on nonverbal tasks. The only hint of a consistent finding is in facial recognition, stemming from the work of Italian laboratories (Umiltà, Brizzolara, Tabossi and Fairweather, 1978). McGlone's review of the same material is much more selective, and reaches the conclusion that the most parsimonious explanation for the reported findings is that there is less functional brain asymmetry in females.

Turning to dichotic listening, there have been fewer studies, but no clearer result. Even of the studies reviewed by McGlone, nine out of fourteen found no effect of sex, and even when an effect is found, for example in the dichotic presentation of consonant-vowel syllables, some studies have found a stronger right ear advantage for females (Dorman and Porter, 1975) and others for males (Harshman, Remington and Krashen, 1974; Lake and Bryden, 1976).

Matters are complicated by the presence of differences in sensory and perceptual performance between the sexes, and by the suggestion that there may be differences between males and females in cognitive strategy. The idea here is that females prefer to adopt 'verbal strategies', and males 'nonverbal' ones (Bryden, 1978). Incidentally, Metzger and Antes in 1976 showed that instructing subjects explicitly to adopt a certain strategy had a general effect on performance, but it did not affect the basic pattern of cerebral asymmetry inferred to underlie task performance. However, the concept of differential strategy utilization is still often discussed as either a cause or an effect of fundamental differences in cerebral lateralization. Strategy adoption, as a sex-linked factor, clearly could have the observed effects on task performance (and criticisms of the mechanism, for example in Harshman *et al.* have often confused within-individual effects with the effects which might be seen when the results of a group of subjects are collated). However, the operation of this mechanism has yet to be experimentally demonstrated, rather than proposed as a *post hoc* explanation.

What view are we therefore to take? Is it that there really are sex differences in brain organization, but that they are subtle and often masked by other sources of variability in task performance? The within-sex variability is perhaps large in comparison with the mean between-sex difference, and the more substantial effects of individual differences in memory function may also swamp any other effects which might be present. That so few studies are designed with the intent of studying sex differences may also explain why so few find these effects on subsequent analysis. We may adopt the position of McGlone and believe that the effects are elusive, although real, and that when they can be demonstrated they show that females have a less lateralized brain. Alternatively, we may follow Fairweather and consider that the evidence is too thin and inconsistent to allow us to include sex in any theory of cerebral laterality (or laterality in any theory of sex differences). My personal inclination is for the latter position. Sex differences have not to date been shown convincingly as present either in the effects of clinical lesions or in the neuropsychological performance of normal subjects. We have to await the accumulation of further evidence to prove this view too cautious.

HANDEDNESS

Handedness is one of the most obvious ways in which the performance of some people differs from that of the majority. Although the precise figure depends on how left handedness is defined, most surveys find that between about 8 and 12 per cent of the population is left handed. This figure seems typical of most contemporary cultures, and to have been invariant through recorded history. There is even evidence that in prehistoric man roughly this proportion was sinistral.

The study of sinistrality is a major topic in its own right, with sociological, culture and even religious aspects. There have been many theories about the origins of left handedness, but ever since asymmetries in the nervous system were first recognized, the major theories have all linked handedness in some way with cerebral laterality (see Corballis and Beale, 1976; Hardyck and Petrinovich, 1977; Herron, 1980).

Against this background, the contribution of genetic factors to the determination of handedness has never been denied. Left handed children are commonly the children of left handed parents, and it can be shown that this is not merely due to cultural transmission. In fact it has been found that left handed parents may more strongly discourage sinistrality in their children because of their awareness of its disadvantages. In recent years there has been a debate between two opposing theories: that of Annett (1978) and that of Levy and Nagylaki (1972). Much of this debate is relatively technical, and the Levy-Nagylaki model is well specified. However, although a more specific model, it seems to account less well for all the available data than Annett's model. The latter is known as the 'right shift' model, because it involves the inheritance of a single factor which shifts handedness towards right preference. Of individuals who do not inherit the factor, half will be of each handedness by random chance variation; among those who do inherit the factor, most, although not all, will be right handed. One of the simplest predictions of this model is that of the children of two left handed parents (who in most cases cannot inherit the right shift factor), almost half will be left handed. This, and more complex, predictions seem to be borne out fairly well by the data.

Much of the research on handedness assumes that the measurement of handedness is a simple matter. It is not. There is no true dichotomy between right and left handers. Although the majority of people perform all skilled actions preferentially with the right hand, the remainder of the population form a continuum out to 'pure' left handedness. Much of the discussion about handedness fails to take this adequately into account. It is, however, recognized in the questionnaires generally employed to assess handedness (Annett, 1970; Bryden, 1977; McFarland and Anderson, 1980).

As a final general point, it should be remembered that handedness occurs in a general setting of biological asymmetries. Although the link with some of these may not appear very direct, for example the hair-whorl on the crown of the head, fingerprints, nostril size and the arrangement of the male testicles, the association with others, such as sighting dominance (which eye you use for a telescope) or footedness, may be more clear. However, while all these phenomena show a statistical relationship with handedness due to an underlying general biological factor, none shows a very direct relation. For example, ocular dominance has less connection with handedness than is often assumed. The association, if any, is a very complex one (Birkett, 1977; Porac and Coren, 1976).

Handedness and Cerebral Dominance

It is now unfashionable to speak of 'cerebral dominance' as a general factor determining laterality, although contemporary theories continue to use the idea quite freely under a number of guises. They may speak of 'dominance for speech' or 'dominance for phoneme discrimination' or whatever specific function is being considered, but in fact all theories involving handedness imply a general factor determining the overall pattern of laterality. There are four ways in which this factor might be linked with handedness:

1. *Pathological left handedness.* This idea has a very long history and is simply that stress or trauma in early life, especially around birth, may result in left handedness. The observation of an unusually high rate of left handedness among many groups of abnormal children and adults, especially those with some dysfunction of the central nervous system, has always been used as an argument to support this idea. If we accept that intelligence is normally distributed in the population (and psychologists arrange that measured IQ, follows this theoretical statistical distribution), there are more left handed people at the lower end of the range than would be expected by statistical variation. This can be explained by the depression of intelligence as a result of accident or pathology. In the same way, handedness is thought to be affected by early damage or injury. This argument reveals the

cultural bias which has often linked sinistrality ('sinister') to weakness and even evil, and we might well question whether the depression of intelligence can be considered a parallel to a shift from right to left handedness. However, pathology is still an important factor in some explanations of left handedness, and there is no doubt that severe abnormal states can be associated with disorders of the nervous system and may result in a variety of atypical patterns of handedness. There is much more doubt whether less severe birth stress and trauma, which do not produce any overt abnormality, can be considered to lead to a shift in hand preference. The evidence about this is discussed below.

2. *The contralateral rule.* This concept is much more simply stated and underlies many popular accounts and discussions of handedness. The concept is that speech dominance is always located in the hemisphere contralateral to the preferred hand. Stated another way, if almost all right handers have left hemisphere speech dominance, then left handers must have right speech dominance. Curiously, although it has never received much support from the scientific research, the idea often crops up in discussions by anthropologists, palaeontologists and biologists of the development of language, tool use and manual skill, when speech lateralization in the evolution of language is often linked to asymmetries of skilled performance. To be fair, it is not necessarily implied that the relation between speech lateralization and skilled manual performance must also hold for left handers, but such a relation is often assumed, so that the mirror image nature of left preferrent performance is extended to a mirror image model of the nervous system.

3. *Bilateralization.* This is probably the most popular position adopted, but is also the most vague. It states that left handers, who include 'mixed' handers either implicitly or explicitly, have a lesser degree of lateralization than the right handed, just as we have seen argued for females. Occasionally the small group of 'pure' left handers are excluded (and then follow the contralateral rule), but this is not generally the case. The reasons for this relative bilateralization are rarely clearly stated, and it is more common for this position to emerge from a review of the available evidence on lateralization of function and handedness.

4. *The right shift model.* Annett (1982) has recently argued that the right shift model of genetic determination of handedness predicts a pattern of cerebral asymmetry for the left handed which is distinct from the bilateralization model. Annett very clearly demonstrates how the strictness of the criterion for what we would consider left

handedness has an important effect on the pattern of cerebral asymmetry to be expected for that group. If the criterion is strict, so that only the more extreme sinistrals are included, then very few will have the right shift factor, and just over half will have left hemisphere speech. As the criterion becomes more lax, more individuals will be included who have the right shift factor, and the proportion with left hemisphere speech will rise as a result since the right shift factor is, of course, considered not only to increase the probability of right handedness, but at the same time of left hemisphere speech. The direct association between speech lateralization and hand preference is still evident, if less directly determined.

All these models make predictions about the pattern of asymmetry to be observed in clinical phenomona and in laboratory performance. The predictions to be made from the pathological model are least clear, but are generally taken to imply some reversal, perhaps with a degree of disorganization, of observed laterality. The contralateral rule predicts reversed patterns of asymmetry, and the bilateralization model that no asymmetry will be observed. Annett's model predicts a reduced degree of the normal pattern to be found with right handers. It would seem, therefore, easy to test between these different predictions. In practice it is not. The pathological model admits results indicating a weak degree of asymmetry, especially if they are in the 'reversed' direction. The bilateralization model admits all results which show any weak degree of laterality in either direction, allowing for sampling bias, errors of measurement, and so on. The right shift model is compatible, on the same grounds, with no asymmetry and even weak reversal, and with a strict criterion of sinistrality, it becomes practically indistinguishable from the bilateralization model. Nevertheless, we must try to evaluate these models in the light of the available evidence.

Two final factors must be mentioned before we turn to the evidence. One is *familial sinistrality*, that is, whether the individual has any relatives who are left handed. This factor is often included as an added dimension in studies of laterality, although its theoretical significance is not always clear; it should, of course, distinguish between 'inherited' and 'pathological' handedness, if such a distinction were to prove valid. It is sometimes linked to the second factor, the *strength* of handedness. This variable can be extracted from questionnaire responses or from measures of lateral dexterity or performance speed. Although Searleman, Tweedy and Springer (1979), for example, have shown strength of handedness and familial sinistrality to be unrelated, it is still often assumed that left handers with sinistral relatives are purely or extremely left handed, and hence right handers with sinistral relatives must be less clearly right handed than those without. It is expected that these variables will be found in the laterality observed on experimental tasks.

The Evidence about Left Handed Brains

The first question to be answered is whether the concept of pathological left handedness receives any significant support. Bakan (1977) has been one of the foremost proponents of this idea, and has defended it against a number of criticisms. He has also shown that there is an excess of left handers among first and late (fourth or later) positions in birth order, which he claims links sinistrality with birth stress. He goes further and specifically proposes that the left handedness results from damage to the left hemisphere pyramidal motor pathways following perinatal anoxia. Nevertheless, other workers have failed to support Bakan's findings. For example, Hicks, Elliott, Garbesi and Martin (1979) constructed a study which they considered would give the greatest chance of replicating the Bakan results. They found, however, that the relationship between handedness and a combination of factors known to be associated with high risk birth was 'trivial'. Annett and Ockwell (1980) found only the weakest relationship for daughters but none for sons, while Leiber and Axelrod (1981) found the slightest of links for sons but none for daughters. The current situation is that the gravest doubt is cast upon the validity of a contribution of birth stress to the determination of handedness.

Turning to the clinical evidence, two methods have already been introduced (see p. 127). The Wada technique by which sodium amytal is introduced into the carotid artery, so interrupting function in the hemisphere on the same side as the injection for a brief period, has given us some data on the speech lateralization of left handers. Rasmussen and Milner's 1975 data has already appeared in Table 7.1, and shows that of the left handers studied, about 70 per cent had left hemisphere speech, 15 per cent right hemisphere speech and 15 per cent had speech bilaterally represented.

The second method mentioned in Chapter 7 was the study of the frequency and severity of aphasia following unilateral lesions of the left or right hemisphere. This is a complicated issue when studied in detail, but Satz's analysis of the studies reported between 1935 and 1973 is probably the clearest summary for our purposes. In its most recent form (Carter, Hoheneggar and Satz, 1980), it suggests a model in which 24 per cent of left handers have left sided speech, none right sided speech and 76 per cent bilateral speech.

A third, although less important, method might also be mentioned: the study of unilateral ECT (Warrington and Pratt, 1973, 1981). ECT (electroconvulsive therapy) for depression is now often administered unilaterally to avoid some of the undesired after-effects of bilateral treatment, which may include interference with verbal memory. Such interference is minimized if the shock is given only on the side which is not dominant for speech. The studies which established this aspect of the unilateral method, and the early treatments which may be given to either side in order to establish speech laterality, also yield information which is of relevance here. What the studies suggest is that left sided speech is to be found in about 70 per cent of left handers, in line with the Wada technique results. Incidentally, Warrington and Pratt found that neither dichotic listening indices nor the hand used for writing could be used to determine speech laterality with any confidence.

What are we to make of this clinically derived evidence? There are problems associated with each of the methods discussed. All are concerned with abnormal subjects, and the general problems of comparing the effects of clinical lesions in different groups apply to the aphasia evidence. The Wada technique is also highly stressful for the patient and imposes severe practical limitations upon testing. The inferences drawn from the study of ECT are particularly indirect, and depressed patients may well have an abnormal pattern of cerebral lateralization (see Chapter 15). Criteria for left handedness also differ between studies. Finally, it is probable that the nature of the testing and the way that responses are scored make a definite finding of right or left lateralization more likely for the Wada and ECT methods than for the aphasia assessments. So, bearing in mind this point, we might conclude that very few, if any, left handers have right hemisphere speech, at least a third have clear left hemisphere speech, and the remainder, between a half and two thirds, have relatively bilateral speech in which the greater contribution comes from the left hemisphere.

What about the evidence from experimental neuropsychology? The work of Geffen and colleagues on a dichotic listening test which would predict speech laterality, and their encouraging results, were discussed in Chapter 11 (see p. 217). The studies of this group have included left handers, and have shown that a left ear advantage or no advantage is more common among left handers than right handers, although handedness did not affect the relative magnitude of the asymmetry. Familial sinistrality in male left handers increased the probability of finding a right ear advantage, and therefore left hemisphere speech (Geffen and Traub, 1979, 1980).

There are a very considerable number of studies using the dichotic listening and divided visual field techniques which have included handedness as a subject variable. Rather as with sex, it has been easy to add handedness as a variable in a study never designed to investigate this factor and the result has been equally unsatisfactory. Happily, there are some valuable reviews of this rather baffling literature: Annett (1982), Hardyck (1977), Hardyck and Petrinovich (1977), and Levy (1980). Both Annett and Hardyck include a tabulation of the most prominent studies and their results. Unhappily, however, the reveiws do not entirely agree in their conclusions.

Annett shows that the usual kind of divided visual field study, using verbal stimuli and obtaining a right visual field advantage for right handers, generally produces no asymmetry in left handers. Of the 15 studies quoted, only one found a left field superiority, while two found the right field to be superior. The picture was much the same for the 13 nonverbal studies cited. Most showed a left field advantage for right handers, but no asymmetry for left handers. For this group, two studies found a left, and three a right, visual field advantage. Familial sinistrality was reviewed independently in 19 studies and the variable was considered to add 'nothing substantial' to the results. It was occasionally found to reduce the lateral advantage of right handers, and to be linked with a trend to reversed asymmetry in left handers, but these effects were neither strong nor clear. Annett concludes that on visual tasks, left handers show no overall asymmetry, especially if left handedness is strictly defined.

Hardyck, by contrast, considers familial sinistrality of significance, and his review leads to a model in which the right handed without sinistral relatives are the most strongly lateralized. Left handers with sinistral relatives are the most bilateral. Right handers with left handed relatives and left handers without left handed relatives are intermediate and show weak (but not reversed) lateralization.

Levy reaches yet a different conclusion. She considers that a few sinistrals have strong right hemisphere language (although this is based principally upon the clinical evidence), but that the majority show weaker left hemisphere language in comparison with right handed subjects. (This is having discounted the small number of sinistrals whose left handedness can be attributed to major early disruption of the left hemisphere, and whose speech functions are then controlled from the right hemisphere.)

In so far as all these studies can be seen to present a common view, they suggest that very few if any left handers have right hemisphere speech. When the latter is observed in individual subjects, it is more commonly in a clinical than an experimental context. It may well be that the small number of cases of reversed dominance results from abnormal processes, and that in normal subjects right hemisphere speech is a rare phenomenon. All the reports agree that the majority of left handers will show weak or relatively bilateral left hemisphere speech lateralization. (The proportion of these individuals whose tendency to left sided speech will be sufficiently pronounced to consider them to have clear left speech dominance will depend on the criteria for dominance, and will probably also be influenced by the criteria adopted for left handedness.) There seems a clear agreement, therefore, that left handedness is in general associated with a reduced degree of cerebral lateralization.

Having reached this conclusion it is not surprising that there are reports, as we have already noted, of a weak relationship between handedness and speech laterality as assessed by dichotic listening (Searleman, 1980); that left handers show greater variability across occasions of testing (Hines, Fennell, Bowers and Satz, 1980); and that for left handers there is no clear correlation between the results of visual and auditory tests (Hines and Satz, 1974).

The conclusion concerning familial sinistrality is less clear. While it seems to have been agreed that the existence of sinistral relatives is likely to be associated with a shift away from strong left hemisphere speech, it has not been agreed how important is the contribution of this variable.

In terms of the four models with which we started, pathological processes appear to provide a significant explanation in only a very small number of cases, and they cannot be considered relevant to any general explanation of left handedness. There is also no evidence to support the operation of the contralateral rule. However, the evidence is broadly in agreement with both the bilateralization and the right shift models. As we noted, it is very difficult to devise a critical test between these two models given present techniques. The clinical evidence would marginally favour the bilateralization model because of the large proportion reported to have clear left sided speech. However, it could be argued that this is not entirely incompatible, given certain methodological considerations, with the right shift model. Annett has shown that the experimental evidence can fit very well with the right shift model, and if this model is accepted to explain the inheritance of handedness, then it also seems to serve fairly well as an interpretation of observations of cerebral laterality in different handedness groups. It certainly seems that this, or some other version of the general bilateralization model, provides a good description of how left handed brains differ from right handed ones.

Differences in Cerebral Mechanisms

While most workers have been content to present the empirical evidence of performance differences between left and right handers, a few have asked how these differences might be expressed in cognitive operations. Semmes (1968) developed an influential model of hemispheric function, suggesting that organization was 'focal' in the left hemisphere and 'diffuse' in the right hemisphere, with consequent advantages for verbal and spatial processes respectively. She admitted, however, that the model could not account for the cerebral organization found in many left handers.

Levy (1974) developed a model based upon a different dichotomy, between 'analytic' and 'global' processing. Within this model, left handers are specifically catered for, and are considered to have bilateral representation of the functions based upon analytic processes normally located in the left hemisphere in right handers. However, while speech, language, writing and calculation are represented in both hemispheres, there is no corresponding bilateralization of 'normal' right hemisphere functions. These suffer in left handers by being crowded out by the verbal functions. Levy has more recently expanded this model to include sex differences in cerebral organization and orientation of writing hand (see p. 263) (Levy, 1980; Levy and Gur, 1980). This theory has become quite complex. Nevertheless, it still contains the idea that left handedness generally indicates a bilateralization of certain functions, which is in turn seen in a superior level of these abilities. The functions for which no fully specialized hemisphere exists will show a deficiency in performance. Handedness is, however, only one factor among others, including birth stress, genetic factors and fetal sex hormones, which may be linked with a depression in the level of ability.

A different model was proposed by Beaumont (1974). This was that left handers showed a general diffuseness of cerebral organization in all functions in comparison with the relative focal organization of the right handed. This was considered to lead to an advantage on certain cognitive functions, but a deficiency on others. The more complex the integration required by the task, the greater the advantage for the left hander, irrespective of whether the task was 'verbal' or 'spatial'. This model was supported by evidence from divided visual field studies.

These last two models have been reviewed by Hardyck (1977). He finds more support for Beaumont's than for Levy's model, but rightly criticizes the lack of an independent criterion of task complexity. His second criticism, that a more diffuse system must imply longer processing times of complex tasks, does not really follow from the model. However, he himself develops a new form of the model, which does have certain advantages over its predecessor. Hardyck's idea is that the most bilateral individuals, left handers with sinistral relatives, will employ more interhemispheric processing. This idea can be extended to generate specific predictions about certain tasks, for instance, that left handers will have an advantage for identity judgements in divided visual field performance, and will make more errors with mirror image stimuli. This model fits well with much of the data, and deserves more attention than it has attracted. In particular, tests of some of the specific predictions would be welcome.

Are Left Handers Less Able?

An issue related to that of the cognitive mechanisms which may distinguish left and right handers is whether left handers are less proficient in certain abilities. Levy (1969) had reported that sinistrals were inferior on nonverbal or 'performance' intelligence subtests, such as are found in the Wechsler Adult Intelligence Scale (WAIS), and this finding was confirmed by Miller (1971) using different tests. That left handers could have such a fundamental handicap was greeted with some scepticism, and it was argued that the populations studied were in some way unusual. In both studies they were students, who are generally selected for their verbal abilities. This might have biased the results in that the left handers examined may have been in some respects atypical of the majority of left handers in the pattern of their abilities.

The doubt cast on these studies was strengthened by the findings of three large-scale studies of the general population: the Oxfordshire Villages Survey in Britain (Newcombe and Ratcliff, 1973); a study of 7,119 schoolchildren in the United States (Roberts and Engle, 1974); a survey of 7,688 children tested by Hardyck, Petrinovich and Goldman (1976). These studies found no evidence that handedness was in any way related to the pattern of verbal and performance abilities. In view of the serious implications which such a handicap would have for left handers, this has been thought to be the more reasonable result.

Nevertheless, some evidence continues to appear of such differences between handedness groups. Bradshaw, Nettleton and Taylor (1981) again found the WAIS Performance deficit among sinistral students, particularly among those with left handed relatives. Hicks and Beveridge (1978) confirmed some of their earlier work by finding that left handers were inferior to right handers on a general factor of intelligence, and although Heim and Watts (1976) did not find differences in the level of ability on three intellectual factors, they did find a specific deficit in numerical ability. This last study was of a large sample of 2,165 nine- to twenty-year-olds. Lastly, a specific deficit in reading abilities was reported by Cohen and Freeman (1978). Left handers were found to be poorer at silent reading, although they had adequate comprehension. They also suffered more, while reading out loud, from visual distortion introduced into the text, although they were less affected by linguistic distortion. This suggests a different strategy in the left handed for reading, based more on visual analysis, which in some situations may prove less efficient.

It therefore appears that while there is no good evidence for a general and serious deficit in the intellectual abilities of left handers, we cannot discount that in certain groups of sinistrals there may be a limited range of functions which are impaired in comparison with right handers. How widespread and significant such a handicap may be has not yet been satisfactorily determined.

Writing Posture

A final topic which has attracted a great deal of interest recently has been that of writing posture. Levy and Reid (1978) reported that speech lateralization, as shown by a divided visual field task, could be predicted by the hand and posture used for writing. They divided hand postures into the 'normal' and the 'inverted'. Although the criteria for this division has never been quite clear, in the normal position the pen points to the top of the page whilst writing. In the inverted posture it points towards the bottom. Inverted postures are rare in right handers, but are common among the left handed. In terms of speech lateralization, the normal posture was associated with speech control contralateral to the hand of writing, while the inverted posture indicated ipsilateral speech localization. Right normals and left inverts therefore must have left sided speech, while left normals must have right sided speech. If this model were supported, then it would be of tremendous value in providing a simple means of assessing speech laterality. Levy and Reid's data were most encouraging.

Unhappily, as seems the normal course in this area, subsequent studies did not unanimously support the model. Two have clearly supported it, and two have failed to provide any support, and indirect evidence has been found to support the model in only two out of three relevant studies. Finding partial support for the model, McKeever and Hoff (1979) attempted to develop it by introducing the idea of intrahemispheric disconnection of left hemisphere visual and manual motor areas. An additional problem is that the model does not seem to work when lateralization is assessed in the auditory modality by dichotic listening, rather than by a divided visual field task (Beaumont and McCarthy, 1981; McKeever and Van Deventer, 1980). This is at best an embarrassment for the model.

While there may well be something of significance about writing posture which can provide information about handedness and cerebral organization, the main findings have not as yet been clearly established. The difficulty of measuring writing posture has not helped to generate clear replicable results. What *is* clear is that on current evidence writing posture does not comprise a valid index of cerebral lateralization in individual subjects. Its initial exciting promise has yet to be fulfilled.

CONCLUSION

The study of individual differences in cerebral organization is an important area of research, particularly in view of the practical necessity in clinical applications of being able to establish the pattern of laterality in an individual patient. Of the two principal variables investigated, the findings with respect to the first, sex, are too inconsistent to allow of clear conclusions and the cautious reader should accept that definite sex differences have yet to be demonstrated. However, the second variable, handedness, shows more consistent findings in that left handedness appears to be associated with an abnormal pattern of cerebral lateralization, with most left handers having a relative bilateralization of function. This may be mediated through a relatively diffuse functional system which requires greater interhemispheric intercommunication in the left handed. Although there is still some suspicion that left handers may suffer distinct cognitive handicaps, large studies have generally failed to support this conclusion. Writing posture seems to reflect certain aspects of cerebral function, but cannot be used as an index of speech lateralization at the present time.

FURTHER READING

The best introduction to the topic of sex differences in cerebral organization is to be found in:

Fairweather, H., 'Sex Differences: Little Reason for Females to Play Midfield', in J. G. Beaumont, ed., *Divided Visual Field Studies of Cerebral Organisation* (London, Academic Press, 1982).

McGlone, J., 'Sex Differences in Human Brain Asymmetry', *Behavioral and Brain Sciences*, 3 (1980), 215–263. This includes associated commentaries.

On handedness, further reading might include:

Hardyck, C. and Petrinovich, L. F., 'Left-handedness', *Psychological Bulletin*, 84 (1977), 385–404.

Herron, J., ed., *Neuropsychology of Left-Handedness* (New York, Academic Press, 1980).

REFERENCES

Annett, M., 'A Classification of Hand Preference by Association Analysis', *British Journal of Psychology*, 61 (1970), 303–321.

Annett, M., 'A Single Gene Explanation of Right and Left Handedness and Brainedness' (Coventry, Lanchester Polytechnic, 1978).

Annett, M., 'Handedness', in J. G. Beaumont, ed., *Divided Visual Field Studies of Cerebral Organisation* (London, Academic Press, 1982).

Annett, M. and Ockwell, A., 'Birth Order, Birth Stress and Handedness', *Cortex*, 16 (1980), 181–188.

Bakan, P., 'Left Handedness and Birth Order Revisited', *Neuropsychologia*, 15 (1977), 837–840.

Beaumont, J. G., 'Handedness and Hemisphere Function', in S. J. Dimond and J. G. Beaumont, eds., *Hemisphere Function in the Human Brain* (London, Elek Science, 1974).

Beaumont, J. G. and McCarthy, R., 'Dichotic Ear Asymmetry and Writing Posture', *Neuropsychologia*, 19 (1981), 469–472.

Birkett, P., 'Measures of Laterality and Theories of Hemispheric Processes', *Neuropsychologia*, 15 (1977), 693–696.

Bradshaw, J. and Gates, A., 'Visual Field Differences in Verbal Tasks: Effects of Task Familiarity and Sex of Subject', *Brain and Language*, 5 (1978), 166–187.

Bradshaw, J., Nettleton, N. C. and Taylor, M. J., 'Right Hemisphere Language and Cognitive Deficit in Sinistrals?', *Neuropsychologia*, 19 (1981), 113–132.

Bryden, M. P., 'Response Bias and Hemispheric Differences in Dot Localization', *Perception and Psychophysics*, 19 (1976), 23–28.

Bryden, M. P., 'Measuring Handedness with Questionnaires', *Neuropsychologia*, 15 (1977), 617–624.

Bryden, M. P., 'Strategy Effects in the Assessment of Hemispheric Asymmetry', in G. Underwood, ed., *Strategies of Information Processing* (London, Academic Press, 1978).

Buffery, A. W. H. and Gray, J. A., 'Sex Differences in the Development of Perceptual and Linguistic Skills', In C. Ounsted and D. C. Taylor, eds., *Gender Differences: their Ontogeny and Significance* (London, Churchill-Livingstone, 1972).

Carter, R. L., Hohenegger, M. and Satz, P., 'Handedness and Aphasia: an Inferential Method for Determining the Mode of Cerebral Speech Specialisation', *Neuropsychologia*, 18 (1980), 569–574.

Cohen, G. and Freeman, R., 'Individual Differences in Reading Strategies in Relation to Handedness and Cerebral Asymmetry', in J. Requin, ed., *Attention and Performance, VII* (Hillsdale, N. J., Lawrence Erlbaum Associates, 1978).

Corballis, M. C. and Beale, I. L., *The Psychology of Left and Right* (Hillsdale, N. J., Lawrence Erlbaum Associates, 1976).

Davidoff, J., 'Hemispheric Differences in Dot Detection', *Cortex*, 13 (1977), 434–444.

Dorman, M. and Porter, R., 'Hemispheric Lateralization for Speech Perception in Stutterers', *Cortex*, 11 (1975), 181–185.

Fairweather, H., 'Sex Differences in Cognition', *Cognition*, 4 (1976), 231–280.

Fairweather, H., 'Sex Differences: Little Reason for Females to Play Midfield', in J. G. Beaumont, ed., *Divided Visual Field Studies of Cerebral Organisation* (London, Academic Press, 1982).

Geffen, G. and Traub, E., 'Preferred Hand and Familial Sinistrality in Dichotic Monitoring', *Neuropsychologia*, 17 (1979), 527–531.

Geffen, G. and Traub, E., 'The Effects of Duration of Stimulation, Preferred Hand and Familial Sinistrality in Dichotic Monitoring', *Cortex*, 16 (1980), 83–94.

Hannay, H. J. and Boyer, C., 'Sex Differences in Hemispheric Asymmetry Revisited', *Perceptual and Motor Skills*, 47 (1978), 317–321.

Hardyck, C., 'A Model of Individual Differences in Hemispheric Functioning', in H. Whitaker and H. A Whitaker, eds., *Studies in Neurolinguistics*, vol. 3 (London, Academic Press, 1977).

Hardyck, C. and Petrinovich, L. F., 'Left-handedness', *Psychological Bulletin*, 84 (1977), 385–404.

Hardyck, C., Petrinovich, L. F. and Goldman, R. D., 'Left-handedness and Cognitive Deficit', *Cortex*, 12 (1976), 266–279.

Harshman, R., Remington, R. and Krashen, D., 'Sex, Language and the Brain. Part II: Evidence from Dichotic Listening for Adult Sex Differences in Verbal Lateralization', paper presented to UCLA Conference on Human Brain Function, Los Angeles (1974).

Heim, A. W. and Watts, K. P., 'Handedness and Cognitive Bias', *Quarterly Journal of Experimental Psychology*, 28 (1976), 355–360.

Herron, J., ed., *Neuropsychology of Left-Handedness* (New York, Academic Press, 1980).

Hicks, R. A. and Beveridge, R., 'Handedness and Intelligence', *Cortex*, 14 (1978), 304–307.

Hicks, R. A., Elliott, D., Garbesi, L. and Martin, S., 'Multiple Birth Risk Factors and the Distribution of Handedness', *Cortex*, 15 (1979), 135–137.

Hines, D. and Satz, P., 'Cross-modal Asymmetries in Perception Related to Asymmetry in Cerebral Function', *Neuropsychologia*, 12 (1974), 239–247.

Hines, D., Fennell, E. B., Bowers, D. and Satz, P., 'Left Handers Show Greater Test-retest Variability in Auditory and Visual Asymmetry', *Brain and Language*, 10 (1980), 208–211.

Hutt, C., *Males and Females* (London, Penguin, 1972).

Kail, R. and Siegel, A., 'Sex and Hemispheric Differences in the Recall of Verbal and Spatial Information', *Cortex*, 14 (1978), 557–563.

Lake, D. and Bryden, M. P., 'Handedness and Sex Differences in Hemispheric Asymmetry', *Brain and Language*, 3 (1976), 266–282.

Leiber, L. and Axelrod, S., 'Not All Sinistrality is Pathological', *Cortex*, 17 (1981), 259–271.

Levy, J., 'Possible Basis for the Evolution of Lateral Specialization of the Human Brain', *Nature*, 224 (1969), 614–615.

Levy, J., 'Psychological Implications of Biological Asymmetry', in S. J. Dimond and J. G. Beaumont, eds., *Hemisphere Function in the Human Brain* (London, Elek Science, 1974).

Levy, J., 'Cerebral Asymmetry and the Psychology of Man', in M. C. Wittrock, ed., *The Brain and Psychology* (New York, Academic Press, 1980).

Levy, J. and Gur, R. C., 'Individual Differences in Psychoneurological Organization', in J. Herron, ed., *Neuropsychology of Left-Handedness* (New York, Academic Press, 1980).

Levy, J. and Nagylaki, T., 'A model for the Genetics of Handedness', *Genetics*, 72 (1972), 117–128.

Levy, J. and Reid, M., 'Variations in Cerebral Organization as a Function of Handedness, Hand Posture in Writing, and Sex', *Journal of Experimental Psychology: General*, 107 (1978), 119–144.

Maccoby, E. E. and Jacklin, C. N., *The Psychology of Sex Differences* (Stanford, Calif., University of Stanford Press, 1974).

McFarland, K. and Anderson, J., 'Factor Stability of the Edinburgh Handedness Inventory as a Function of Test-retest Performance, Age and Sex', *British Journal of Psychology*, 71 (1980), 135–142.

McGlone, J., 'Sex Differences in Functional Brain Asymmetry', *Cortex*, 14 (1978), 122–128.

McGlone, J., 'Sex Differences in Human Brain Asymmetry', *Behavioral and Brain Sciences*, 3 (1980), 215–263.

McKeever, W. F. and Hoff, A. L., 'Evidence of a Possible Isolation of Left Hemisphere Visual and Motor Areas in Sinistrals Employing an Inverted Handwriting Posture', *Neuropsychologia*, 17 (1979), 445–455.

McKeever, W. F. and Van Deventer, A., 'Visual and Auditory Language Processing Asymmetries: Influences of Handedness, Familial Sinistrality and Sex', *Cortex*, 13 (1977), 225–241.

McKeever, W. F. and Van Deventer, A., 'Inverted Handwriting Position, Language Laterality and the Levy-Nagylaki Genetic Model of Handedness and Cerebral Organisation', *Neuropsychologia*, 18 (1980), 99–102.

Metzger, R. and Antes, J., 'Sex and Coding Strategy Effects on Reaction Time to Hemispheric Probes', *Memory and Cognition*, 4 (1976), 167–171.

Miller, E., 'Handedness and the Pattern of Human Ability', *British Journal of Psychology*, 62 (1971), 111–112.

Newcombe, F. and Ratcliff, G., 'Handedness, Speech Lateralisation and Ability', *Neuropsychologia*, 11 (1973), 399–407.

Porac, C. and Coren, S., 'The Dominant Eye', *Psychological Bulletin*, 83 (1976), 880–897.

Rasmussen, T. and Milner, B., 'Clinical and Surgical Studies of the Cerebral Speech Areas in Man', in K. J. Zülch, O. Creutzfeldt and G. C. Galbraith, eds., *Cerebral Localization* (Berlin, Springer-Verlag, 1975).

Rizzolatti, G. and Buchtel, H. A., 'Hemispheric Superiority in Reaction Time to Faces: a Sex Difference', *Cortex*, 13 (1977), 300–305.

Roberts, J. and Engle, A., 'Family Background, Early Development and Intelligence of Children 6–11 years', *Data from the National Health Survey, Series 11, No. 142* (DHEW Publication No. (HRA) 75–1624. Washington, D. C., GPO, 1974).

Sasanuma, S. and Kobayashi, Y., 'Tachistoscopic Recognition of Line Orientation', *Neuropsychologia*, 16 (1978), 239–242.

Searleman, A., 'Subject Variables and Cerebral Organisation for Language', *Cortex*, 16 (1980), 239–254.

Searleman, A., Tweedy, J. and Springer, S. P., 'Interrelationships among Subject Variables Believed to Predict Cerebral Organisation', *Brain and Language*, 7 (1979), 267–276.

Semmes, J., 'Hemispheric Specialization: a Possible Clue to Mechanism', *Neuropsychologia*, 6 (1968), 11–26.

Umiltà, C., Brizzolara, D., Tabossi, P. and Fairweather, H., 'Factors Affecting Face Recognition in the Cerebral Hemispheres: Familiarity and Naming', in J. Requin, ed., *Attention and Performance, VII* (Hillsdale, N. J., Lawrence Erlbaum Associates, 1978).

Warrington, E. K. and Pratt, R. T. C., 'Language Laterality in Left-handers Assessed by Unilateral ECT', *Neuropscyhologia*, 11 (1973), 423–428.

Warrington, E. K. and Pratt, R. T. C., 'The Significance of Laterality Effects', *Journal of Neurology, Neurosurgery and Psychiatry*, 44 (1981), 193–196.

IV

Applications

CHAPTER 14

Neuropsychological Practice

The neuropsychologist who applies his knowledge of the functions of the brain to clinical practice is likely to find that his major role is assessment of patients. The assessment is usually to assist in the diagnosis and localization of any cerebral pathology, but it may also be to establish a patient's current functional status to act as a basis for the design of his remedial or rehabilitative therapy, and to monitor his progress of treatment and recovery.

Neuropsychologists are becoming increasingly active in the design and execution of therapy programmes, contributing their specialized knowledge of the structure of human abilities, of the psychological aspects of training, and of specific behavioural methods, to the efforts of the remedial team. Nevertheless, although more clinical time is being devoted to such activities, the major concern of most clinical neuropsychologists is to contribute their peculiar skills in the assessment of cognitive abilities. In any clinic, neuropsychologists will be asked to see particular patients, and will typically be expected to provide an opinion on one of three questions: (1) whether the patient is suffering from any cerebral pathology, its nature, and whether focal or diffuse; (2) if focal cerebral pathology is present, which behavioural functions have been affected and what localization these imply; and (3) how the patient can best be helped in his return towards normal functioning.

The way in which answers might be sought to these three questions is sketched out below, but a general point should first be made. In trying to introduce as clearly as possible the relation between lesions and deficits, and the procedures of assessment and treatment, there is a danger that neuropsychological practice may seem to be simply a matter of following a well-charted routine. Nothing could be further from the truth. Neuropsychological practice involves sensitive and emphatic insight into the patient's problems, and a creative and questioning intellectual approach to his dysfunction, no less than in any other area of clinical psychology. As a naive graduate student I expected neurological patients to be much easier to deal with than psychiatric patients – after all they were only medically ill, like people with broken legs or liver complaints; they would, I thought, be cooperative, well-motivated and grateful for my help. My view of all types of patient has since matured. Many neurological patients are indeed a pleasure to meet, but, largely as a result of their neurological state, some may be poorly motivated, distractible and irritable. They often tire easily and suffer from headaches, causing bad temper, and consultation requires patience and empathy. Any assessment may have to be spread, in brief sessions, over many days. This makes clinical practice no less challenging and rewarding, but it is as well to remember the difficult conditions under which much assessment and therapy is carried out when reading the following sections.

TESTING FOR BRAIN DAMAGE

This is one of the classic demands directed to clinical psychologists or specialized neuropsychologists. It is, however, the demand which is least easy to satisfy. When psychologists are asked to give opinions as to whether a particular patient shows any form of brain damage or not, they are likely to refuse to answer so general a question, or at least to feel little confidence in their ability to answer it.

The difficulty arises with the assumption that there is some validity in the notion of a generalized phenomenon which can be called '*brain damage*'. It should by now be clear that there are a variety of pathological processes which can result in cerebral lesions: trauma from blows which may or may not pierce the skull (*open* or *closed* head injuries); tumours; cerebral diseases; poisoning by toxic substances; strokes; brain haemorrhages; and the side-effects of disorders of other bodily systems. These pathological processes may result in a diffuse pattern of lesions throughout the brain, or in more or less localized or focal lesions. The lesions may be in continuous progressive development, slow or rapid; or they may be static, the result of a single traumatic event. They may be chronic, of long-standing, or acute and recently acquired. Lesions of course affect different hemispheres and different lobes of the brain, and the evidence presented in Section II showed how these variables could be related to different resulting deficits. Also take into account the patient's age, his premorbid level of achievements and abilities, and his current motivation, and it will be easy to see what a dramatic range of behavioural disturbances, in both variety and severity, may follow damage to the brain.

Much time and effort were devoted during the decade following the Second World War to trying to establish some single factor which would characterize 'brain damage'; it was hoped that by measuring such a factor it would be possible readily to determine the presence or absence of brain damage. The result of this research was, in essence, that no single factor could be identified. The only single aspect of psychological function which has any claim to be generally affected by any cerebral pathology is psychomotor speed. This is the speed with which simple tasks, usually requiring some active motor participation in response, can be carried out. It involves both speed of thinking and speed of motor execution. This might be useful were it not that this factor is equally affected by most functional psychiatric states, ruling out its application to the detection of brain damage.

The problem of *screening* for the presence of brain damage is nonetheless a practical clinical issue, and a number of single tests are employed to test for the presence of brain damage. Heaton, Baade and Johnson (1978) have usefully reviewed studies of the performance of these tests in making what is often the most difficult discrimination: between organic cerebral dysfunction and psychiatric states. They found that if chronic and process schizophrenics (those with long lasting and severe psychotic illnesses) were included, then the tests performed very poorly. If, however, these patients were excluded, then the median success rate for determining brain damage was about 75 per cent. The tests, in descending rank of success, included the Bender Gestalt Test (success enhanced by use of the Background Interference procedure), the Benton Visual Retention Test, the Trail Making Task, and the Memory for Designs test. The ability of these tests to discriminate between the brain damaged and psychiatric patients, excluding the chronic and process schizophrenics, was about equivalent to their ability to distinguish between the brain damaged and normals. It is a matter of opinion whether you regard these tests as successful and justified for use in clinical practice, but it is obvious that discrimination rates in the region of 75 per cent leave very considerable room for improvement.

An additional factor must also be taken into account in assessing the utility of these and other assessment tests: the effect of *base rates*. There is an interesting statistical phenomenon (most lucidly explained in Vernon (1964)) which results in the ability of a test result to identify a certain characteristic being dependent on the base rate of that characteristic, the base rate being the proportion of individuals in the tested population who possess the characteristic. Discrimination will be best when the characteristic occurs in 50 per cent of the population, and will decline dramatically as the base rate falls. In research studies which as part of their design employ equally-sized groups of those with and without brain damage, the success of a test to pick out the brain damaged will be considerably greater than when trying to screen for brain damage in a population where such damage might be expectected to occur in, perhaps, only 20 per cent of cases. Care should be taken that the base rates of the research studies match those of the target clinical populations.

It is also the case that when the old are to be tested, and determination of *cerebral dementia* in the old is a difficult and yet clinically important problem, the tests which are often employed may perform even less well. The Newcastle-upon-Tyne study (Savage, Britton, Bolton and Hall, 1973), found that indices derived from the Weschsler Adult Intelligence Scale (WAIS) tended to identify only a third to a half of the organic patients, at the same time misclassifying up to a third of normal subjects or psychiatric patients as organic. The Allen Index, which takes the difference between the summed scaled scores for the Information and Comprehension subtests and for the Digit Span and Digit Symbol subtests, correctly identified 52 per cent of the organics, but went on to declare 48 per cent of the psychiatric patients and 62 per cent of the normals as brain damaged! Two more specialized tests, a paired associate learning test and the Modified New Word Learning Test, performed rather better, but not at a satisfactory level. It is sometimes pointed out that in screening, false positives are less serious than false negatives because they will result in further investigation, following which pathology will be ruled out, rather than resulting in pathology being missed. This is to some extent true, but it depends somewhat on the context. In the case of the aged where organic and functional illnesses are most difficult to distinguish, it might well mean that a patient failed to receive treatment for a remediable functional psychiatric illness on the assumption that the problem was a progressive untreatable cerebral dementia.

Battery tests, which we shall shortly discuss, have also been used to detect generalized brain damage. They have had rather better success than the single tests, the Halstead-Reitan Battery showing a general level of discrimination of about 80 per cent (Boll, 1981), and the Luria-Nebraska of about 86 per cent, for the presence of brain damage. This is to some extent because they sample a broad range of psychological functions, and therefore have a greater opportunity to pick up whatever signs of dysfunction are present. The improved success comes at the expense of very lengthy testing which makes these procedures impractical as a general screening device for the presence of brain damage.

Before moving on to discuss the examination of specific functions, some of the difficulties which underlie the assessment of behavioural deficits should be pointed out. Two logical approaches can be taken to testing: direct and indirect. In *direct testing*, the patient's performance is measured premorbidly and then again following the onset of the lesion. This is the ideal state of affairs, but it is rarely possible. Occasionally, particularly in the case of servicemen, there will be recent formal assessments of intelligence and cognitive abilities which form an accurate baseline against which to measure subsequent decline. However, when this information is not available, the only direct approach is by repeated testing, perhaps weekly or monthly. Leaving aside the problems of teasing out the effects of familiarity with the test instrument, repeated testing may enable the development of the functional state to be charted but it will not give any information by which to assess the extent of decline from premorbid abilities.

As the direct approach is often not feasible, an *indirect approach* must be adopted. One version of this is to find some index by which the patient's premorbid level of functioning can be inferred. At one time it was thought that vocabulary ability was not affected by cerebral damage. This idea was based upon a further notion that vocabulary ability remains unaffected when other abilities decline during normal ageing (which is, incidentally, not true when stated this simply). It was argued that if brain dysfunction was like normal ageing, then vocabulary would remain stable and could be used as a pointer to premorbid intelligence. It is not surprising that this method has not been found to be valid. Vocabulary is, of course, affected by some cerebral lesions, and the way in which it is affected depends on the previous levels of ability and education; even hospitalization, in itself, is known to produce a decline in vocabulary ability. This approach has therefore fallen out of favour. However, one recent development, the New Adult Reading Test (Nelson and O'Connell, 1978), which is a simple test of the patient's ability to read a list of words, has been shown to predict with reasonable accuracy the premorbid intelligence level of dementing adults, and is being used in some clinics. It remains to be seen whether this develops into a useful and popular test.

The only approach which remains to the neuropsychologist, and another indirect one, is the use of inferences from the patient's history. It is possible to piece together from the patient's educational attainments, his occupational choice and success, and his pastimes and interests, a fairly accurate picture of the level and pattern of the patient's cognitive abilities. It will be easier in some cases than others, particularly if examinations have recently been passed, or particular occupations successfully taken up. However, it is all that the clinician often has to work with, and presents yet another challenge to his professional skill to develop an accurate and valid assessment from the information which he is able to collect, both by direct observation and by indirect inference.

THE ASSESSMENT OF SPECIFIC FUNCTIONS

It was noted in Chapter 1 that there are three distinct traditions in the approach to neuropsychological assessment of specific functions. These traditions are: behavioural neurology; the use of neuropsychological batteries; and the individual-centred normative approach. They can loosely be said to typify clinical neuropsychology in the Soviet Union, the United States, and Britain respectively.

Behavioural Neurology

This approach derives from the influential work of the Russian neuropsychologist A. R. Luria and is individual-centred and clinical in nature. The goal of neuropsychological assessment is not a quantitative measurement of the patient's difficulties, but a qualitative analysis and description of his problems. Rather than employing psychometric procedures to identify abnormal performance by statistical means, with reference to a normal population, the emphasis is on behaviours which any normal individual of the age, background and general ability of the patient should be able to perform. When such behaviours cannot be generated, then a deficit has been demonstrated. Particular attention is paid to the qualitative aspects of *how* a task is performed, instead of merely to the absolute level of performance which is observed.

The neuropsychological examination has four essential aspects. First, the psychologist begins from his knowledge of the different types of dysfunction which follow cerebral lesions, that is, he begins from a *model* of the organization of the brain. Secondly, in order to locate the areas of dysfunction to be investigated in depth, the initial stages of examination explore in a preliminary fashion the optic, auditory and kinaesthetic processes together with motor behaviour. Thirdly, in analysing the behavioural deficits observed, a distinction is maintained between deficits which follow from a primary failure in the system under investigation, and those which are a secondary result of some more general fundamental failure. Last, the examination must include tests of complex integrated activity, such as speech, reading, writing, comprehension and problem solving. The aim is a careful qualitative analysis of the entire range of the patient's activity, of the difficulties which he experiences, and the mistakes which he makes.

The investigation therefore begins with a general evaluation of the basic 'individual analysers' (optic, auditory, and so on) of Luria's model, considered in terms of the levels of direct sensory reaction, mnestic organization, and complex mediated operations. The tests available are short and are selected for their appropriateness to the patient. There is no rigid pattern of administration or scoring. The investigation then moves into a second phase designed to investigate in detail the problems of the individual patient, a period of individualized qualitative exploration.

Whilst maintaining a high regard for the insightful and persuasive nature of much of Luria's model, and an admiration for Luria's clinical skills, most Western psychologists have found this approach difficult to apply. However, considerable assistance to those attempting to employ the approach was given by Christensen's publication of a systematized version of the tests used in Luria's clinic (Christensen, 1974). While only covering the initial stages of the investigation, it provides a source of materials and procedures for use in assessment. The text is divided into main sections such as the Investigation of Acoustico-motor Organization, of Higher Cutaneous and Kinaesthetic Functions, of Impressive Speech, and so on. Each of these is divided into subsections for which a number of simple test procedures are supplied. The Investigation of Acoustico-motor Organization is broken down into the investigation of perception and the reproduction of pitch relationships, and the perception and reproduction of rhythmic structures. The first of these is further subdivided into the perception of pitch and the reproduction of pitch relationships and musical melodies; the second into perception and evaluation of acoustic signals and motor performances of rhythmic groups. For each of about three or four dysfunctions which might be observed under each of these subdivisions, a lesion site is suggested. For example, in motor performance of rhythmic groups, using the four little tests of rhythmic reproduction suggested, if the patient does not fully apprehend the incorrectness of his performance, a right temporal lesion is indicated, but a lesion of the frontotemporal division of the cortex is indicated if the patient exhibits marked incoordination in all tests. This version does not reflect fully the philosophy behind Luria's work but it conveys something of the character and flexibility of the approach. For a good description of the application of Luria's approach, the paper by Luria and Majovsky (1977) is a useful introduction to the fuller account in Luria (1980).

The advantages of Luria's method are first that it is based upon an explicit theoretical foundation, his model of cerebral organization, although this model (as noted on p. 59, for example) has not always been supported by empirical evidence. Secondly, it emphasizes the qualitative aspects of performance and is flexible in approaching the diagnosis of functional deficits. Particularly in view of our imperfect knowledge of cerebral organization and function, this latter aspect might be expected to result in greater accuracy and finer resolution in the final description of a patient's difficulties.

The disadvantage is that the system depends almost entirely upon the clinical acumen and skill of the neuropsychologist. In the hands of Luria, the results are impressive, as the published case reports demonstrate. However, the approach demands a comprehensive grasp of the details of Luria's complex theoretical model. There are no rigorous investigations of the validity of the procedures in routine application, and the result, in the West, has been some suspicion of the 'clinical-analytical' approach, and a reluctance to apply it in regular practice.

Neuropsychological Batteries

The strict psychometric approach, in complete contrast with behavioural neurology, has been more popular in the United States than elsewhere. While it would be false to give the impression that this is the only approach adopted there, it is the only region where the employment of neuropsychological batteries has been taken up with any enthusiasm, and if anything, the trend is towards increasing popularity.

Historically, there have been a number of batteries which have been widely used in clinical practice. However, two are currently of major importance: the Halstead-Reitan Neuropsychological Battery and the Luria-Nebraska Neuropsychological Battery.

The *Halstead-Reitan Neuropsychological Battery* has been gradually developed by Reitan and co-workers over a number of years from tests originally selected, on a largely pragmatic basis, by Halstead in the 1940s. The exact tests which make up the battery vary a little from clinic to clinic, but the tests seek to cover as comprehensive a range of behavioural functions as is possible. The Halstead Category Test (see

Fig. 3.1) is a concept attainment task involving learning, memory, mental efficiency and adaptability. The Tactual Performance Test is a formboard test, with repeated presentations in which improvement in speed can be observed, culminating in a blindfold trial in which the patient must remember the location of the holes which take each shape. The Rhythm Test is drawn from the Seashore Tests of Musical Ability (see p. 72), and the Speech-Sounds Perception Test involves multiple-choice identification of auditorily presented nonsense words. The Finger Oscillation Test examines simple motor speed. Most versions of the battery include all the above tests.

Also employed are the 'allied procedures', comprising: the Trail Making Test in which numbered or lettered circles are to be joined in sequence, or by alternating letters and numbers, by a pencil line; a Strength of Grip Test; and the Sensory-Perceptual Examination of tactile, visual and auditory modalities. To these are added three tests of tactile perception and a modified form of the Halstead-Wepman Aphasia Screening Test. The full WAIS is often also given.

It will be appreciated that this battery takes a long time to administer. Even with uninterrupted testing a period of six to eight hours is required, and with a distractible or easily fatigued patient testing may have to be undertaken over many days. Nevertheless, the battery has been widely used, and a great deal is known about its reliability, validity and psychometric structure. The battery, in common with most procedures, has some difficulty in identifying chronic schizophrenics as psychiatric patients, but otherwise the results are quite impressive. Reitan, working from the test protocols alone, without any additional information about the patient, is able to identify the presence of brain damage, distinguish diffuse from focal lesions, and lateralize and localize focal lesions, with an accuracy of around 80 per cent. This may to some extent reflect Reitan's clinical skills, but even relatively untrained personnel can show remarkable diagnostic success using the battery. There has been extensive investigation of the performance of the battery when applied to criterion groups of brain damaged and psychiatric patients and normal subjects in a long series of studies for validation and cross-validation (in which diagnostic criteria established in one research sample are tested out upon an independent sample).

One particularly interesting development has been the creation of a computer-supported automated diagnostic process which operates by a number of classificatory keys from the set of 41 scores yielded by the full battery (Russell, Neuringer and Goldstein, 1970). This program had an accuracy rate of 88 per cent for detecting brain damage,

80 per cent for lateralizing left and right hemisphere lesions, and 62 per cent for identifying diffuse lesions. This compares well with traditional methods, and the computer agreed with clinical neurologists and neuropsychologists as often as they agreed with each other.

In favour of this battery, then, is the extensive evaluation of its validity which has been published. It covers a broad range of functions, and has the ability to identify complex test patterns and relationships across a number of tests, which may typify certain specific conditions. Nevertheless, the test carries a heavy penalty in the time taken in administration, and it does not cover all possible neurological deficits. Its heavy reliance on motor performance also rules out its use with certain patients. It has, however, proved a useful instrument, and may form the basis of further improved versions.

The second, and much more recently developed, battery is that generally known as the *Luria-Nebraska Neuropsychological Battery*, more formally referred to as the Standardized Version of Luria's Neuropsychological Techniques. This is just what it is, an attempt to take Luria's procedures and assemble a battery of normatively based tests from them.

The battery is formed of 269 items which cover the main components of the Luria Investigation as described, for example, by Christensen (see p. 277). These components comprise: motor function; rhythmic and pitch skills; tactile functions; visual (spatial) functions; receptive speech; expressive speech; writing; reading; arithmetic; memory; and intellectual processes. Each item is scored according to formal protocols. Summary Pathognomic, Left Hemisphere and Right Hemisphere scores are calculated, and a profile across the individual scales may be drawn.

There is much less research available on the Luria-Nebraska battery than the Halstead-Reitan battery. Nevertheless, reports to date are extremely encouraging and suggest that it is at least as powerful in identifying both the presence and the type of brain damage. A recently published cross-validation study (Golden *et al.*, 1981) found that the presence of brain damage was correctly diagnosed in 86 per cent of cases, the lateralization was correct in 78 per cent, localization in 92 per cent, and the quadrant of the brain in which the lesion was situated was correctly identified in 84 per cent of cases.

This battery does have the advantage that it takes considerably less time to administer than the Halstead-Reitan, at around two and a half hours, and it relates more directly to the patient's problems on a clinical level. However, it requires that the user be aware of Luria's formal model, and the greatest clinical value will only be derived from it when qualitative as well as quantitative aspects of performance are taken into account. The authors of the test (principally Charles Golden) specifically state that the test depends upon both the standardized and qualitative interpretive systems which the battery can provide. Nevertheless, this battery is being taken up with some enthusiasm, particularly in North America, and we have yet to see how well it will appear in the light of continuing research and evaluation. (Several books give clinical case examples of the use of both these batteries, and are listed at the end of the chapter.)

The Individual-Centred Normative Approach

This approach, typical of clinical practice in Britain, stands between the two approaches already described. It relies to some extent on a formal psychometric approach, but it emphasizes the need to tailor the assessment to the nature of a particular patient's difficulties. British neuropsychologists have generally considered batteries to be inefficient, wasteful of time and resources, and unlikely to provide a full and accurate description of the dysfunction under investigation. The aim of formulating such a description, which goes beyond a simple diagnostic classification to an understanding of the behavioural deficits in psychological terms, has always been kept firmly in view.

The strategy of assessment has therefore been, as in the Russian approach, to conduct a broad general survey of the patient's functions, identifying areas of difficulty, and pursuing an analysis of these particular areas. Each investigation thus becomes an individual examination of the possibly unique state which the patient exhibits. Unlike the Russian approach, however, the particular tests employed are rooted in the empirical tradition. Performance is carefully analysed and scored, and reference made, whenever possible, to established norms against which to judge the patient's performance. Where individual experiments are set up to test some hypothesis about the patient's cognitive state, then attention is paid to the scientific design of the procedures, and there will be a formal statistical evaluation of the results.

The procedure of neuropsychological consultation, after collection of informal data about the patient's complaint, and a preliminary interview with the patient, might often begin with the WAIS (Filskov and Leli, 1981; McFie, 1975). Although never designed with such an application in mind, the quality of this test and the range of functions which it examines make it the most popular instrument for detailed general evaluation of intellectual functions. The degree to which a neuropsychologist may be willing to infer deficits from the pattern of results on the WAIS varies widely, and few are likely to consider it a sufficient assessment, although a great deal can be inferred by a skilled clinician from this test alone.

Having identified the general areas of difficulty, and undertaken tests of primary sensory functions if appropriate, the neuropsychologist will have begun to formulate hypotheses about the nature of the deficit, and perhaps the lesion site. The next stage is to employ specific individual testing procedures to evaluate these hypotheses. The tests are of the type described in Chapters 3 to 6 when discussing the effects of specific lesions, and include the assessment of language function, which was discussed on pp. 141–142. Because these tests have been shown to be affected by lesions of certain areas, then as a corollary the tests can be used to locate the sites of unidentified lesions. There are an enormous number of such tests available. Lezak (1976) in her valuable and comprehensive guide to neuropsychological assessment lists about 300, but most clinicians will routinely use perhaps a couple of dozen, calling on less popular tests when an unusual or baffling case is encountered.

For example, if a frontal lesion is suspected, there are three areas of function which are likely to be examined. Concept attainment and abstraction may be tested with the Wisconsin Card Sorting Test (Fig. 3.3), the Halstead Category Test (Fig. 3.1), the Colour-Form Sorting Test or the Milan Sorting Test. Planning and the integrated execution of complex actions may be investigated with the Porteus Mazes (Fig. 3.5), the Trail Making Test or by arithmetical problem solving. Finally the Verbal Fluency Test might be used to check upon 'frontal' aspects of verbal function. There will, however, be wide variation in the practice of individual neuropsychologists (Goldstein, 1974; Warrington, 1970).

Because these tests are insufficient to provide a comprehensive coverage of behavioural functions, the gaps will be filled by the development of special experiments to investigate individual hypotheses about the deficits under examination. If a patient's poor motor performance is thought to be due to poor kinaesthetic feedback, then artificial feedback could be introduced under experimental conditions to see if performance improves. If the problem is thought to be due to a deficit of verbal memory, then additional cues could be used to determine the level of the patient's performance. As another example, a patient's difficulty in performing mental arithmetic could be examined by presenting problems in different forms, verbally encoded or formally abstract, in written or mental form, in order to tease out whether the difficulty is one of abstracting the problem, of employing an appropriate strategy for solution, or of undertaking the mechanics of computation. The possibilities are only limited by the ingenuity of the neuropsychologist and the sophistication of his model of cognitive processes.

It must be remembered that the investigation aims not only to classify the lesion, but also to understand the patient's difficulty in psychological terms. This form of cognitive analysis (Kinsbourne, 1971) attempts to specify the dysfunction in terms of the rate and accuracy of information processing, and the operation of the normal repertoire of cognitive strategies. The component processes are identified and measures of the efficiency of each employed. This psychological analysis can in turn be related to areas of localized cerebral function, but it can also form a basis for the management, treatment and rehabilitation of the patient. This would be lacking from a simple diagnosis of the lesion and its site. An excellent demonstration of how the cognitive psychologist's knowledge of reading processes can help in assessing patients, and of how data from the clinic can be fed back to develop our understanding of normal function, has been provided by Patterson (1981).

This approach relies heavily on the skills and insight of the individual clinician. There is the risk that areas of function will be neglected, or that complex patterns of functional interaction will be missed. Nevertheless it seems the most intelligent approach to neuropsychological assessment, if practised by capable and sensitive clinicians.

REHABILITATION

I wish that it were possible to devote a full chapter to treatment and rehabilitation, but unfortunately this would not be justified. While there are encouraging developments, neuropsychologists have not traditionally been heavily involved in therapy for brain damaged patients.

Part of the difficulty has been in formulating a model of *how function is reinstated*, when that does occur. As there is no significant regrowth of damaged tissue in the central nervous system, what process results in lost functions being regained? There are at least four ways in which this might happen. Firstly, recovery may result from the reinstatement of function at its original site, in tissue which has not been irreversibly damaged but only temporarily upset by processes associated with the acute effects of the lesion. Secondly, recovery may result from the adoption of the function of the damaged area of cortex by an area which did not originally serve it. Some have considered that this process of neural relocation might be fundamentally programmed into the system. Thirdly, there may simply be adaptation to the deficit. As most high level performance can be achieved by the mobilization of a variety of component processes, it may be possible to learn to perform the old skills by new processes which avoid the site of dysfunction in the system. Finally, some have thought that recovery reflects the original tissue regaining control of functions which have been temporarily taken away by other sites during the acute phase of the illness (LeVere, 1980; Finger, 1978). Without an accepted model of how recovery is achieved, it is difficult to plan a rational programme of therapy which will be both effective and efficient.

The progress of recovery, unaided or with physical and occupational therapy only, can last over a very long period, and improvement continuing over at least six years has been recorded in some studies. Nevertheless, it is generally accepted that the most important period of recovery, if it is going to occur, is during the first year following injury, and especially during the first six months. There have, however, been few formal studies of the course of recovery. The exceptions have been long-term studies of the war-injured over periods of up to thirty years (Newcombe, 1969; Teuber, 1975), which show certain deficits persisting throughout that period, and recent studies of the psychosocial effects of closed head injury (Bond, 1975; Humphrey, 1980; Levin *et al.*, 1979; Miller, 1979). These studies have shown great variation in the social functioning regained by the patients, related in part to the severity of the injury, but also to the patient's premorbid personality and intelligence.

There is growing interest, however, in a number of forms of therapeutic intervention by neuropsychologists. Aphasia therapy has already been discussed (see p. 142), and forms an important aspect of this work. In more general terms, training has been the dominant strategy employed. This has sometimes been within the context of a belief that practice of a skill might actually play some part in the direct physiological reinstatement of that function, and is sometimes known as 'brain function therapy' (Buffery, 1977; Powell, 1981). More often, the approach has been simply behavioural, in that it is accepted that the patient cannot perform a certain activity, and psychological knowledge of learning is applied to teach him to perform it.

The kind of contribution that the psychologist can bring to the design of *training programmes* is in performing task analyses and constructing appropriate training routines (Golden, 1981). This is where the cognitive analysis carried out during assessment can be of great value. The components of the dysfunctional skill must be recognized if the training is to be accurately directed at the dysfunctional processes. Once the components have been identified, they can be practised within tasks in which the level of difficulty can be varied, and the errors committed by the patient controlled. Emphasis should also be placed upon careful monitoring of the patient's progress, and of providing him with immediate, direct and clear feedback about his performance. In addition, biofeedback (for example, of neuromuscular activity) has sometimes been used to aid the patient in maintaining an accurate internal representation of his performance and its effects.

Attempts have also been made to introduce new *cognitive strategies* to the patient. For example, the patient with a verbal memory deficit may be taught to use explicit visual-imagery associations and nonverbal mnemonics to improve his performance. Similarly, patients may be encouraged to deepen their encoding of stimuli, by thinking directly about associations with the material, constructing appropriate cues and practising regular rehearsal, so that words are less likely to be forgotten and may be retrieved when recall is attempted (Crovitz, 1979; Lewinsohn, Danaher and Kikel, 1977).

Specific *behavioural methods* have also been explored, using operant, or occasionally classical, conditioning techniques. Existing behaviour may be shaped or new behaviour established by the use of explicit reinforcement strategies, the patient being rewarded for the appropriate performance of some target behaviour. Inappropriate behaviour can similarly be reduced by the withdrawal of rewards, or by punishment regimes. Perhaps the most dramatic application has been the attempt to reduce the frequency of epileptic seizures by operant conditioning, which was found to be at least partly effective (Cott, Pavloski and Black, 1979). Some general success has been achieved with these methods, although they have not been widely used (Wood and Eames, 1981). While they are thought by some to devalue the humanity of the patient, they may be useful where there is poor social communication or where there are motivational deficiencies.

Finally, 'reality orientation therapy' should be mentioned (Miller, 1977). This form of milieu therapy has been successfully used with elderly demented patients, and is designed to provide artificially the basic information which the patient requires in order to conduct sensible interaction and generate appropriate behaviour. A simple example is to greet Mrs Brown, wandering about the ward at 2 am, with 'Hello Mrs Brown, you are in Barchester Hospital, and it's two o'clock in the morning. You ought to be in bed, asleep. Can I help you, dear?', rather than simply 'What's the matter, dear?', which does not assist the patient to maintain appropriate orientation for time and place, and behave accordingly. The rationale for this form of therapy is clear.

In general, therefore, there is beginning to be an increasing interest in neuropsychological ways of helping brain damaged patients. What is now needed is the systematic development and study of these methods, so that really effective help may be provided for the handicaps which these patients suffer.

CONCLUSION

The efforts of the neuropsychologist are of course only one element in the operation of a clinical team. Besides the neuropsychologist, and the neurologist or neurosurgeon who heads a team of medical staff, there are radiographers, electroencephalographers, pathologists and biomedical laboratory staff, medical physicists, speech and occupational therapists, medical social workers and of course the nursing staff. A psychiatrist, specializing in 'liaison psychiatry', may well also bring his special skills into play. The diagnostic information, and the recommendations for management and treatment which the neuropsychologist makes will therefore be evaluated in the light of findings and opinions contributed by other members of the team. The level of accuracy of neuropsychological assessment may seem disappointingly low, and there is undoubtedly considerable room for improvement in the validity of assessment procedures, but taken in the context of other medical and physical investigations, it can contribute crucial information to the understanding of the patient's condition.

A variety of general approaches and specific procedures have been used in determining the presence of brain damage and in assessing its nature and location. Many of these methods show a moderate degree of success, and are of undoubted clinical value, but at present none seems outstanding in accuracy or efficiency. Much work remains to be done to refine the instruments available for use within the neuropsychological clinic.

The increasing interest in treatment and rehabilitation, which has yet to be supported by the basic research necessary to make it really effective, promises new developments in the work of neuropsychologists and a sensible expansion of their clinical contribution.

FURTHER READING

The best general texts which cover the clinical applications discussed in this chapter are:

Filskov, S. B. and Boll, T. J., eds., *Handbook of Clinical Neuropsychology* (New York, John Wiley, 1981).

Golden, C. J., *Diagnosis and Rehabilitation in Clinical Neuropsychology*, 2nd edition (Springfield, Illinois, Charles, C. Thomas, 1981).

With reference to more specific aspects of assessment:

Christensen, A.-L., *Luria's Neuropsychological Investigation: Text* (Copenhagen, Munksgaard, 1974).

Golden, C. J., *Clinical Interpretation of Objective Psychological Tests* (New York: Grune and Stratton, 1979). This is wide-ranging and includes clinical case examples.

Golden, C. J., Osmon, D. C., Moses, J. A. Jr. and Berg, R. A., *Interpretation of the Halstead-Reitan Neuropsychological Test Battery*. (New York, Grune and Stratton, 1981). This includes copious case material.

Lezak, M. D., *Neuropsychological Assessment* (New York, Oxford University Press, 1976). An authoritative guide to general procedures and specific tests.

Luria, A. R., *Higher Cortical Functions in Man*, 2nd edition (New York, Basic Books, 1980). Useful for the Russian approach.

See Chapter 7 for references to aphasia therapy, but on recovery and rehabilitation the most useful texts are:

CIBA, *Outcome of Severe Damage to the Central Nervous System*, CIBA Symposium 34 (new series), (Amsterdam, Elsevier, 1975).

Finger, S., ed., *Recovery from Brain Damage: Research and Theory* (New York, Plenum Press, 1978).

Powell, G. E., *Brain Function Therapy* (London, Gower, 1981).

REFERENCES

Boll, T. J., 'The Halstead-Reitan Neuropsychology Battery', in S. B. Filskov and T. J. Boll, eds., *Handbook of Clinical Neuropsychology* (New York, John Wiley, 1981).

Bond, M. R., 'Assessment of Psychosocial Outcome after Severe Head Injury', in CIBA, *Outcome of Severe Damage to the Central Nervous System*, CIBA Symposium 34 (new series), (Amsterdam, Elsevier, 1975).

Applications

Buffery, A. W., 'Clinical Neuropsychology: Review and Preview', in S. Rachman, ed., *Contributions to Medical Psychology* (Oxford, Pergamon, 1977).

Christensen, A.-L. *Luria's Neuropsychological Investigation: Text* (Copenhagen, Munksgaard, 1974).

Cott, A., Pavloski, R. P. and Black, A. H., 'Reducing Epileptic Seizures through Operant Conditioning of Central Nervous System Activity: Procedural Variables', *Science*, 203 (1979), 73–75.

Crovitz, H. F., 'Memory Retraining in Brain-Damaged Patients: the Airplane List', *Cortex*, 15 (1979), 131–134.

Filskov, S. B. and Leli, D. A., 'Assessment of the Individual in Neuropsychological Practice', in S. B. Filskov and T. J. Boll, eds., *Handbook of Clinical Neuropsychology* (New York, John Wiley, 1981).

Finger, S., ed., *Recovery from Brain Damage: Research and Theory* (New York, Plenum Press, 1978).

Golden, C. J., *Diagnosis and Rehabilitation in Clinical Neuropsychology*, 2nd edition (Springfield, Illinois, Charles, C. Thomas, 1981).

Golden, C. J., Osmon, D. C., Moses, J. A. Jr and Berg, R. A., *Interpretation of the Halstead-Reitan Neuropsychological Test Battery* (New York, Grune and Stratton, 1981).

Goldstein, G., 'The Use of Clinical Neuropsychological Methods in the Lateralisation of Brain Lesions', in S. J. Dimond and J. G. Beaumont, eds., *Hemisphere Function in the Human Brain* (London, Elek Science, 1974).

Heaton, R. K., Baade, L. E. and Johnson, K. L., 'Neuropsychological Test Results Associated with Psychiatric Disorder in Adults', *Psychological Bulletin*, 85 (1978), 141–162.

Humphrey, M., 'Social Recovery During the Year Following Severe Head Injury', *Journal of Neurology, Neurosurgery and Psychiatry*, 43 (1980), 798–802.

Kinsbourne, M., 'Cognitive Deficit: Experimental Analysis', in J. L. McGaugh, ed., *Psychobiology* (New York, Academic Press, 1971).

Levin, H. S., Grossman, R. G., Rose, J. E. and Teasdale, G., 'Long-term Neuropsychological Outcome of Closed Head Injury', *Journal of Neurosurgery*, 50 (1979), 412–422.

Lewinsohn, P. M., Danaher, B. G. and Kikel, S., 'Visual Imagery as a Mnemonic Aid for Brain-injured Persons', *Journal of Consulting and Clinical Psychology*, 45 (1977), 717–723.

Lezak, M. D., *Neuropsychological Assessment* (New York, Oxford University Press, 1976).

LeVere, T. E., 'Recovery of Function after Brain Damage: a Theory of the Behavioural Deficit', *Physiological Psychology*, 8 (1980), 297–308.

Luria, A. R., *Higher Cortical Functions in Man*, 2nd edition (New York, Basic Books, 1980).

Luria, A. R. and Majovski, L. V., 'Basic Approaches Used in American and Soviet Clinical Neuropsychology', *American Psychologist*, 32 (1977) 959–968.

McFie, J., *Assessment of Organic Intellectual Impairment* (London, Academic Press, 1975).

Miller, E., 'The Management of Dementia: a Review of Some Possibilities', *British Journal of Social and Clinical Psychology*, 16 (1977), 77–83.

Miller, E., 'The Long-term Consequences of Head Injury: a Discussion of the Evidence with Special Reference to the Preparation of Legal Reports', *British Journal of Social and Clinical Psychology*, 18 (1979), 87–98.

Nelson, H. E. and O'Connell, A., 'Dementia: the Estimation of Premorbid Intelligence Levels Using the New Adult Reading Test', *Cortex*, 14 (1978), 234–244.

Newcombe, F., *Missile Wounds of the Brain* (Oxford, Oxford University Press, 1969).

Patterson, K. E., 'Neuropsychological Approaches to the Study of Reading', *British Journal of Psychology*, 72 (1981), 151–174.

Powell, G. E., *Brain Function Therapy* (London, Gower, 1981).

Russell, E. W., Neuringer, C. and Goldstein, G., *Assessment of Brain Damage: a Neuropsychological Key Approach* (New York, John Wiley, 1970).

Savage, R. D., Britton, P. G., Bolton, N. and Hall, E. H., *Intellectual Functioning in the Aged* (London, Methuen, 1973).

Teuber, H.-L., 'Recovery of Function after Brain Injury in Man', in CIBA, *Outcome of Severe Damage to the Central Nervous System*, CIBA Symposium 34 (new series), (Amsterdam, Elsevier, 1975).

Vernon, P. E., *Personality Assessment* (London, Methuen, 1964).

Warrington, E. K., 'Neurological Deficits', in P. Mittler, ed., *The Psychological Assessment of Mental and Physical Handicaps* (London, Methuen, 1970).

Wood, R. L. and Eames, P., 'Application of Behaviour Modification in the Rehabilitation of Traumatically Brain-injured Adults', in G. Davey, ed., *Applications of Conditioning Theory* (London, Methuen, 1981).

CHAPTER 15

Psychiatry and Neuropsychology

Less than a decade ago, I submitted an academic paper to a highly respected psychiatric journal on the subject of hemisphere laterality and schizophrenia. The anonymous, but presumably eminent, reviewer rejected the paper not principally on the merit of its contents but because he considered that to look for abnormal brain organization in schizophrenics was an outdated and futile exercise, of no interest to current psychiatry.

In *A Pelican at Blandings*, published in 1969, P. G. Wodehouse has Galahad Threepwood say: 'That was the night you were so disturbed because she hummed and giggled, giving you the impression that something had gone wrong with the two hemispheres of her brain and the broad band of transversely running fibres known as the corpus callosum and that she was, in your crisp phrase, potty.'

Wodehouse seems to have been the more prophetic of the two in view of the dramatic increase in interest in neuropsychological variables in psychiatry over the past ten years. Neurologists and psychiatrists have always been interested in mental states which result from cerebral pathology, the area known as neuropsychiatry or organic psychiatry, but this interest has now been extended to disorders which would not traditionally fall within this field, such as schizophrenia and affective psychosis.

NEUROPSYCHIATRY

It has been clear for a very long time that abnormal mental states can follow from damage to the brain. Some of the changes associated with focal lesions which were discussed in Section II are obviously of a psychiatric nature, and there are in addition changes which follow from diffuse brain diseases, and from generalized trauma associated with blows to the head.

It should, however, be remembered that not all neurological conditions involving the brain produce psychiatric symptoms. In a large study of over 3,500 war veterans with brain injuries, about a third of whom had penetrating wounds, lasting cognitive impairment was present in only 2 per cent, character changes in 18 per cent, psychosis in 8 per cent and severe neurosis in 11 per cent (Hillbom, 1960). The incidence of mental changes following the development of tumours is rather higher, in the range of approximately 50 to 80 per cent among patients in various studies, but on the other hand the incidence of cognitive and psychiatric sequelae after closed head injuries producing concussion and temporary amnesia is remarkably low. Such cases do nevertheless occur.

The variety of psychiatric conditions associated with organic states is a special area of study in its own right, particular patterns of psychiatric impairment being associated with, for example, the various cerebral diseases (see Lishman, 1978). However, there are a number of general symptoms which are often seen to accompany organic nervous disease. Patients frequently show some disturbance of consciousness, varying from mild inattention to disorientation, delirium, unconsciousness and coma. Sleep may also be disturbed, either in quantity, in pattern or in the electrical rhythms recorded through the night. Impairment of memory is also common, patients tire easily, and tend to perseverate in their thoughts or their activity. They are often irritable, exhibit frequent changes in emotion, and their behaviour may also be relatively disinhibited.

Some of these symptoms have been found to be associated in the *post-concussional syndrome* (sometimes called post-traumatic neurosis) which is characterized by severe headache, giddiness and blackouts, fatigue and difficulty in concentrating, loss of confidence, depression, anxiety, irritability and intolerance of noise. Patients may also complain of insomnia and show a reasonable but particular concern for, and awareness of, their head.

Epilepsy might also be expected to be associated with psychiatric disorders. However, although epilepsy is a common after-effect of cerebral trauma or disease, epileptics in general show relatively low rates of psychiatric disorder. Studies of the incidence of mental abnormality in epileptics commonly find that only about 5 per cent are ever diagnosed as suffering from a serious psychiatric condition. This compares with a rate of about 1 per cent for the general population. There does however, seem to be a much clearer relationship between temporal lobe epilepsy and psychiatric disorder. This form is found disproportionately among epileptics admitted to mental hospitals.

The abnormal behaviour can take the form of psychiatric symptoms following fits, or less commonly of a chronic psychotic state rather similar to paranoid schizophrenia.

A particular form of personality, typified by stubbornness, concreteness, lack of spontaneity, egocentricity and unctuosity has also been described as typical of epileptics. However, these descriptions were based upon institutionalized epileptics, not those living in the general community (as most are), and it seems probable that any personality changes which do occur can be regarded as secondary reactions to being handicapped by epilepsy, rather than as primary effects mediated by changes in cerebral systems.

Cerebral *dementia* is, of course, invariably accompanied by psychiatric changes. Dementia, seen most commonly in the aged but also in certain presenile degenerative diseases, involves the generalized and progressive loss of cortical tissue from the brain. Most dementias are, at present, irreversible. As the cortex is lost, then mental functions decline progressively. There is a global deterioration of memory, thinking, motor performance, emotional responsiveness and social behaviour. As the illness develops, speech may be affected, behaviour becomes increasingly unreasonable and often disruptive, until finally the control of basic and vital processes becomes disorganized. It is a distressing and pathetic progression familiar to many with ageing relatives.

Finally, of course, it should be remembered that there are a range of specific psychiatric effects which can follow damage to the brain, and these will depend upon the site of the lesion, its speed of development, the nature of the pathology, and particular characteristics of the individual patient.

This, very briefly, is the subject matter of organic psychiatry, and is comprised of *organic* states or reaction-types. In traditional psychiatry these have always been distinguished from *functional* states. Although the distinction is not entirely clear-cut, functional states are those where no clear physical pathology can be established. Whether this is because they do not follow from physical pathology, or because we are ignorant of the physical basis of each condition, is a matter for debate, but the distinction has nevertheless been traditionally maintained. Functional disorders have generally been accepted to include the major psychotic states of schizophrenia and manic-depressive illness. However, there has been a need to re-examine this distinction, particularly in the light of new evidence which suggests that abnormal neuropsychological organization might be shown to be typical of certain of these disorders.

A word should be said here about the psychiatric terms referred to in this chapter. A distinction is usually made between neuroses and psychoses. In the *neuroses*, which are less severe and usually require no more than out-patient treatment, the patient maintains contact with reality and has some insight into his problems. The symptoms are likely to be anxiety, depression or avoidance behaviour, but without hallucinations or extreme deviations in thought, mood or action. *Psychoses* are more serious and generally require admission to hospital. The symptoms may be primarily in mood (manic-depressive or affective psychosis: mania being intense excitement and overactivity, depression a state of mute, expressionless and perhaps agitated withdrawal) or in changes in thought or action (hallucinations, delusions, bizarre behaviour) in states usually termed schizophrenic. These psychotic patients generally have little contact with reality and limited awareness of their own condition. (If you feel uncertain about the distinctions being made here, it would be worth reading the section on abnormal psychology in an introductory psychology text.)

FUNCTIONAL STATES AND LATERALITY

Some general points should be made before considering in detail the studies of lateral cerebral organization in psychiatric patients. The first is that a rather simple model of psychiatric disorder is often assumed, in which mental illness is seen as exactly like a physical disease. It has long been recognized that there are problems with this view, particularly in accounting for the effects which psychological and social variables have upon abnormal behaviour. Secondly, although considerable advances have been made in recent years, there is still considerable unreliability in the use of psychiatric diagnostic labels. Some terms, particularly 'schizophrenia', are rather loosely used and encompass a variety of rather different disorders. Thirdly, scientific rigour is lacking in many of the studies. Clinical studies are difficult to conduct, but in comparison with the experimental studies discussed in Section III, research with psychiatric patients has been methodologically of poor quality. Little care has been taken over the specification of patient groups, over the measurement of cerebral asymmetries, and over the interpretation of data collected. A variety of experimental findings have been squeezed uncomfortably into a mould formed by the researchers' expectations. The findings, and the strong claims made for them, must be treated with some caution, although the research questions remain of considerable interest and importance.

Studies of lateral cerebral organization in psychiatric patients seem to have been undertaken in a number of laboratories at about the same time, but one important influence was the work of Flor-Henry. Early on he observed that different psychiatric symptoms appeared to be associated with left- and right-sided temporal lobe epilepsy. A great variety of forms of evidence are now quoted in support of laterality differences in functional psychiatric states, but many of the early observations were also of this kind, concerned with lateralized organic states or lateralized symptoms and signs.

Lateralized symptoms

Among lateralized signs in psychiatric patients are conversion symptoms, in which disturbance is expressed by some overt physical manifestation, such as hysterical paralysis or loss of sensation. Such 'conversions' have been reported to be found more commonly on the left than on the right, especially in females (Galin, Diamond and Braff, 1977), although in another study, of 759 cases with conversion symptoms, only 29 showed lateralization, and among these, 12 were left- and 17 right-sided (Bishop, Mobley and Farr, 1978). Other studies have found at best only marginal significance for a left-sided preponderance of psychogenic symptoms. Fleminger, McClure and Dalton (1980) used an interesting Suggestion Test to show that suggestion would operate more powerfully upon left-sided responses. They did indeed find such an effect, but not only for the psychiatric patients they studied, but also for the psychiatric nurses they used as controls.

Pain has also been reported to be more frequent or intense on the left side, especially when it can be considered psychogenic in origin. The inference is that the increased pain is associated with a more 'emotional' right hemisphere. However, some of the most careful studies have failed to find any asymmetry, in particular a study of a large sample of patients attending a pain clinic, using data which was not collected with any intention that it should be analysed for lateral asymmetry (Hall, 1981).

An alternative approach has been to examine the performance of psychiatric patients on standard neuropsychological test batteries to see what kind of organic dysfunction such performance might suggest. Flor-Henry, with others (1981), used a Reitan-type battery with hysterical and schizophrenic patients. The results were complex, but it was argued that they supported a model of bilateral frontal pathology being associated with hysteria, but with greater importance being placed upon a dominant (left) hemisphere dysfunction. Hysteria, it was argued, can be viewed as a special form of schizophrenia in this context. Similar results, of schizophrenia being linked with dominant hemisphere dysfunction, particularly of the temporal and temporal-parietal regions, were also found by Taylor and co-workers using an aphasia test and Smith's neuropsychological test battery (Taylor, Greenspan and Abrams, 1979; Taylor, Redfield and Abrams, 1981). Not only were Kronfol *et al.* (1978) able to show, using standard tests, a right hemisphere abnormality in depressed patients before treatment, but they were also able to show that unilateral ECT (see p. 258), administered to either side of the head, improved 'right hemisphere' performance on the tests.

In this context, a study by Hommes and Panhuysen (1971) using the Wada technique with depressed patients has been much quoted. They found that there was a negative relationship between the depth of depression and the degree of left hemisphere speech dominance. They also found that the injection of sodium amytal resulted in improved mood, whether the injection was to the left or right, but especially when it was on the left. They concluded that normal mood regulation depends on the integrity of left hemisphere functional dominance, although their results have also been taken by others to implicate a *right* hemisphere dysfunction in depressed mood.

Physiological processes

The study of electroconvulsive therapy has already been mentioned above and in the context of laterality research, and the findings can be turned around to provide evidence for lateralized brain dysfunction in depressive conditions.

A second physiological approach has been to look at electro-physiological parameters. It has long been known that psychiatric patients may show mild abnormalities in their EEG. Abrams and Taylor (1980), for instance, found 44 of 159 psychiatric patients with functional psychoses to have clinical EEG abnormalities, and these were more commonly observed in the left temporal region, and in those patients who had 'formal thought disorder'.

Some studies have taken a more systematic approach to the study of on-going EEG, and Flor-Henry *et al.* (1979) found atypical brain function in the left frontal region in obsessive-compulsive patients. Similar results, of greater left hemisphere variability of alpha in paranoid schizophrenia and greater right hemisphere variability in depression, have also been reported (Rochford, Weinapple and Goldstein, 1981). Coherence studies (see p. 230) have yielded rather complex results, but have if anything tended to suggest a deficit in interhemispheric integration, rather than a lateralized dysfunction in one of the hemispheres (Shaw *et al.*, 1979; Weller and Montagu, 1979).

As might be expected, evoked potentials (see p. 231) have been studied as well as on-going EEG. Some studies have supported a left hemisphere dysfunction in schizophrenia (Roemer *et al.*, 1978; Shagass *et al.*, 1980), although this last study also found evidence of a similar left hemisphere dysfunction for depression, rather than the right-sided dysfunction which was expected. The hypothesis of a failure in interhemispheric communication was supported by the study of Jones and Miller (1981), examining somatosensory evoked potentials, which found no difference in the latency of components following ipsilateral or contralateral stimulation.

Finally, it seems relevant to note two drug studies. Carr (1978) has reported evidence that Piracetam, which is known to facilitate interhemispheric neural transmission, had the effect of improving certain aspects of schizophrenic performance, including scores on certain memory and learning tasks. Chlorpromazine, which is one of the major tranquillizers used in the control of schizophrenic symptoms, has also been shown to decrease lateral asymmetry in auditory temporal discrimination (Hammond and Gruzelier, 1978).

None of this evidence seems of great significance taken alone, but it all contributes to a general picture of disturbed cerebral organization which might characterize some psychiatric patients.

Experimental tasks

Beaumont and Dimond (1973) were the first to use the divided visual field technique with psychiatric patients. They examined within- and between-hemisphere matching using a variety of stimuli, and found evidence for some degree of lateralized dysfunction, but also for a more significant deficit in interhemispheric communication. Some later workers have found a similar effect (Pic'l, Magaro and Wade, 1979), but others have found clearer evidence for a specific lateralized deficit (Gur, 1978; Tucker *et al.*, 1978). Colbourn (1982) has thoroughly reviewed the DVF studies with psychiatric patients, and concludes that it is possible to interpret the findings in terms of a left hemisphere dysfunction being associated with schizophrenia, although the findings for other conditions are much less clear. However, he goes on to point out that other interpretations of the evidence should also be examined.

Dichotic listening has been employed rather more often than the visual techniques. Here again the evidence has been rather confused. However, it again falls roughly into two areas. There are those who argue for a lateralized deficit from the ear differences which have been obtained. Bruder and Yozawitz (1979) found evidence for a right hemisphere abnormality in patients with affective disorders, but no evidence of an abnormality in schizophrenia. With a similar group of patients, an abnormal pattern of lateralization, which returned towards normal with ECT treatment, was also found by Moscovitch, Strauss and Olds (1981). Schizophrenics were found to have an enhanced right ear advantage in the study of Nachshon (1980), and Tucker *et al.* (1978) also found a right ear attentional bias in patients with anxiety syndrome.

Other workers have interpreted their findings differently. Lishman with others (1978), studying recently recovered psychotic patients, found evidence of abnormal auditory laterality, but concluded that this was more typical of an interhemispheric integration deficit than of a left hemisphere dysfunction. Against the general trend, Wexler and Heninger (1979) found increasing laterality to be associated with a decreasing probability of psychotic thought and behaviour, so that they formulated their view of the schizophrenic deficit in terms of a failure of interhemispheric inhibition. Lastly, Walker, Hoppes and Emory (1981) have reanalysed the data of Nachshon's study and argue that it really supports a hypothesis of faulty interhemispheric transfer.

Any conclusion with respect to auditory laterality has been considerably complicated by the finding of Gruzelier and Hammond (1979) of asymmetries in hearing thresholds, with diurnal variation, in schizophrenic patients.

There are also studies of lateral performance asymmetry in the tactile modality, but they all point towards a deficit in intermanual transfer and integration, rather than specific lateralized deficits (Carr, 1980; Dimond *et al.*, 1980).

A relatively high level of agreement has also been shown by studies of lateral eye movements. These have, in general, found a tendency for an increase in rightward conjugate lateral eye movements (or a reduction in left movements) in schizophrenia (Gur, 1978; Schweitzer, 1979; Tomer *et al.*, 1979; Tucker *et al.*, 1978). The interpretation placed upon these findings has generally been that this demonstrates the presence of some abnormal process originating from the dominant left hemisphere.

It should also be noted that there have been reports of abnormal distributions of hand preference within psychiatric groups. The overall results have been, however, somewhat unclear. Some workers (Gur, 1977; Lishman and McMeekan, 1976) have reported an increase in left handedness among schizophrenic patients. Alternately, some have found an excess of right handers among these patients (Taylor, Dalton and Fleminger, 1980). There are undoubtedly difficulties in assessing the handedness of psychiatric patients by quesionnaire measures, and this may contribute to some of the variability in the findings.

By now you may feel thoroughly confused by the variety of studies and the diversity of the findings. A whole range of different methods of investigation has been used with all kinds of different patients, and the result has been a very complex set of research data. This rather selective survey of the studies, with rather more references than usual, has been presented in order to illustrate just how difficult it can be to make sense of some particular field of investigation. However, we must try and make what sense we can out of the research, and it seems useful to do this in the light of the two major theoretical hypotheses which have been adopted.

Theoretical Models

Three types of model have been proposed to link lateral asymmetry with functional psychiatric disorder. The first was proposed by Galin (1974, 1977), and is the only one to be based upon *psychodynamic* concepts. Galin derived his ideas from split-brain research and argued that psychiatric states might be likened to the activity of the disconnected right hemisphere. Specifically, the right hemisphere could be associated with the Freudian 'primary process' and by its relative disconnection from the conscious, speaking left hemisphere could be the source of unconscious processes and repression. This is an intriguing theory, but partly because a psychodynamic approach is not fashionable in contemporary psychiatry, certainly among those psychiatrists likely to be interested in biological correlates of mental illness, then relatively little attention has been paid to Galin's ideas.

The other two theoretical models will probably already be apparent from the sketch of the research evidence given above. These are of *specific lateralized cerebral dysfunction* and of *impaired interhemispheric integration*. The concept of a specific dysfunction has been more actively promoted, especially by Flor-Henry (Gruzelier and Flor-Henry, 1979; Flor-Henry, 1978, 1979). Flor-Henry has based his theories on extremely diverse evidence, of the kind which has been cited already, and while the theory is fairly complex, it boils down to the idea that functional disturbances can be linked with dysfunction of the frontal and temporal regions of the brain. If the abnormality is on the dominant side, then the illness will be of a schizophrenic nature. If the abnormality is on the nondominant side, then the disorder will be an affective one with symptoms of depression more likely than symptoms of mania. Flor-Henry, supported by others, argues quite directly that the research evidence unequivocally supports his theoretical model.

The alternative model, which stems from the work of Dimond (Beaumont and Dimond, 1973; Dimond, 1980; Dimond *et al.*, 1980), proposes that certain functional states, principally schizophrenia, can be viewed as a disconnection syndrome. The psychiatric symptoms are associated with a failure of interhemispheric transfer across the corpus callosum. In this it reflects Galin's model, but is formulated in terms of information-handling processes rather than psychodynamic mechanisms. It has not been claimed that such a model can explain all the evidence which is sometimes cited for neuropsychological effects in psychiatric illness, but it is proposed as a more satisfactory explanation of many of the findings using well-controlled experimental tasks with schizophrenic patients. As we have seen, the results of a number of studies provide clear support for such a model.

Before assessing the relative validity of these models, one or two methodological and analytical points should be noted. In this book it has often been necessary to stand back and consider methodological issues before assessing the value of any conclusions that might be drawn, and it often seems that the methodological difficulties overshadow the significance of the outcome of the research. This is, simply, part of the nature of neuropsychology at present, and whether it stems from the immaturity of this field of research or the complexity of the processes under investigation is difficult to say.

There are a whole host of procedural problems which I do not intend to spell out at length. These include the difficulties of undertaking laterality research and of obtaining laterality measurements, which have been discussed in preceding chapters. Added to these are the problems of undertaking clinical studies, and particular problems associated with psychiatric research. It is difficult to standardize the diagnostic procedures employed to classify groups of psychiatric patients; in addition most have been institutionalized for varying periods, and almost all are being treated with a variety of powerful drugs acting upon the central nervous system. These problems have been extensively discussed in a number of recent reviews (Colbourn, 1982; Marin and Tucker, 1981; Merrin, 1981).

One problem which cannot go undiscussed, however, is the difficulty of interpreting abnormal lateral asymmetries. This is particularly relevant when considering a model of specific lateralized dysfunction. The problem is that once the concepts of interhemispheric inhibition or overactivation are introduced into the discussion of research findings, then almost any model of lateralized dysfunction can be supported by *post hoc* interpretation of the results. Let me take two studies as examples. This is not to spotlight these studies as examples of bad science – in fact both seem well-conducted and yield valuable data – but they are useful to illustrate the problems which are frequently encountered in interpretation of the findings.

Gruzelier and Hammond (1980) examined schizophrenic performance in a dichotic listening task. Among other findings they found that in the serial position effect with digit pairs of equal loudness, there was a tendency for the left ear to lack primacy in report. They discussed this as evidence in support of the expected *left* hemisphere processing impairment. Their argument was, roughly, that as the reporting processes rely upon verbal encoding, which can be considered a left hemisphere activity, then even though the effect was at the left ear, it demonstrated a left hemisphere impairment. They may be correct, and I have taken their result out of the context of their other findings, but it still seems that the result could as easily be taken as direct evidence of an alternative right hemisphere deficit.

In a second study, Gur (1979) asked schizophrenics to judge pairs of altered pictures which were presented simultaneously or successively. Control subjects did better overall, and were equally fast in the simultaneous and successive conditions. The schizophrenics were faster in the successive than the simultaneous condition. Gur argues that this pattern of performance is typical of right brain damaged subjects, which must therefore be evidence for *left* hemisphere overactivation in schizophrenics. Even assuming that the parallel with brain damage allows a valid inference to be drawn, the conclusion might obviously just as well be that the schizophrenics have a defective right hemisphere.

So what conclusions may be drawn about laterality and functional psychiatric states? Of the most recent scholarly reviews, one concludes that despite the methodological difficulties, there is consistent support for a model of left hemisphere overactivation or dysfunction in schizophrenia (Newlin, Carpenter and Golden, 1981). Three other reviews, however, are driven to the view that there is no consistent support for any of the models proposed, and each makes certain recommendations which are designed to improve the quality of research in this field (Marin and Tucker, 1981; Merrin, 1981; Wexler, 1980).

My own view is that this last position is the only possible conclusion at the present. Many of the theoretical discussions have been far too selective in the evidence that they have considered, and most have indulged quite shamelessly in *post hoc* interpretation which has been in line only with the hypotheses being promoted. The basic research evidence is still too sketchy to allow any clear conclusions to be drawn, and it is certainly much too early to proclaim that functional psychiatric states can be explained in terms of abnormal neuropsychological processes. There are a variety of other psychological models of psychotic behaviour, for instance in terms of an attentional disturbance associated with heightened arousal, and many of these models are more powerful in explaining the data than the neuropsychological theories. Whether neuropsychological models will come to reflect models cast in other conceptual terms, and derived from different levels of behavioural analysis, remains to be seen, but the thought undoubtedly provides at least one avenue for future research.

CONCLUSION

Neuropsychology has been able to make an increasingly valuable contribution to the study of the mental sequelae of organic pathological processes in the area known as neuropsychiatry or organic psychiatry. The psychiatric effects of gross damage to the brain have long been recognized, and neuropsychology is able to clarify and illuminate the processes involved by developing its own models of the processes which underlie brain-behaviour relationships.

Almost no clear conclusions have emerged from the recent upsurge of interest in the neuropsychological concomitants of functional psychiatric states. There has been a refreshing re-evaluation of the processes which might contribute to schizophrenic and affective psychotic disorders. Many exciting theoretical models have been formulated, but despite the growing research effort, it is still too early to say whether a particular neuropsychological dysfunction can be identified as accompanying a given functional state. This area is nevertheless one of the most exciting and challenging of any in contemporary neuropsychology.

The problems and difficulties which arise when we attempt practical applications of neuropsychology illustrate not only the fundamental deficiencies of our knowledge but also the importance of understanding how physical systems generate the highest levels of thinking, feeling and consciousness. We have made considerable progress in unravelling the nature of brain-behaviour processes, and yet there is much still to be discovered, not only about the details of functional relationships, but about the fundamental principles which govern the operation of those functions. To discover the answers involves an attack upon essential philosophical issues, a rigorous and creative approach to experimental design, and a questioning and critical appraisal in the construction of theories. The answers – and they will be found – will be of fundamental importance for our understanding, not only of disordered behaviour, but also of everyday human action and of the essence of the humanity of man.

FURTHER READING

On the topic of neuropsychiatry, a readable general introduction and an excellent reference source are respectively:

Trimble, M. R., *Neuropsychiatry* (Chichester, John Wiley, 1981).
Lishman, W. A., *Organic Psychiatry* (Oxford, Blackwell Scientific Publications, 1978).

Further reading on laterality and functional disorders is to be found in:

Gruzelier, J. and Flor-Henry, P., *Hemisphere Asymmetries of Function in Psychopathology* (Amsterdam, Elsevier/North Holland, 1979).
Marin, R. S. and Tucker, G. J., 'Psychopathology and Hemispheric Dysfunction: a Review', *Journal of Nervous and Mental Disease*, 169 (1981), 546–557.
Merrin, E. L., 'Schizophrenia and Brain Asymmetry: an Evaluation of Evidence for Dominant Lobe Dysfunction', *Journal of Nervous and Mental Disease*, 169 (1981), 405–416.

REFERENCES

Abrams, R. and Taylor, M. A., 'Psychopathology and the EEG', *Biological Psychiatry*, 15 (1980), 871–878.
Beaumont, J. G. and Dimond, S. J., 'Brain Disconnection and Schizophrenia', *British Journal of Psychiatry*, 123 (1973), 661–662.
Bishop, E. R., Mobley, M. C. and Farr, W. F., 'Lateralization of Conversion Symptoms', *Comprehensive Psychiatry*, 19 (1978), 393–396.
Bruder, G. E. and Yozawitz, A., 'Central Auditory Processing and Lateralization in Psychiatric Patients', in J. Gruzelier and P. Flor-Henry, eds., *Hemisphere Asymmetries of Function in Psychopathology* (Amsterdam, Elsevier/North Holland, 1979).
Carr, S. A., 'The Effects of Piracetam (UCB 6225) on Interhemispheric Transfer and Memory in Chronic Schizophrenics', *Bulletin of the British Psychological Society*, 31 (1978), 64–65.
Carr, S. A., 'Interhemispheric Transfer of Stereognostic Information in Chronic Schizophrenics', *British Journal of Psychiatry*, 136 (1980), 53–58.

Colbourn, C. J., 'Divided Visual Field Studies of Psychiatric Patients', in J. G. Beaumont, ed., *Divided Visual Field Studies of Cerebral Organisation* (London, Academic Press, 1982).

Dimond, S. J., *Neuropsychology* (London, Butterworth, 1980).

Dimond, S. J., Scammell, R., Pryce, I. J., Huws, D. and Gray, C., 'Some Failures of Intermanual and Cross-lateral Transfer in Chronic Schizophrenia', *Journal of Abnormal Psychology*, 89 (1980), 505–509.

Fleminger, J. J., McClure, G. M. and Dalton, R., 'Lateral Response to Suggestion in Relation to Handedness and the Side of Psychogenic Symptoms', *British Journal of Psychiatry*, 136 (1980), 562–566.

Flor-Henry, P., 'Gender, Hemispheric Specialisation and Psychopathology', *Social Science and Medicine*, 12 (1978), 155–162.

Flor-Henry, P., 'On Certain Aspects of the Localisation of the Cerebral Systems Regulating and Determining Emotion', *Biological Psychiatry*, 14 (1979), 677–698.

Flor-Henry, P., Yeudall, L. T., Koles, Z. J. and Howarth, B. G., 'Neuropsychological and Power Spectral EEG Investigations of the Obsessive-compulsive Syndrome', *Biological Psychiatry*, 14 (1979), 119–130.

Flor-Henry, P., Fromm-Auch, D., Tapper, M. and Schopflocher, D., 'A Neuropsychological Study of the Stable Syndrome of Hysteria', *Biological Psychiatry*, 16 (1981), 601–626.

Galin, D., 'Implications for Psychiatry of Left and Right Cerebral Specialization', *Archives of General Psychiatry*, 31 (1974), 572–583.

Galin, D., 'Lateral Specialisation and Psychiatric Issues', *Annals of the New York Academy of Sciences*, 299 (1977), 397–411.

Galin, D., Diamond, R. and Braff, D., 'Lateralisation of Conversion Symptoms: More Frequent on the Left', *American Journal of Psychiatry*, 134 (1977), 578–580.

Gruzelier, J. and Flor-Henry, P., *Hemisphere Asymmetries of Function in Psychopathology* (Amsterdam, Elsevier/North Holland, 1979).

Gruzelier, J. H. and Hammond, N. V., 'Gains, Losses and Lateral Differences in the Hearing of Schizophrenic Patients', *British Journal of Psychology*, 70 (1979), 319–330.

Gruzelier, J. H. and Hammond, N. V., 'Lateralised Deficits and Drug Influences on the Dichotic Listening of Schizophrenic Patients', *Biological Psychiatry*, 15 (1980), 759–779.

Gur, R. E., 'Motoric Laterality Imbalance in Schizophrenia: a Possible Concomitant of Left Hemispheric Dysfunction', *Archives of General Psychiatry*, 34 (1977), 33–37.

Gur, R. E., 'Left Hemisphere Dysfunction and Left Hemisphere Overactivation in Schizophrenia', *Journal of Abnormal Psychology*, 87 (1978), 226–238.

Gur, R. E., 'Cognitive Concomitants of Hemispheric Dysfunction in Schizophrenia', *Archives of General Psychiatry*, 36 (1979), 269–277.

Hall, W. D., 'Does Pain Occur More on the Left?', *Bulletin of the British Psychological Society*, 34 (1981), 23.

Hammond, N. V. and Gruzelier, J. H., 'Laterality, Attention and Rate Effects in the Auditory Temporal Discrimination of Chronic Schizophrenics: the Effect of Treatment with Chlorpromazine', *Quarterly Journal of Experimental Psychology*, 30 (1978), 91–103.

Hillbom, E., 'After-effects of Brain Injuries', *Acta Psychiatrica et Neurologica Scandinavica*, suppl. 60 (1960), 36–47.

Hommes, O. R. and Panhuysen, L. H. H. M., 'Depression and Cerebral Dominance', *Psychiatria Neurologia Neurochirurgia*, 74 (1971), 259–270.

Jones, G. H. and Miller, J. J., 'Functional Tests of the Corpus Callosum in Schizophrenia', *British Journal of Psychiatry*, 139 (1981), 553–557.

Kronfol, Z., Hamsher, K. de S., Digre, K. and Waziri, R., 'Depression and Hemispheric Functions: Changes Associated with Unilateral ECT', *British Journal of Psychiatry*, 132 (1978), 560–567.

Lishman, W. A., *Organic Psychiatry* (Oxford, Blackwell Scientific Publications, 1978).

Lishman, W. A. and McMeekan, E. R. L., 'Hand Preference Patterns in Psychiatric Patients', *British Journal of Psychiatry*, 129 (1976), 158–166.

Lishman, W. A., Toone, B. K., Colbourn, C. J., McMeekan, E. R. L. and Mance, R. M., 'Dichotic Listening in Psychotic Patients', *British Journal of Psychiatry*, 132 (1978), 333–341.

Marin, R. S. and Tucker, G. J., 'Psychopathology and Hemispheric Dysfunction: a Review', *Journal of Nervous and Mental Disease*, 169 (1981), 546–557.

Merrin, E. L., 'Schizophrenia and Brain Asymmetry: an Evaluation of Evidence for Dominant Lobe Dysfunction', *Journal of Nervous and Mental Disease*, 169 (1981), 405–416.

Moscovitch, M., Strauss, E. and Olds, J., 'Handedness and Dichotic Listening Performance in Patients with Unipolar Endogenous Depression Who Received ECT', *American Journal of Psychiatry*, 138 (1981), 988–990.

Nachshon, I., 'Hemispheric Dysfunctioning in Schizophrenia', *Journal of Nervous and Mental Disease*, 168 (1980), 241–242.

Newlin, D. B., Carpenter, B. and Golden, C. J., 'Hemispheric Asymmetries in Schizophrenia', *Biological Psychiatry*, 16 (1981), 561–582.

Pic'l, A. K., Magaro, P. A. and Wade, E. A., 'Hemispheric Functioning in Paranoid and Nonparanoid Schizophrenia', *Biological Psychiatry*, 14 (1979), 891–903.

Rochford, J. M., Weinapple, M. and Goldstein, L., 'The Quantitative Hemispheric EEG in Adolescent Psychiatric Patients with Depression or Paranoid Symptomatology', *Biological Psychiatry*, 16 (1981), 47–54.

Roemer, R. A., Shagass, C., Straumanis, J. J. and Amadeo, M., 'Pattern Evoked Potential Measurements Suggesting Lateralised Hemisphere Dysfunction in Chronic Schizophrenics', *Biological Psychiatry*, 13 (1978), 185–202.

Schweitzer, L., 'Differences in Cerebral Lateralisation among Schizophrenics and Depressed Patients', *Biological Psychiatry*, 14 (1979), 721–733.

Shagass, C., Roemer, R. A., Straumanis, J. J. and Amadeo, M., 'Evoked Potential Evidence of Lateralised Hemispheric Dysfunction in Depressive Psychosis', *Electroencephalography and Clinical Neurophysiology*, 49 (1980), 26P.

Shaw, J. C., Brooks, S., Colter, N. and O'Connor, K. P., 'A Comparison of Schizophrenic and Neurotic Patients Using EEG Power and Coherence Spectra', in J. Gruzelier and P. Flor-Henry, eds., *Hemisphere Asymmetries of Function in Psychopathology* (Amsterdam, Elsevier/North Holland, 1979).

Taylor, M. A., Greenspan, B. and Abrams, R., 'Lateralised Neuropsychological Dysfunction in Affective Disorder and Schizophrenia', *American Journal of Psychiatry*, 136 (1979), 1031–1034.

Taylor, M. A., Redfield, J. and Abrams, R., 'Neuropsychological Dysfunction in Schizophrenia and Affective Disease', *Biological Psychiatry*, 16 (1981), 467–478.

Taylor, P. J., Dalton, R. and Fleminger, J. J., 'Handedness in Schizophrenia', *British Journal of Psychiatry*, 136 (1980), 375–383.

Tomer, R., Mintz, M., Levi, A. and Myslobodsky, M. S., 'Reactive Gaze Laterality in Schizophrenic Patients', *Biological Psychology*, 9 (1979), 115–127.

Tucker, D. M., Antes, J. R., Stenslie, C. E. and Barnhardt, T. M., 'Anxiety and Lateral Cerebral Function', *Journal of Abnormal Psychology*, 87 (1978), 380–383.

Walker, E., Hoppes, E. and Emory, E., 'A Reinterpretation of Findings on Hemispheric Dysfunction in Schizophrenia', *Journal of Nervous and Mental Disease*, 169 (1981), 378–380.

Weller, M. and Montagu, J. D., 'Electroencephalographic Coherence in Schizophrenia: a Preliminary Study, in J. Gruzelier and P. Flor-Henry, eds., *Hemisphere Asymmetries of Function in Psychopathology* (Amsterdam, Elsevier/North Holland, 1979).

Wexler, B. E., 'Cerebral Laterality and Psychiatry: a Review of the Literature', *American Journal of Psychiatry*, 137 (1980), 279–291.

Wexler, B. E. and Heninger, G. R., 'Alterations in Cerebral Laterality During Acute Psychotic Illness', *Archives of General Psychiatry*, 36 (1979), 278–288.

Wodehouse, P. G., *A Pelican at Blandings* (London, Herbert Jenkins, 1969).

Name Index

Saron, C. 237, 245
Sasanuma, S. 251, 268
Satz, P. 127, 128, 145, 146, 218, 222, 257, 260, 266, 267
Savage, C. W. 176, 182
Savage, R. D. 274, 289
Savodnik, I. 182, 183
Scammell, R. 303
Schaffer, R. E. 246
Schmit, V. 199, 205
Schmitt, F. O. 182, 223
Schoonover, R. A. 182
Schopflocher, D. 303
Schott, B. 183
Schuell, H. 143, 146
Schurr, P. 155, 162
Schweitzer, L. 297, 304
Scoville, W. B. 154
Searleman, A. 172, 182, 218, 224, 256, 260, 268
Segalowitz, S. J. 195, 206, 222
Selnes, O. A. 133, 147
Semmes, J. 59, 67, 90, 91, 96, 110, 261, 268
Severn, J. Millot 9
Shagass, C. 296, 304
Shallice, T. 106, 110
Shalman, D. C. 75, 87
Shaw, J. C. 230, 244, 247, 296, 304
Shucard, D. W. 241, 247
Shucard, J. L. 241, 247
Sidtis, J. 171, 183, 208, 224
Siegel, A. 251, 267
Signoret, J. L. 57, 66
Silverberg, R. 119, 124
Simmel, M. L. 147
Simson, R. 240, 246
Smith, J. C. 241, 245
Smith, J. S. 161
Smith, W. L. 161, 167, 182, 204
Smylie, C. S. 177, 181
Snyder, M. 237, 245
Sparks, R. 143, 146
Spellacy, F. 210, 224
Sperry, R. W. 165, 166, 169, 172, 175, 177, 181, 182, 183, 184
Spinnler, H. 120, 125
Springer, S. P. 21, 167, 171, 174, 182, 183, 208, 211, 212, 221, 224, 256, 268
Spurzheim, J. C. 9
Stachowiak, F.-J. 143, 147
Steele Russell, I. 182
Steklis, H. D. 145
Stenslie, C. E. 305
Stevens, R. 181
Stierman, I. 217, 223
Straumanis, J. J. 304
Strauss, E. 297, 304
Studdert-Kennedy, M. 216, 224
Sullivan, M. 146
Swanson, J. M. 193, 206, 239, 246
Sweet, W. H. 152, 162
Swencionis, C. 237, 247
Swenson, W. M. 152, 161

Tabossi, P. 251, 268

Tanguay, P. E. 240, 241, 247
Tapper, M. 303
Tassinari, G. 189, 204
Taub, J. M. 240, 241, 247
Taylor, A. M. 92, 110
Taylor, D. C. 266
Taylor, L. 53, 67
Taylor, M. A. 295, 302, 305
Taylor, M. J. 215, 222, 263, 265
Taylor, M. L. 143, 147
Taylor, N. 237, 245
Taylor, P. J. 298, 305
Teasdale, G. 288
Teng, E. L. 217, 224
Terbeck, D. 214, 223
Teuber, H.-L. 10, 49, 59, 60, 65, 67, 76, 87, 90, 96, 109, 110, 116, 125, 284, 289
Thatcher, R. W. 229, 240, 248
Tomer, R. 297, 305
Toone, B. K. 304
Tooth, G. C. 154, 162
Torjussen, T. 121, 125
Traub, E. 217, 223, 259, 266
Trevarthen, C. 169, 172, 173, 175, 178, 182, 183
Trimble, M. R. 302
Tucker, D. M. 238, 248, 296, 297, 305
Tucker, G. J. 152, 160, 162, 299, 300, 302, 304
Tueting, P. 234, 244, 245
Tweedy, J. 256, 268
Tzeng, O. J. L. 195, 205

Umiltà, C. 201, 204, 251, 268
Underwood, G. 181, 204, 222, 266

Valenstein, E. S. 66, 109, 144, 145, 146, 154, 159, 161, 162, 181
Van Allen, M. 149, 161
Vanderplas, J. M. 191
Van Deventer, A. 251, 264, 267, 268
Van Hoff, M. W. 182
Van Huijzen, C. 42
Van Wagenen, W. P. 165, 167
Varney, N. R. 117, 124
Vernon, P. E. 273, 289
Vetter, R. R. 214, 223
Vignolo, L. A. 73, 87
Vilkki, J. 149, 162
Vinken, P. J. 109, 110
Vogel, P. 165, 166, 174
Volpe, B. T. 177, 181
Voogd, J. 42

Wada, J. A. 241, 245
Wade, E. A. 296, 304
Waldeier, H. 238, 245
Walker, E. 297, 305
Wallace, P. M. 42, 160
Walsh, K. W. 21, 55, 66, 67
Walter, R. D. 162
Wang, W. S.-Y. 195, 205
Ward, T. B. 196, 206

Warren, J. M. 67
Warrington, E. K. 78, 87, 92, 93, 106, 110, 120, 125, 258, 268, 282, 289
Watson, P. J. 149, 162
Watts, J. W. 153, 161
Watts, K. P. 263, 266
Waziri, R. 304
Webster, R. 190, 205
Weidner, W. E. 74, 87
Weigl, E. 143, 147
Weinapple, M. 295, 304
Weinberger, A. 220, 222
Weinstein, E. A. 99, 110
Weinstein, S. 59, 67, 90, 96, 110
Weisenberg, T. 129, 147
Weiskrantz, L. 78, 87, 109, 120, 125
Weiss, M. S. 212, 224
Weller, M. 296, 305
Weniger, D. 143, 147
Wepman, J. M. 143, 147
Wernicke, C. 9
Wexler, B. E. 297, 300, 305
Whishaw, I. Q. 21, 65, 66, 87
Whitaker, H. 125, 145, 266
Whitaker, H. A. 125, 133, 145, 146, 147, 167, 183, 212, 222, 266
White, M. J. 191, 206
Whitty, C. W. M. 86, 87
Wiener, M. S. 237, 246
Wiesel, T. N. 112, 125
Wilson, A. 210, 224
Wilson, D. H. 166, 167, 171, 174, 177, 181, 182, 183, 208, 224
Witelson, S. F. 220, 224
Wittrock, M. C. 21, 145, 182, 222, 267
Wodehouse, P. G. 290, 305
Wolff, H. G. 49
Wood, C. C. 240, 248
Wood, R. L. 285, 289
Woods, D. L. 242, 244, 246
Worden, F. G. 182, 223
Wyke, M. 213, 224

Yahr, M. D. 152, 161
Yarbus, A. L. 57, 67
Yeager, C. L. 246
Yeudall, L. T. 303
Yingling, C. D. 246
Young, A. W. 186, 187, 192, 204, 206, 221, 245
Yozawitz, A. 297, 302
Yund, E. W. 208, 222

Zaidel, D. 177, 183
Zaidel, E. 172, 175, 177, 183, 186, 206
Zangwill, O. L. 10, 86, 87, 99, 107, 110, 133, 147
Zatorre, R. J. 214, 224
Zeitlin, G. M. 246
Zülch, K. J. 146, 147, 182, 268
Zurif, E. B. 72, 87, 143, 146, 183, 211, 224

Subject Index